The Civil War and Reconstruction

Uncovering the Past: Documentary Readers in American History
Series Editors: Steven Lawson and Nancy Hewitt

The books in this series introduce students in American history courses to two important dimensions of historical analysis. They enable students to engage actively in historical interpretation, and they further students' understanding of the interplay between social and political forces in historical developments.

Consisting of primary sources and an introductory essay, these readers are aimed at the major courses in the American history curriculum, as outlined further below. Each book in the series will be approximately 225–50 pages, including a 25–30 page introduction addressing key issues and questions about the subject under consideration, a discussion of sources and methodology, and a bibliography of suggested secondary readings.

Published

Stanley Harrold
The Civil War and Reconstruction: A Documentary Reader

Paul G. E. Clemens
The Colonial Era: A Documentary Reader

In preparation

Camilla Townsend
American Indian History: A Documentary Reader

Brian Ward
The 1960s: A Documentary Reader

Robert Ingalls and David Johnson
The United States Since 1945: A Documentary Reader

Sean Adams
The Early American Republic: A Documentary Reader

The Civil War and Reconstruction

A Documentary Reader

Edited by
Stanley Harrold

Blackwell Publishing

BLACKWELL PUBLISHING

350 Main Street, Malden, MA 02148-5020, USA
9600 Garsington Road, Oxford OX4 2DQ, UK
550 Swanston Street, Carlton, Victoria 3053, Australia

The right of Stanley Harrold to be identified as the Author of the Editorial Material in this Work has been asserted in accordance with the UK Copyright, Designs, and Patents Act 1988.

Designations used by companies to distinguish their products are often claimed as trademarks. All brand names and product names used in this book are trade names, service marks, trademarks, or registered trademarks of their respective owners. The publisher is not associated with any product or vendor mentioned in this book.

This publication is designed to provide accurate and authoritative information in regard to the subject matter covered. It is sold on the understanding that the publisher is not engaged in rendering professional services. If professional advice or other expert assistance is required, the services of a competent professional should be sought.

First published 2008 by Blackwell Publishing Ltd

2 2012

Library of Congress Cataloging-in-Publication Data

The Civil War and Reconstruction : a documentary reader / edited by Stanley Harrold.
　　p. cm. — (Uncovering the past : documentary readers in American history; [1])
　　Includes bibliographical references and index.
　　ISBN 978-1-4051-5663-9 (hardcover : alk. paper) — ISBN 978-1-4051-5664-6 (pbk. : alk. paper)
　　1. United States—History—Civil War, 1861–1865—Sources. 2. Reconstruction (U.S. history,
1865–1877)—Sources. 3. United States—History—1849–1877—Sources. I. Harrold, Stanley.
　　E464.C445 2008
　　973.7′14–dc22

　　　　　　　　　　　　　　　　　　2007024938

A catalogue record for this title is available from the British Library.

Set in 10/12.5pt Sabon
by SPi Publisher Services, Pondicherry, India
Printed in the UK

The publisher's policy is to use permanent paper from mills that operate a sustainable forestry policy, and which has been manufactured from pulp processed using acid-free and elementary chlorine-free practices. Furthermore, the publisher ensures that the text paper and cover board used have met acceptable environmental accreditation standards.

For further information on
Blackwell Publishing, visit our website:
www.blackwellpublishing.com

For Meredith and Randall

Contents

Figures

Series Editors' Preface

Primary sources have become an essential component in the teaching of history to undergraduates. They engage students in the process of historical interpretation and analysis and help them understand that facts do not speak for themselves. Rather, students see how historians construct narratives that recreate the past. Most students assume that the pursuit of knowledge is a solitary endeavor; yet historians constantly interact with their peers, building upon previous research and arguing among themselves over the interpretation of documents and their larger meaning. The documentary readers in this series highlight the value of this collaborative creative process and encourage students to participate in it.

Each book in the series introduces students in American history courses to two important dimensions of historical analysis. They enable students to engage actively in historical interpretation, and they further students' understanding of the interplay among social, cultural, economic, and political forces in historical developments In pursuit of these goals, the documents in each text embrace a broad range of sources, including such items as illustrations of material artifacts, letters and diaries, sermons, maps, photographs, song lyrics, selections from fiction and memoirs, legal statutes, court decisions, presidential orders, speeches, and political cartoons.

Each volume in the series is edited by a specialist in the field who is concerned with undergraduate teaching. The goal is not to offer a comprehensive selection of material but to provide items that reflect major themes and debates; that illustrate significant social, cultural, political, and economic dimensions of an era or subject; and that inform, intrigue and inspire undergraduate students. The editor of each volume has written an introduction that discusses the central questions that have occupied historians in this field and the ways historians have used primary sources to answer them. In addition, each introductory essay contains an explanation of the kinds of materials available to investigate a particular subject, the methods by which scholars analyze them, and the considerations that go into interpreting them. Each source selection is introduced by a short headnote that gives students the necessary information and a context for understanding the document. Also, each section of the volume includes questions to guide student reading and stimulate classroom discussion.

Stanley Harrold's *Civil War and Reconstruction* offers an array of documents dealing with the causes of the Civil War, the fighting of the war, the effects on the homefront, and the efforts to fashion a Reconstruction policy that would provide African Americans with equal civil and political rights. He also provides a lucid introduction to the vast literature on this period and concise but rich headnotes that locate specific documents in this larger context. This volume incorporates the views of northerners and southerners, African Americans and whites, slaves and free blacks, soldiers and civilians, and women and men. The sources allow students to analyze the views of politicians, journalists, diarists, political cartoonists, Confederate and Union troops, generals, preachers, reformers, newly emancipated African Americans, songwriters, and photographers as they grappled with the bloodiest war in American history and the dramatic debates that erupted in its aftermath.

Steven F. Lawson and Nancy A. Hewitt, Series Editors

Acknowledgments

Selecting and editing more than 60 documents pertaining to the Civil War and Reconstruction era proved to be an enjoyable and enlightening task. It would have been far less enjoyable, however, without the help, advice, and encouragement provided by a number of people. For their help in locating many of the documents that appear in this volume, I thank the staffs of several departments at the University of South Carolina's Thomas Cooper Library. Among them are the Government Information, Microforms, and Newspapers Department; the Interlibrary Loan Department; and the Rare Books and Special Collections Department. I extend thanks for similar help to the staff at the South Caroliniana Library. *Uncovering the Past* series editors Nancy A. Hewitt and Steven F. Lawson and the anonymous experts who read my proposal and manuscript deserve especial credit for helping me to determine which out of thousands of documents are most useful in understanding people and events during the Civil War and Reconstruction. Nancy and Steven also established the general framework for this volume and have offered their assistance throughout the project. Emily and Judy Harrold – as usual – provided technical assistance, and my colleague William C. Hine read the manuscript version of the collection and made suggestions concerning the introduction and headnotes that improved my prose. Finally, I thank Peter Coveney, Emily L. Martin, Deirdre Ilkson, and others at Blackwell Publishing for their insight, support, and commitment to their craft.

S. H., Orangeburg, SC, December 12, 2006

Introduction

The Civil War and the years of Reconstruction that followed are linked in American history. They overlap in time, as the war stretched from 1861 to Union victory in 1865, and the effort to rebuild and reshape the defeated South lasted from 1863 to 1877. The two eras also overlap thematically. The war's two central issues, national unity versus southern independence and black freedom versus slavery, shaped Reconstruction as well. Yet American memory and culture treat the two differently. The Civil War is a popular topic. There is a huge market for Civil War books, movies, and television dramas. There are numerous biographies of Union and Confederate leaders, histories of military units, and accounts of battles. There is a great demand for Civil War novels. Reenacting the battles is a widespread hobby that attracts media attention. Despite the war's terrible levels of death and destruction, Americans celebrate the conflict as a glorious reflection of the nation's bravery, patriotism, and honor.

In contrast Reconstruction attracts little interest beyond the ranks of professional historians. In part this is because it has acquired a more complex and darker legacy than the war. Although it was ostensibly a rebuilding process with noble goals for national unity and racial justice, Reconstruction foundered amid racism, terrorism, and charges of corruption. For many years it appeared to have been a time when white southerners endured exploitation and insult under the plundering rule of African Americans and northern carpetbaggers. Currently historians portray it as an era in which northern politicians and public opinion allowed a white southern reaction to destroy black aspirations for freedom and equal rights. Taken together, as they should be, the Civil War and Reconstruction invite students to analyze how the two eras are related, go beyond entrenched assumptions, and use evidence to reach their own conclusions.

The origins of the Civil War and Reconstruction lay in the establishment, during the seventeenth century, of race-based slavery in Great Britain's North American colonies. From the 1780s, antislavery sentiment associated with the American Revolution and modernizing economic forces led to slavery's gradual abolition in the North. Meanwhile, stimulated by the rise of cotton production during the 1790s, slavery grew stronger in the South. During the early nineteenth century white southerners became increasingly committed to it. They embraced slavery not only as essential to their agricultural economy but to controlling a growing black population. In contrast, by the 1850s most northerners regarded slavery as an economic and political evil that threatened their interests. Many northerners also held slavery to be a moral evil and a radical minority of antislavery activists, called abolitionists, demanded its immediate termination.

As early as the 1820s a few southerners responded to northern opposition to slavery by threatening that their states would withdraw (or secede) from the Union. By the 1850s, secessionist sentiment thrived in the South, as the powerful Republican Party organized in the North against the expansion of slavery and increasing numbers of northerners helped escaping slaves avoid recapture. When in 1860 Republican candidate Abraham Lincoln won the presidential election, the seven states of the Deep South seceded from the Union. In February 1861 they established the Confederate States of America under a constitution that explicitly recognized the legality of slavery. War began that April as Confederate forces attacked and captured Union-occupied Fort Sumter in Charleston Harbor. Within a month four of the Upper South states had withdrawn from the Union to join the Confederacy.

Americans fought the Civil War on momentous geographical and human scales. There were three theaters of combat stretching across the South from the Atlantic Ocean to the Far West. The Eastern Theater included the region between the East Coast and the Appalachian Mountains. The Western Theater spanned the distance between the Appalachians and the Mississippi River. The Trans-Mississippi Theater included the entire region west of the Mississippi. About 1,600,000 men served in Union armed forces and about 1,000,000 in Confederate. Each side lost about one-third of its soldiers in killed and wounded. Everyone realized that the Union enjoyed greatly superior population and manufacturing resources. In the long run these strengths provided it with an overwhelming strategic advantage. But the Confederacy's defensive posture and its effective military commanders made it competitive. Confederate leaders also vainly hoped northern men would not fight well and that Britain, France, and other European powers would intervene on their behalf.

Each side had its largest armies in the portion of the Eastern Theater located between the Confederate capital at Richmond, Virginia, and the Union capital at Washington. The biggest battles occurred there. Nevertheless Union armies in the Western Theater made the fastest progress. They split the Confederacy in two with the capture of Vicksburg in July 1863 and opened the way for General William Tecumseh Sherman's invasion of the Deep South in 1864. Confederate armies won impressive victories and mounted offensive campaigns into Union territory in 1862 and 1863. But the Union advances in the West, the defeat of Robert E. Lee's Army of Northern Virginia at Gettysburg, Pennsylvania, in July 1863, and an ever more effective Union naval blockade of southern ports, decided the outcome. Pressed relentlessly by the Union Army of the Potomac, commanded by Ulysses S. Grant, Lee surrendered at Appomattox, Virginia, on April 9, 1865. Before the last major Confederate army followed Lee's example, a Confederate agent named John Wilkes Booth assassinated Lincoln.

From the war's beginning in 1861 antislavery northerners, including abolitionists and Radical Republican politicians and journalists, urged that the North fight to emancipate the slaves as well as to preserve the Union. In the South many slaves used wartime disruptions to free themselves by escaping to Union lines. In January 1863 Lincoln's Emancipation Proclamation made abolition a Union war aim, and nearly 200,000 black men fought in Union armed forces to achieve that goal, which was accomplished with the ratification of the Thirteenth Amendment in December 1865. Meanwhile, black southerners – with support from northern black leaders, abolitionists, large segments of the Republican Party, and northern public opinion – pressed for citizenship rights.

Most white southerners, led by former slaveholders, resisted these efforts. The former Confederate states passed Black Codes designed to keep African Americans on plantations in semi-slavery. Presidential Reconstruction, under Lincoln and Andrew Johnson, contributed to that effort by emphasizing rapid creation of loyal state governments, which would decide the fate of former slaves. By the time of his death, Lincoln appeared to have become more favorable to federal support for black citizenship. Johnson, however, who succeeded Lincoln, was a southern Democrat who opposed genuine freedom for African Americans. In contrast, Radical Republican congressmen, for a variety of reasons, insisted on federal protection for black rights in the South. Led by Radicals, Congress took control of Reconstruction in 1867. It passed the Fourteenth and Fifteenth Amendments (ratified respectively in 1868 and 1870), which provided constitutional guarantees for black citizenship and voting rights for black men. When Johnson resisted these efforts, Congress impeached him. In May 1868 the Radicals came within one vote of removing him from office.

Congressional (or Radical) Reconstruction in the South varied from state to state in duration and degree. From the late 1860s and into the late 1870s, many black men served in southern state governments (and several served in Congress). With short-lived help from the United States Freedmen's Bureau and the US Army, African Americans established churches, schools, and other institutions. Southern state governments under Radical control attempted to modernize and diversify economies and to build transportation and governmental infrastructures that had either been destroyed during, or had not existed prior to, the Civil War. But neither Congress nor northern public opinion supported plans for extensive land reform that might have provided former slaves with the economic independence they required to counteract movements designed to deprive them of political influence.

Beginning in 1868, amid terrorist tactics carried out by the Ku Klux Klan and similar organizations, white reactionaries – known as Redeemers – worked through state Democratic parties to drive African Americans from politics. A Republican-controlled Congress and Ulysses S. Grant's Republican presidential administration (1869–77) resisted these efforts. But a variety of factors, including racism, a desire to placate former Confederates, and states' rights sentiments among US Supreme Court justices, allowed most of the South to return to white Democratic rule by the mid-1870s. A disputed presidential election in 1876 led to the withdrawal of federal troops from the South and the fall (in South Carolina, Florida, and Louisiana) of the last state governments in which black men participated. African Americans lost most of what they had gained as a result of the Civil War. During the 1890s racial separatism and inequality gained legal and constitutional sanction across the South.

Historians address a variety of questions related to the Civil War and Reconstruction. Some questions (such as what caused the war and why the North won) are perennial and attract wide interest. The staying power of these questions demonstrates the centrality of the Civil War in American history. Other questions that have risen within the last 30 years – involving Reconstruction as well as the war – reflect changes in American society that inspire new scholarly perspectives.

The debate over what caused the Civil War (or what it was about) has attracted the most attention. Documents produced by abolitionists, Republicans, and slaveholders agree that slavery caused sectional strife. Secession conventions and Confederate leaders, before and during the war, boasted that they left the Union to protect slavery and white supremacy. After the war, former Confederates changed their minds. Rather than slavery, they maintained, northern aggression against southern state rights and economic interests caused the war. For much of the twentieth century, most American historians agreed. More recently southern Neoconfederates, who refer to the Civil War as the "War for Southern Independence" and – more provocatively – the "War of Northern Aggression," maintain that northern economic, cultural, and political imperialism (not slavery) caused it. Rather than credit the statements of secessionist leaders that they fought to defend slavery, Neoconfederates emphasize statements by northerners who attempted in early 1861 to hold the Union together by deemphasizing the slavery issue. Among the more prominent of these statements is Lincoln's promise in his First Inaugural Address of March 1861 to enforce the Fugitive Slave Law and accept a constitutional amendment protecting slavery in the southern states.

Yet, for over forty years, professional historians have almost universally traced the war's origins to slavery and the determination of white southerners to defend it. Like most northerners of the 1850s, Lincoln favored the "ultimate extinction" of slavery. While most white southerners believed that slavery had to expand into new territories to survive, Lincoln and other Republicans opposed that expansion. Lincoln declared in 1858 that the Union could not endure "half *slave* and half *free*." Had most of the slave states not seceded, his administration would have acted against slavery within the national domain and worked to create an antislavery party in the South. Facing a permanent loss of power in the national government and what they regarded as a decidedly antislavery president, southern leaders dismissed Lincoln's reassurances. They believed that to protect slavery they had to take their states out of the Union.

The related question of whether or not the Civil War could have been avoided is as old as the question of its causes. Lincoln's "House Divided" speech and William H. Seward's "Irrepressible Conflict," speech argue that basic differences between the free-labor North and slave-labor South could never be reconciled. For many years thereafter, historians agreed that these differences made war inevitable. Still, in early 1861 President Lincoln and Secretary of State Seward hoped to avoid war. Years earlier northern Democratic leader Stephen A. Douglas had contended that antislavery and proslavery extremists, rather than fundamental differences, drove the sections apart. During the early twentieth century a generation of historians, who denied that slavery was evil, emphasized what (white) Americans held in common, and rejected ideology as a historical force, argued as Douglas had that the Civil War was "repressible." As dedicated centrists, they contended that "fanatics" and a "blundering generation" of politicians led the United States into a "needless war." More recently historians have returned to emphasizing essential differences between northern and southern labor systems, clashing ideologies, divisions of power within a federal system, and cultural differences including a volatile tradition of "southern honor," as predisposing the sections toward war. They, nevertheless, stress that there was nothing inevitable about *when* the war might begin.

Historians ask many questions concerning the Civil War itself. How did it shape America economically, culturally, constitutionally, and racially? What battles, tactics, and generals were most important? Was it the world's last traditional war or its first modern war? How did soldiers experience the war? How did it affect the northern and southern homefronts? What precedents did the war set concerning civil liberties? Why was it transformed from a war to save the Union to a war to abolish slavery? What was Lincoln's significance?

In 1927 Charles and Mary Beard contended that Civil War production demands transformed the North (and thereby the United States) into an industrial nation. In the Beards' interpretation, the war placed a new class of industrialists in control of national policy, as the Republican Party became the political representative of American capitalism. The war replaced a dominant slaveholding aristocracy with a new commercial one. By the 1960s, historians had begun to regard this interpretation as too narrowly focused. They showed that industrialization had begun in the North well before the Civil War, that an economic revolution was underway during the 1850s, that the war may have retarded some economic development, and that in many respects it expanded egalitarianism.

Historians are more in accord concerning the relationship of the Civil War to the Constitution. They agree that the war, rather than legislative or judicial action, decided that the central government is superior to the state governments, that state sovereignty does not include power to nullify laws passed by Congress, interpret the Constitution, or leave the Union. Historians, however, disagree concerning whether or not these are positive developments. Most historians since the late nineteenth century, reflecting liberal and nationalist perspectives, have regarded constitutional change as a prerequisite for the emergence of the United States as a world power and as necessary for the establishment of equal rights for its citizens. In contrast archconservatives, libertarians, and some romantic liberals (most of whom are not historians) consider the North's victory as the death of a decentralized Jeffersonian republic and the birth of a centralized empire, with all its attendant threats to individual liberty. In the Confederacy Governor Joseph E. Brown of Georgia and others feared that war would lead to centralized military despotism. Similarly, historians have long debated Lincoln's suspension of the writ of habeas corpus and arrest during the war of about

15,000 civilians. Some of them were Confederate guerillas or spies but most were, like Clement L. Vallandigham, Peace Democrats ("Copperheads") who wrote or spoke against northern war policies.

The Civil War is known as "the last gentleman's war" *and* the "first modern war." Those who emphasize *gentlemanly* aspects point out that, although Confederate troops on at least six occasions massacred black prisoners and prisoner-of-war camps were often hell-holes, each side generally treated the other with respect. Civilian casualties were few compared to twentieth and twenty-first century wars. In regard to tactics, the Civil War was both traditional and innovative. Union and Confederate generals looked back to the Napoleonic era for instruction. They stressed close-order assaults and the massed firepower of muskets. Yet the Union and Confederate governments anticipated twentieth-century total war in mobilizing their economies, passing conscription laws, and restricting civil liberties. They used railroads to move troops and by 1864 trench warfare developed to the southeast of Petersburg, Virginia – foreshadowing World War I.

Since the 1960s historians have sought to place the war's political and military events in broader social contexts, to go beyond concentration on government officials, generals, tactics, and strategy in order to view events "from the bottom up." They ask questions designed to reveal the experiences of average people, including enlisted soldiers, nurses, and civilians. Historian James M. McPherson asks why did the soldiers fight? He concludes that knowledge of the issues that divided the country and loyalty to their comrades motivated them. Historians also investigate the lives and motives of the few women who disguised themselves as men in order to enlist. They investigate how the war affected African Americans, foreign immigrants, urban workers, poorer white southerners, women, and children. They ask how these groups helped shape the war's character. In other words, what was the connection between organized warfare and broader social forces? How did the battlefield and the homefront affect each other? In recent years, historians have also considered the relationship between the Civil War and Reconstruction and events in the Far West. How did the war and its aftermath impact westward expansion? How did American Indians of the Great Plains and Rocky Mountains experience the period between 1861 and 1877?

Perhaps most controversial has been determining the relationship of African Americans to the war. A frequent question is "Who freed the slaves?" Not long ago the obvious answers were Abraham Lincoln and Union armies. But recently some historians have maintained that the slaves themselves were responsible. By leaving their masters as the war began and crossing Union lines they created an issue of their status – slave, free, or something in between (what Union General Benjamin F. Butler called "contrabands"). As the Union's need for black workers, and later black soldiers, became clear, pressure on Lincoln, from black abolitionist Frederick Douglass and others, to make emancipation a war aim and to enlist black troops, mounted. Meanwhile white Union soldiers – despite their racial bias – recognized the contribution of slave labor to the Confederate war effort and helped spread a demand in the North for emancipation. It was within this context that Lincoln gradually came to accept the practical and moral expediency of transforming the goal of the war from preserving the Union as it had been to achieving a "new birth of freedom." Many historians still regard Lincoln as essential to the decision, but no longer overlook the role of slaves in bringing it about.

Historians also ask a variety of questions about Reconstruction. They recognize that the Republican Party failed to gain its stated objectives of citizenship rights for African Americans and transformation of the southern economy into one more like the North's. They ask why these failures occurred and why the North so quickly lost interest in the South and the former slaves. Early in the twentieth century, William Dunning and his students maintained that Reconstruction failed because "negro rule" led to radicalism, corruption, and ineptitude in the postwar Republican regimes that governed the former Confederate states. According to the Dunning School, it was for the best that these governments failed, that African Americans lost the rights they had gained, and that white Democrats "redeemed" the South for their race.

In 1935 the black scholar W. E. B. DuBois challenged this interpretation. He maintained that Reconstruction's black leaders were mostly competent and effective rather than ignorant and corrupt. By the 1950s and 1960s historians interpreted Reconstruction as a noble experiment in which black and white Republicans attempted to rebuild a shattered southern economy, create a civil infrastructure, and establish black rights within an integrated polity. They charged that reactionary forces in the South and a fundamentally racist northern public opinion, distracted by issues closer to home, destroyed this effort. During the 1970s, another reassessment began that reflects a perspective greatly altered from that which prevailed at the start of the twentieth century. Histories of Reconstruction written since the 1970s contend (as Albion W. Tourgee had in 1879) that the postwar Republican effort to transform the South failed because it was too conservative. Radical Republican policies were too shortsighted, white southern Republicans too limited by their racism, and the Freedmen's Bureau too accommodating to former masters' determination to keep black workers on plantations.

Over the past four decades, historians have asked new questions about the role of African Americans in Reconstruction. They have found that former slaves had a central role in shaping a radical agenda for change. As the war ended, black southerners asserted their rights as citizens. From 1868 they participated in state constitutional conventions and state governments that expanded public education and other government services. They served in state militias and some of them acquired land. Although Reconstruction failed to protect black rights effectively during the 1860s and 1870s and conditions deteriorated thereafter, historians have for many years noted that the ratification of the Fourteenth and Fifteenth Amendments, designed respectively to protect black civil rights and voting rights, were momentous achievements. Despite decades of ineffectiveness, they became the constitutional foundation for the twentieth-century civil rights movement. Reconstruction also left a positive legacy in the strengthening of black institutions, including families, schools, and churches, out of which later civil rights struggles drew strength.

Why have historians disagreed among themselves in answering questions about the Civil War and Reconstruction? In part it is because as time has passed their interests, concerns, ideologies, and research priorities have changed. Concerted research into the roles of African Americans and women, for example, is recent and provides fresh insight into old issues. In addition modern historians' answers to questions about the Civil War and Reconstruction are strongly influenced by an expanded search for the testimony of people who lived through these eras. The more perspectives the testimony provides, the more sophisticated become historians' accounts. But because the testimony is often contradictory different interpretations arise. Historians must evaluate the conflicting claims from northern and southern leaders concerning which section was the aggressor in the war. They must also analyze why white Union soldiers often regarded black soldiers as ineffective, while black soldiers and their white officers indicated otherwise.

The most important factor in the varied and often complex answers to questions about the Civil War and Reconstruction is the vast number of primary documents (eyewitness testimony) that exists concerning these momentous events. The documents take a variety of forms. They range from military and governmental records to songs that soldiers and civilians sang; from speeches, proclamations, and legislative acts to newspaper reports, private letters, and memoirs; from political cartoons to photographs; from Lincoln's extraordinary Gettysburg Address to mundane Sanitary Commission reports. Much of this material has been published.

Government records are especially important in revealing the war's causes, its military and political aspects, and the phases of Reconstruction. The *Congressional Globe* and its successor, the *Congressional Record* (which began publication in 1873) contain speeches delivered in Congress. There are also a variety of official documents published by the House of Representatives and the US Senate, including committee reports and the publications of executive departments and bureaus. Presidential documents are available in James D. Richardson, ed., *A Compilation of the Messages and Papers of the Presidents* (1897). US Supreme Court decisions are in *United States Reports* and the decisions of lower federal courts in *Federal Cases*. In 1904–5 the US Congress published the *Journal of the Congress of the Confederate States of America 1861–1865* in seven volumes. A more complete version, entitled *Proceedings of the Confederate Congress* was published between 1923 and 1959 as volumes 44 through 52 of the *Southern Historical Society Papers*. There are also Richardson's *A Compilation of the Messages and Papers of the Confederacy* (1905) and Rembert W. Patrick, ed., *The Opinions of the Confederate Attorneys General 1861–1865* (1950). Between 1880 and 1901, the US government published accounts of military engagements in *War of the Rebellion: Official Records of the Union and Confederate Armies* (128 vols.). For naval warfare there is *Official Records of the Union and Confederate Navies in the War of the Rebellion*, published between 1894 and 1901 in 31 volumes. In addition there are voluminous state government publications pertaining to the Civil War and Reconstruction. They include codes, statutes, constitutions, legislative journals, governors' messages, and court reports.

Nongovernmental published primary sources provide more personal, and often more universal, perspectives on the war and the period that followed. Many of them describe the experiences of enlisted men, African Americans, women, and noncombatants who are underrepresented in official records. Among such sources are regimental histories, collected letters and collected works, diaries, reminiscences, autobiographies, and a huge number of contemporary newspapers and magazines.

The white men who led the Union and Confederacy were the first of their era to have their writings collected. Among several collections of Lincoln's works, Roy P. Basler et al., eds., *The Collected Works of Abraham Lincoln* (9 vols., 1953–55) is considered definitive. There is also Haskell M. Monroe et al., eds., *The Papers of Jefferson Davis*, published in six volumes between 1974 and 1989. More recent are collections of the writings of abolitionists and feminists. There are *The Papers of William Lloyd Garrison*, edited by Walter M. Merrill and Louis Ruchames (6 vols., 1971–81), *The Frederick Douglass Papers*, edited by John W. Blassingame and others (7 vols., 1979–99), and

C. Peter Ripley et al., eds., *The Black Abolitionist Papers* (5 vols., 1985). In 1981 Ellen Carol DuBois edited *Elizabeth Cady Stanton, Susan B. Anthony: Correspondence, Writings, Speeches.*

Published diaries include not only those of such prominent government officials as Salmon P. Chase, who served as Lincoln's Treasury secretary and later as Chief Justice of the US Supreme Court, and Secretary of the Navy, Gideon Welles, but enlisted soldiers and civilians as well. One of the more notable of the latter is Mary Chesnut's *A Diary from Dixie* (1905). Others include war reporter William Henry Russell's *My Diary North and South* (1863) and John B. Jones's *A Rebel War Clerk's Diary at the Confederate Capital* (1866). The best of the Civil War reminiscences, and the only one that achieves literary greatness, is Ulysses S. Grant's *Personal Memoirs* (1885–86). There are many others.

Documentary sources for the black experience during the Civil War and Reconstruction have become more accessible during recent years. In addition to the *Douglass* and *Black Abolitionist* papers, there is the impressive and very useful *Freedom: A Documentary History of Emancipation* (1982–93), edited in four volumes by Ira Berlin and others. There are also several collections of letters from black enlisted men. They include Virginia M. Adams, ed., *On the Altar of Freedom: A Black Soldier's Civil War Letters from the Front* (1991); Noah Andre Trudeau, ed., *Voices from the 55th Massachusetts Volunteers 1861–1865* (1996); and Edwin S. Redkey, ed., *A Grand Army of Black Men: Letters from African-American Soldiers in the Union Army* (1997).

Except in Congress and state legislatures, women participated in every aspect of the Civil War and Reconstruction. A very few women disguised themselves as men in order to serve in Union or Confederate armies. More commonly women, black and white, served as army nurses, as aid workers in black refugee camps, as fundraisers, and as teachers and missionaries in the Union-occupied South. Some women, North and South, worked in munitions factories during the war. Many more replaced men as government clerks and secretaries or took on masculine duties as heads of households and plantation supervisors. Documents pertaining to their lives are available in a variety of venues, although there is no comprehensive documentary history of women during either period. Sarah Rosetta Wakeman served in the 153d Regiment, New York Volunteers. She sent letters home that are published in Lauren Cook Burgess, ed., *An Uncommon Soldier* (1994). Katharine Wormeley describes her work with wounded soldiers as a Sanitary Commission employee in *The Cruel Side of War* (1898). There are numerous diaries and memoirs of women who experienced the war years as noncombatants. *The Cormany Diaries* (1982) are remarkable in that the book consists of the diaries of a husband and wife. He was a Union enlisted man, and she was an impoverished mother living in the southeastern portion of Pennsylvania, invaded in 1863 by the Army of Northern Virginia. More documents produced by Confederate women have been published than those produced by Union women. Belle Boyd and Rose O'Neal Greenhow provide accounts of their activities as Confederate spies in Washington, DC and their subsequent imprisonment. There are also many published diaries and journals of women living in the South during the war and Reconstruction. *The War the Women Lived: Female Voices from the Confederate South*, edited by Walter Sullivan (1995) provides a sampling.

Beyond government publications and private accounts, literary, musical, and photographic sources provide important primary documentation. In 1864 Ledyard Bill edited *Lyrics, Incidents, and Sketches of the Rebellion*. There is also *Bugle-echoes: A Collection of Poems of the Civil War, North and South* (1886), edited by Francis Fisher Browne. Much more recent and extensive is *Civil War Poetry: An Anthology* (1997), edited by Paul Negi. The National Archives and Library of Congress have large collections of Civil War era prints and photographs, some of which are available online. There are also many published collections of photographs. Among these are Francis Trevelyan Miller's 10 volume *Photographic History of the Civil War* (1912), *Mathew Brady's Illustrated History of the Civil War* (1978), and William C. Davis's five volume *The Image of War 1861–1865* (1981–84).

Published sources for Reconstruction are less extensive. Two collections of major government documents were published in 1906. They are Edward McPherson, ed., *The Political History of Reconstruction* (2 vols.) and Walter L. Fleming, ed., *A Documentary History of Reconstruction*. Several of the collections of US government and southern state government documents discussed earlier for the Civil War also include Reconstruction. Among contemporary US government publications several are especially useful. Congressional documents include the *Report of the Joint Committee on Reconstruction* (1866) and the *Report of the Select Committee on the Condition of the South* (1875). There is also the 13 volume *Report of the Joint Select Committee to Inquire into the Condition of Affairs in the Late Insurrectionary States* (1872), dealing with the Ku Klux Klan. Executive branch documents include Oliver O. Howard, *Report of the Commissioner of the Bureau of Refugees, Freedmen, and Abandoned Lands* (1867) and John W. Alvord, *Semi-Annual Report[s] on Schools for Freedmen* (1866–70).

As in the case of the Civil War, a variety of private individuals provide eyewitness accounts of the South during Reconstruction that go beyond official reports. *The Journal of Charlotte L. Forten Grimke*, edited by Brenda Stevenson in 1988, provides the views of a black northern woman who undertook missionary work with former slaves in the South Carolina Sea Islands. John David Smith in *Black Voices from Reconstruction 1865–1877* (1996) weaves documents into a narrative history. The reports of white northern military officers, travelers, and reporters also illuminate conditions in the South after the war. John T. Trowbridge's *The South: A Tour of the Battle-Fields and Ruined Cities, a Journey through the Desolated States, and Talks with the People* (1866), and Sidney Andrews's *The South since the War, as Shown by Fourteen Weeks of Travel and Observation in Georgia and the Carolinas* (1866) describe a devastated South. Whitlaw Reid's *After the War: A Southern Tour May 1, 1865 to May 1, 1866* (1866), Robert Somers's *The Southern States since the War 1870–1871* (1871), and Charles Nordhoff's *The Cotton States in the Spring and Summer of 1875* (1876) provide northern travelers' impressions of the Reconstruction era South. James S. Pike's *The Prostrate State: South Carolina under Negro Government* (1875) ridicules Radical rule. It should be balanced by Albion W. Tourgee's *A Fool's Errand: A Novel of the South during Reconstruction* (1879).

Historians analyze documents in a variety of ways. They break them into their component parts. They approach them holistically. They consider the race, class, and gender of their creators. They are aware that the meaning of documents depends on context and that meaning can change as understanding of context changes. Few documents address only one subject or have only one meaning. The Declaration of Sentiments of the American Anti-Slavery Society, for example, reveals a variety of things about the abolitionists. Historians also seek out inconsistencies in documents. Some documents have components that contradict each other. What, for example, should be made of Lincoln's First Inaugural Address, in which his denial that he will coerce southern states seems to contradict his commitment to enforcing United States law within their boundaries? In addition, historians must consider whether a document follows rules of logic, and if it does not, why not. They must judge, as well, whether documents are authentic and truthful. Often what documents omit is as important as what they assert. Historians must appreciate the overall intent of a document's creator in order to answer such questions.

Judging the intent of a person, a group, or a government body is never easy. This is one reason that historians disagree. In his 1865 speech on Reconstruction, for example, was Thaddeus Stevens more concerned with the interests of the Republican Party or with the rights of African Americans?

To resolve such dilemmas, historians place documents in a variety of contexts. They begin by categorizing a document. Is it a diary or journal entry meant only for the author? Is it private communication? Is it a newspaper or magazine article designed for a particular audience? Or is it a public pronouncement influenced by the author's broad assessment of public opinion? Is it an official government or military document? A description of a battle, for example, has different meanings, depending on whether it is an official report, a journalist's description, or part of a private letter from a soldier to his wife.

Documents are always biased. They reflect the temporal, gender, class, ideological, racial, and geographical prejudices of their creators. In analyzing documents, historians must be acutely aware that these biases simultaneously limit and enhance their value. Mary Chesnut's diary is important because it embodies the view of a white southern woman during the first year of the Civil War. But it also reflects a very limited point of view that must be balanced by the views expressed in other documents. Historians recognize that descriptions of the Battle of Gettysburg vary according to whether they are produced by Union or Confederate soldiers, or reporters for northern, southern, or European newspapers. Similarly during Reconstruction, African Americans, white northerners, and white southerners all had biases that shaped their interpretation of events. While white southerners praised the Ku Klux Klan and white northerners regarded it as a political threat, southern African Americans directly experienced its terrorist tactics.

Historians must also consider when and where documents are produced. A report written about an event by someone present, such as Union Colonel Frank J. Haskell's account of the Battle of Gettysburg, is more valuable than a document by a contemporary who was not present or recalled the event long after it took place. A lapse of time between when a person participates in or observes an event and when that person records an impression of the event is an extremely important consideration in analyzing a document. Human memory is fallible. Not only do memories weaken over time, intervening events reshape them. Therefore, while autobiographies, reminiscences, memoirs, and oral histories constitute eyewitness testimony, they are not considered to be as reliable as documents produced during or shortly after an event. When historians rely on long-term memories, they have to be watchful for anachronisms and evolving points of view. As historian David W. Blight emphasizes, Union and Confederate soldiers – who were enemies fighting for causes they believed in during the Civil War – years later looked back on the war as a test of manhood for the nation, in which both sides served admirably.

In every instance, historians have to organize documents chronologically and topically to understand their meaning and interrelationships. Early reports that the Union army was winning the First Battle of Bull Run in 1861, that Lee's Army of Northern Virginia would capture Washington, DC in 1863, that Reconstruction would produce racial justice in the South, have to be interpreted in light of later documents that contradict them.

Historians cannot rely on a single or just a few sources to achieve an understanding of the Civil War, Reconstruction, or any other topic. Instead they create a context based on what other historians have concluded and a multitude of documents. There must be interplay as historians place documents in context and each document has the potential to either confirm or alter the context. Historians also consult the writings of scholars in other disciplines, including cultural anthropology, social psychology, political science, literary criticism, and archeology.

The first step is to develop a working hypothesis about the topic, which may be as broad as the causes of the war and the impact of Reconstruction, or as narrow as the role of a single person or community in the war and its aftermath. A hypothesis must rest on interpretations created by other scholars as well as on primary documents. Familiarity with a variety of interpretations is essential because historians have to understand what others have written about a topic if they are to make an original contribution of their own.

In many cases earlier studies have a positive impact on new work. But even when historians disagree with an existing interpretation, they have to be familiar with it. The Dunning School, for example, serves as a point of reference for more recent scholars who interpret the same Reconstruction documents from a different perspective.

As fields of inquiry emerge, historians seek new or underutilized documents that pertain to their topic. They also approach documents in new ways. As African-American history arose as a major field, the discovery of documents related to the black experience during the Civil War and Reconstruction became a major concern. But the utilization of sources that had long been available – such as antislavery newspapers, Freedmen's Bureau archives, plantation records, and interviews carried out under the Works Progress Administration during the 1930s – was also important. Similarly histories of women during the Civil War and Reconstruction rely on a mixture of newly collected documents and reinterpretations of documents that have long been available. In addition, historians have increasingly turned to paintings, photographs, and other nonliterary sources to enhance their understanding of nearly every aspect of the war and its aftermath.

The collection of Civil War and Reconstruction documents that follows is not exhaustive. Instead it is a representative selection of sources, some of which often appear in more extensive collections. The documents reflect a variety of contemporary points of view and topics of current interest. They may be analyzed from various perspectives and in a variety of contexts. Speeches, official records, and accounts of battles constitute an important part of them. But many of the documents testify to the experiences and perspectives of soldiers in the ranks, noncombatants, and men and women on the homefronts. The goal is to provide the most vital of the official records, while including a broad range of other testimony pertaining to the Civil War and Reconstruction eras. The shorter documents appear in their entirety. The longer documents have been edited for clarity, relevance, and brevity.

Chapter 1   Causes

1. [William Lloyd Garrison]
Declaration of Sentiments of the American Anti-Slavery Society,
December 5, 1833

Organized calls for the general abolition of slavery emerged in the Atlantic World during the late eighteenth century. Quaker and evangelical religious impulses, natural rights doctrines, economic development, and unrest among enslaved African Americans contributed to antislavery sentiment. Principles expressed in the American Declaration of Independence had a leading influence on movements to end slavery in the northern section of the United States and on national efforts to discourage slavery elsewhere. Between 1780 and 1804 all of the states north of the Mason–Dixon Line abolished slavery either gradually or immediately. In 1787 Congress banned slavery in the Northwest Territory, and in 1808 abolished the external slave trade. In December 1816 a group of prominent slaveholders organized the American Colonization Society, claiming as its goals the gradual abolition of slavery in the South and the deportation of former slaves from the United States to Liberia in West Africa. During the 1820s opposition among free African Americans to this plan, on the grounds that it would strengthen rather than weaken slavery by getting rid of its main opponents, had a major impact on a minority of slavery's white northern critics. In 1831 the most outspoken of these, William Lloyd Garrison (1805–79), initiated his weekly newspaper, the Liberator. In December 1833 the organizers of the American Anti-Slavery Society called on Garrison to write the new organization's Declaration of Sentiments. Although few African Americans (or white women) attended this meeting, Garrison vividly portrays a movement dedicated to the immediate peaceful abolition of slavery, without sending former slaves to Liberia, and without compensating former masters.

The Convention assembled in the city of Philadelphia, to organize a National Anti-Slavery Society, promptly seize the opportunity to promulgate the following *Declaration of Sentiments*, as cherished by them in relation to the enslavement of one-sixth portion of the American people.

More than fifty-seven years have elapsed, since a band of patriots convened in this place, to devise measures for the deliverance of this country from a foreign yoke. The corner-stone upon which they found the *Temple of Freedom* was broadly this–: "that all men are created equal; that they are endowed by their Creator with certain inalienable rights; that among these are life, LIBERTY, and the pursuit of happiness." At the sound of their trumpet-call, three millions of people rose up as from the sleep of death, and rushed to the strife of blood; deeming it more glorious to die instantly as freemen, than desirable to live one hour as slaves. – They were few in number – poor in resources; but the honest conviction that *Truth, Justice* and *Right* were on their side, made them invincible.

We have met together for the achievement of an enterprise, without which that of our fathers is incomplete, and which, for its magnitude, solemnity, and probable results upon the destiny of the world, as far transcends theirs as truth does physical force.

Their principles led them to wage war against their oppressors, and to spill human blood like water, in order to be free. *Ours* forbid the doing of evil that good may come, and lead us to reject, and to entreat the oppressed to reject, the use of all carnal weapons for deliverance from bondage – relying solely upon those which are spiritual, and mighty through God to the pulling down of strong holds.

Their measures were physical resistance – the marshalling in arms – the hostile array – the mortal encounter. Ours shall be such only as the opposition of moral purity to moral corruption – the destruction of error by the potency of truth – the overthrow of prejudice by the power of love – and the abolition of slavery by the spirit of repentance.

Their grievances, great as they were, were trifling in comparison with the wrongs and sufferings of those for whom we plead. Our fathers were never slaves – never bought and sold like cattle – never shut out from the light of knowledge and religion – never subjected to the lash of brutal taskmasters.

But those, for whose emancipation we are striving – constituting at the present time at least one-sixth part of our countrymen, – are recognized by the laws, and treated by their fellow beings, as brute beasts; – are plundered daily of the fruits of their toil without redress; – really enjoy no constitutional nor legal protection from licentious and murderous outrages upon their persons; – are ruthlessly torn asunder – the tender babe from the arms of its frantic mother – the heart-broken wife from her weeping husband – at the caprice or pleasure of irresponsible tyrants; – and, for the crime of having a dark complexion, suffer the pangs of hunger, the infliction of stripes, the ignominy of brutal servitude. They are kept in heathenish darkness by laws expressly enacted to make their instruction a criminal offence[.]

These are the prominent circumstances in the condition of more than TWO MILLIONS of our people, the proof of which may be found in thousands of indisputable facts, and in the laws of the slaveholding States.

Hence we maintain –

That, in View of the civil and religious privileges of this nation, the guilt of its oppression is unequaled by any other on the face of the earth; and, therefore,

That it is bound to repent instantly, to undo the heavy burden, to break every yoke, and to let the oppressed go free

We further maintain –

That no man has a right to enslave or imbrute his brother – to hold or acknowledge him, for one moment, as a piece of merchandise – to keep back his hire by fraud – or to brutalize his mind by denying him the means of intellectual, social, and moral improvement.

The right to enjoy liberty is inalienable. To invade it, is to usurp the prerogative of Jehovah, Every man has a right to his own body – to the products of his own labor – to the protection of law – and to the common advantages of society. It is piracy to buy or steal a native African, and subject him to servitude. Surely, the sin is as great to enslave an AMERICAN as an AFRICAN.

Therefore we believe and affirm –

That there is no difference, *in principle*, between the African slave trade and American slavery;

That every American citizen, who retains a human being in involuntary bondage, as his property, is, a MANSTEALER.

That the slaves ought instantly to be set free, and brought under the protection of law;

That all those laws which are now in force, admitting the right of slavery, are . . . before God, utterly null and void; being an audacious usurpation of the Divine prerogative, a daring infringement on the law of nature, a base overthrow of the very foundations of the social compact, a complete extinction of all the relations, endearments and obligations of mankind, and a presumptuous transgression of all the holy commandments – and that therefore they ought to be instantly abrogated.

We further believe and affirm –

That all persons of color who possess the qualifications which are demanded of others, ought to be admitted forthwith to the enjoyment of the same privilege, and the exercise of the same prerogatives, as others; and that the paths of preferment, of wealth and of intelligence, should be opened as widely to them as to persons of a white complexion.

We maintain that no compensation should be given to the planters emancipating their slaves – Because it would be a surrender of the great fundamental principle, that man cannot hold property in man;

Because SLAVERY IS A CRIME, AND THEREFORE IT IS NOT AN ARTICLE TO BE SOLD; ...

Because, if compensation is to be given at all, it should be given to the outraged and guiltless slaves, and not to those who have plundered and abused them.

We regard, as delusive, and cruel and dangerous, any scheme of expatriation which pretends to aid, either directly or indirectly, in the emancipation of the slaves, or to be a substitute for the immediate and total abolition of slavery.

We fully and unanimously recognize the sovereignty of each State, to legislate exclusively on the subject of the slavery which is tolerated within its limits. We concede that Congress, *under the present national compact*, has no right to interfere with any of the slave States, in relation to this momentous subject.

But we maintain that Congress has a right, and is solemnly bound, to suppress the domestic slave trade between the several states, and to abolish slavery in those portions of our territory which the Constitution has placed under its jurisdiction.

We also maintain that there are, at the present time, the highest obligations resting upon the people of the free states to remove slavery by moral and political action, as prescribed in the constitution of the United States. They are now living under a pledge of their tremendous physical force, to fasten the galling fetters of tyranny upon the limbs of millions in the southern States; – they authorize the slave owner to vote for three-fifths of this slaves as property, and thus enable him to perpetuate his oppression; – they support a standing army at the south for its protection; – and they seize the slave, who has escaped into their territories, and send him back to be tortured by an enraged masters or a brutal driver.

This relation to slavery is criminal, and full of danger: IT MUST BE BROKEN UP.

These are our views and principles – these, our designs and measures. With entire confidence in the overruling justice of God, we plant ourselves upon the Declaration of our Independence and the truths of Divine Revelation, as upon the EVERLASTING ROCK.

We shall organize Anti-Slavery Societies, if possible, in every city, town and village in our land.

We shall send forth Agents to lift up the voice of remonstrance, of warning, of entreaty and rebuke.

We shall circulate, unsparingly and extensively, anti-slavery tracts and periodicals.

We shall enlist the PULPIT and the PRESS in the cause of the suffering and the dumb.

We shall aim at a purification of the churches from all participation in the guilt of slavery.

We shall encourage the labor of freemen over that of slaves, by giving a preference to their productions; – and

We shall spare no exertions nor means to bring the whole nation to speedy repentance.

Our trust for victory is solely in GOD. We may be personally defeated, but our principles never. TRUTH, JUSTICE, REASON, HUMANITY, must and will gloriously triumph....

Submitting this DECLARATION to the candid examination of the people of this country, and of the friends of liberty all over the world, we hereby affix our signatures to it; – pledging ourselves that, under the guidance and by the help of Almighty God, we will do all that in us lies, consistently with this Declaration of our principles, to overthrow the most execrable system of slavery that has ever been witnessed upon earth – to deliver our land from its deadliest curse – to wipe out the foulest stain which rests upon our national escutcheon – and to secure to the colored population of the United States, all the rights and privileges which may belong to them as men and as Americans – come what may to our persons, our interests, or our reputations – whether we live to witness the triumph of JUSTICE, LIBERTY and HUMANITY, or perish untimely as martyrs in this great, benevolent and holy cause.

Source: *Liberator*, December 14 (1833).

2. Henry Highland Garnet
Address to the Slaves of the US, August 17, 1843

> *During the late 1830s abolitionists began to doubt that the American
> Anti-Slavery Society's tactics could in themselves produce general
> emancipation. Many of them advocated creating an abolitionist political
> party. A radical minority of these political abolitionists contended that slavery
> could never be legal and that therefore slaves might justly escape or rise up
> against their masters. Among those who embraced this view was Henry
> Highland Garnet (1815–82), a former slave who served as pastor to a black*

church in Troy, New York. His Address to the Slaves, *presented on August 17, 1843 to a black convention held in Buffalo, uses black nationalist themes to call on enslaved men to act against a system that destroyed their natural rights, their immortal souls, and their masculinity. Like other radical political abolitionists, Garnet remained ambivalent concerning the use of force. But his call for slave resistance influenced a generation of black leaders, including Frederick Douglass, whose call of black men to arms during the Civil War echoes Garnet.*

Brethren and Fellow Citizens:

Slavery... afflicts and persecutes you with a fierceness which we might not expect to see in the fiends of hell. But still the Almighty Father of Mercies has left to us a glimmering ray of hope, which shines out like a lone star in a cloudy sky. Mankind are becoming wiser, and better – the oppressor's power is fading, and you, every day, are becoming better informed, and more numerous. Your grievances, brethren, are many. We shall not attempt, in this short address, to present to the world, all the dark catalogue of this nation's sins, which have been committed upon an innocent people. Nor is it indeed, necessary, for you feel them from day to day, and all the civilized world look upon them with amazement.

Two hundred and twenty-seven years ago, the first of our injured race were brought to the shores of America. They came not with glad spirits to select their homes, in the New World. They came not with their own consent, to find an unmolested enjoyment of the blessings of this fruitful soil.... They came with broken hearts, from their beloved native land, and were doomed to unrequited toil, and deep degradation. Nor did the evil of their bondage end at their emancipation by death. Succeeding generations inherited their chains, and millions have come from eternity into time, and have returned again to the world of spirits, cursed, and ruined by American Slavery.

[...]

The colonists threw the blame upon England. They said that the mother country entailed the evil upon them, and that they would rid themselves of it if they could. The world thought they were sincere, and the philanthropic pitied them. But time soon tested their sincerity. In a few years, the colonists grew strong and severed themselves from the British Government. Their Independence was declared, and they took their station among the sovereign powers of the earth. The declaration [of independence] was a glorious document. Sages admired it, and the patriotic of every nation reverenced the godlike sentiments which it contained. When the power of Government returned to their hands, did they emancipate the slaves? No; they rather added new links to our chains. Were they ignorant of the principles of

Liberty? Certainly they were not. The sentiments of their revolutionary orators fell in burning eloquence upon their hearts, and with one voice they cried, LIBERTY OR DEATH. O, what a sentence was that! It ran from soul to soul like electric fire, and nerved the arm of thousands to fight in the holy cause of Freedom. Among the diversity of opinions that are entertained in regard to physical resistance, there are but a few found to gainsay that stern declaration. We are among those who do not.

SLAVERY! How much misery is comprehended in that single word.... In every man's mind the good seeds of liberty are planted, and he who brings his fellow down so low, as to make him contented with a condition of slavery, commits the highest crime against God and man. Brethren, your oppressors aim to do this. They endeavor to make you as much like brutes as possible. When they have blinded the eyes of your mind – when they have embittered the sweet waters of life – when they have shut out the light which shines from the word of God – then, and not till then has American slavery done its perfect work.

TO SUCH DEGRADATION IT IS SINFUL IN THE EXTREME FOR YOU TO MAKE VOLUNTARY SUBMISSION. The divine commandments, you are in duty bound to reverence, and obey. If you do not obey them you will surely meet with the displeasure of the Almighty. He requires you to love him supremely, and your neighbor as yourself – to keep the Sabbath day holy – to search the Scriptures – and bring up your children with respect for his laws, and to worship no other God but him. But slavery sets all these at naught, and hurls defiance in the face of Jehovah.... Your condition does not absolve you from your moral obligation. The diabolical injustice by which your liberties are cloven down, NEITHER GOD, NOR ANGELS, OR JUST MEN, COMMAND YOU TO SUFFER FOR A SINGLE MOMENT. THEREFORE IT IS YOUR SOLEMN AND IMPERATIVE DUTY TO USE EVERY MEANS, BOTH MORAL, INTELLECTUAL, AND PHYSICAL, THAT PROMISE SUCCESS....

[...]

Brethren, the time has come when you must act for yourselves. It is an old and true saying, that "if hereditary bondmen would be free, they must themselves strike the blow." You can plead your own cause, and do the work of emancipation better than any others.... The combined powers of Europe have placed their broad seal of disapprobation upon the African slave trade. But in the slave holding parts of the United States, the trade is as brisk as ever. They buy and sell you as though you were brute beasts. The North has done much – her opinion of slavery in the abstract is known. But in regard to the South, we adopt the opinion of the New York Evangelist – "We have advanced so far, that the cause apparently waits for a more effectual door to be thrown open than has been yet." We are about to

point you to that more effectual door. Look around you, and behold the bosoms of your loving wives, heaving with untold agonies! Hear the cries of your poor children! Remember the stripes your fathers bore. Think of the torture and disgrace of our noble mothers. Think of your wretched sisters, loving virtue and purity, as they are driven into concubinage, and are exposed to the unbridled lusts of incarnate devils. Think of the undying glory that hangs around the ancient name of Africa: – and forget not that you are native-born American citizens, and as such, you are justly entitled to all the rights that are granted to the freest. Think how many tears you have poured out upon the soil which you have cultivated with unrequited toil, and enriched with your blood; and then go to your lordly enslavers, and tell them plainly, that YOU ARE DETERMINED TO BE FREE. Appeal to their sense of justice, and tell them that they have no more right to oppress you, than you have to enslave them. Entreat them to remove the grievous burdens which they have imposed upon you, and to remunerate you for your labor. Promise them renewed diligence in the cultivation of the soil, if they will render to you an equivalent for your services. . . . Tell them in language which they cannot misunderstand, of the exceeding sinfulness of slavery, and of a future judgment, and of the righteous retributions of an indignant God. Inform them that all you desire, is FREEDOM, and that nothing else will suffice. Do this, and for ever after cease to toil for the heartless tyrants, who give you no other reward but stripes and abuse. If they then commence the work of death, they, and not you, will be responsible for the consequences. You had far better all die – *die immediately*, than live slaves, and entail your wretchedness upon your posterity. If you would be free in this generation, here is your only hope. However much you and all of us may desire it, there is not much hope of Redemption without the shedding of blood. If you must bleed, let it all come at once – rather, *die freeman, than live to be slaves.*
[. . .]
We do not advise you to attempt a revolution with the sword, because it would be INEXPEDIENT. Your numbers are too small, and moreover the rising spirit of the age and the spirit of the gospel, are opposed to war and bloodshed. But from this moment cease to labor for tyrants who will not remunerate you. Let every slave throughout the land do this, and the days of slavery are numbered. You cannot be more oppressed than you have been – you cannot suffer greater cruelties than you have already. RATHER DIE FREEMEN, THAN LIVE TO BE SLAVES. Remember that you are THREE MILLIONS.

It is in your power so to torment the God-cursed slaveholders, that they will be glad to let you go free. . . . But you are a patient people. You act as though you were made for the special use of these devils. You act as though your daughters were born to pamper the lusts of your masters and overseers. And worse than all, you tamely submit, while your lords tear your wives from your embraces, and defile them before your eyes. In the name of God we ask, are you men? Where is the blood of your fathers? Has it all run out of your veins? Awake, awake; millions of voices are calling you! Your dead fathers speak to you from their graves. Heaven as with a voice of thunder, calls on you to arise from the dust.

Let your motto be RESISTANCE! RESISTANCE! RESISTANCE! – No oppressed people have ever secured their liberty without resistance. What kind of resistance you had better make, you must decide by the circumstances that surround you, and according to the suggestion of expediency. Brethren, adieu. Trust in the living God. Labor for the peace of the human race, and remember that you are three millions.

Source: Henry Highland Garnet, *Walker's Appeal, with a Brief Sketch of His Life and also Garnet's Address to the Slaves of the United States of America* (New York: [Garnet], 1848), 89–96.

3. John C. Calhoun
Address of the Southern Delegates in Congress to their Constituents, January 22, 1849

In 1849 John C. Calhoun (1782–1850) was a US Senator from South Carolina and a former vice president, secretary of war, and secretary of state. He emerged during the 1830s as America's leading defender of slavery and what he called "southern rights." Calhoun was an insightful, logical, and usually calm writer and speaker. But, in the December 1848 address he wrote for forty-seven other distressed southern Congressmen, he makes an emotional appeal designed to encourage unity among white southerners during a national crisis, which he defines as racial as well as sectional. The American victory in the war against Mexico (1846–48) resulted in a huge territorial acquisition in the Southwest, consisting of what had been the Mexican provinces of California and New Mexico. The House of Representatives twice voted to ban slavery from these territories. Calhoun argues that southerners had an inalienable right to bring their slave property into any US territory. He emphasizes what he presents as a long series of northern aggressions on the South. Calhoun contends that, unless the white South united, northern aggression would result in black freedom and ascendancy in that section. Calhoun died prior to the passage of the Compromise of 1850 that attempted to placate the fears he expresses, but his spirit guided his southern successors during the turbulent decade of the 1850s. His address accurately predicts the white southern interpretation of Reconstruction.

We...address you in discharge of what we believe to be a solemn duty, on the most important subject ever presented for your consideration. We allude to the conflict between the two great sections of the Union, growing out of a difference of feeling and opinion in reference to the relation existing between the two races, the European and the African, which inhabit the southern section, and the acts of aggression and encroachment to which it has led.

The conflict commenced not long after the acknowledgment of our independence, and has gradually increased until it has arrayed the great body of the North against the South on this most vital subject. In the progress of this conflict, aggression has followed aggression, and encroachment, until they have reached a point when a regard for your peace and safety will not permit us to remain longer silent. The object of this address is to give you a clear, correct but brief account of the whole series of aggression and encroachments on your rights with a statement of the dangers to which they expose you. Our object in making it is not to cause excitement, but to put you in full possession of all the facts and circumstances necessary to a full and just conception of a deep-seated disease, which threatens great danger to you and the whole body politic. We act on the impression that in a popular government like ours, a true conception of the actual character and state of a disease is indispensable to effecting a cure....

Not to go further back, the difference of opinion and feeling in reference to the relation between the two races, disclosed itself in the Convention that framed the Constitution, and constituted one of the greatest difficulties in forming it. After many efforts, it was overcome by a compromise, which provided in the first place, that representation and direct taxes shall be apportioned among the States according to their respective numbers; and that, in ascertaining the number of each, five slaves shall be estimated as three free persons. In the next, that slaves escaping into States where slavery does not exist, shall not be discharged from servitude, but shall be delivered up on claim of the party to whom their labor or service is due. In the third place, that Congress shall not prohibit the importation of slaves before the year 1808; but a tax not exceeding ten dollars may be imposed on each imported. And finally, that no capitation or direct tax shall he laid, but in proportion to federal numbers; and that no amendment of the Constitution, prior to 1808, shall affect this provision, nor that relating to the importation of slaves.

So satisfactory were these provisions, that the second, relating to the delivering up of fugitive slaves, was adopted unanimously, and all the rest, except the third, relative to the importation of slaves until 1808, with almost equal unanimity. They recognize the existence of slavery, and make a specific provision for its protection where it was supposed to be the most exposed. They go further, and incorporate it, as an important element, in determining the relative weight of the several States in the Government of the Union, and the respective burden they should bear in laying capitation and direct taxes. It was well understood at the time, that without them the Constitution would not have been adopted by the Southern States, and of course that they constituted elements so essential to the system that it never would have existed without them. The Northern States, knowing all this, ratified the Constitution, thereby pledging their faith, in the most solemn manner, sacredly to observe them. How that faith has been kept and that pledge redeemed we shall next proceed to show.

With few exceptions of no great importance, the South had no cause to complain prior to the year 1819 – a year, it is to be feared, destined to mark a train of events, bringing with them many, and great, and fatal disasters, on the country and its institutions. With it commenced the agitating debate on the question of the admission of Missouri into the Union. We shall pass by for the present this question, others of the same kind, directly growing out of it, and shall proceed to consider the effects of that spirit of discord, which it roused up between the two sections. It first disclosed itself in the North, by hostility to that portion of the Constitution which provides for the delivering up of fugitive slaves. In its progress it led to the adoption of hostile acts, intended to render it of non-effect, and with so much SUCCESS that it may be regarded now as practically expunged from the Constitution....

[...]

The citizens of the South, in their attempt to recover their slaves, now meet, instead of aid and co-operation, resistance in every form; resistance from hostile acts of legislation, intended to baffle and defeat their claims by all sorts of devices, and by interposing every description of impediment – resistance from judges and magistrates – and finally, when all these fail, from mobs, composed of whites and blacks, which, by threats or force, rescue the fugitive slave from the possession of his rightful owner. The attempt to recover a slave, in most of Northern States, cannot now be made without the hazard of insult, heavy pecuniary loss, imprisonment, and even of life itself....

But a provision of the Constitution may be violated indirectly as well as directly; by doing an act in its nature inconsistent with that which is enjoined to be done. Of the form of violation, there is a striking instance connected with the provision under consideration. We allude to secret combinations which are believed to exist in many of the Northern States, whose object is to entice, decoy, entrap, inveigle, and seduce slaves to escape from their owners, and to pass them secretly and rapidly, by means organized for the purpose, into Canada, where they will be beyond the reach of the provision....

[...]

There remains to be noticed another class of aggressive acts of a kindred character, but which instead of striking at an express and specific provision of the Constitution, aims directly at destroying the relation between the two races at the South, by means subversive in their tendency of one of the ends for which the Constitution was established. We refer to the systematic agitation of the question by the Abolitionists, which, commencing about 1835, is still continued in all possible forms. Their avowed intention is to bring about a state of things that will force emancipation on the South. To unite the North in fixed hostility to slavery in the South, and to excite discontent among the slaves with their condition, are among the means employed to effect it. With a view to bring about the former, every means are resorted to in order to render the South, and the relation between the two races there, odious and hateful to the North.... The agitation of the subject of abolition in Congress, and the employment of emissaries are relied on to excite discontent among the slaves.... We regard both object and means to be aggressive and dangerous to the rights of the South, and subversive, as stated, of one of the ends for which the Constitution was established.... What gives a deeper shade to the whole affair, is the fact, that one of the means to effect their object, that of exciting discontent among our slaves, tends directly to subvert what its preamble declares to be one of the ends for which the Constitution was ordained and established: "to ensure domestic tranquility," and that in the only way in which domestic tranquility is likely ever to be disturbed in the South. Certain it is, that an agitation so systematic – having such an object in view, and sought to be carried into execution by such means – would, between independent nations, constitute just cause of remonstrance by the party against which the aggression was directed, and if not heeded, an appeal to arms for redress....

We now return to the question of the admission of Missouri to the Union, and shall proceed to give a brief sketch of the occurrences connected with it, and the consequences to which it has directly led. In the latter part of 1819, the then territory of Missouri applied to Congress, in the usual form, for leave to form a State Constitution and Government, in order to be admitted into the Union. A bill was reported for the purpose, with the usual provisions in such cases. Amendments were offered [by a northern congressman], having for their object to make it a condition for her admission, that her Constitution should have a provision to prohibit slavery. This brought on the agitating debate, which, with the effects that followed, has done so much to alienate the South and North, and endanger our political institutions. Those who objected to the amendments, rested their opposition on the high grounds of the right of self-government. . . .

They claimed that Congress has no right to add this condition, and that to assume it would be tantamount to the assumption of the right to make its entire Constitution and Government; as no limitation could be imposed, as to the extent of the right, if it be admitted that it exists at all. Those who supported the amendment denied these grounds, and claimed the right of Congress to impose, at discretion, what conditions it pleased. In this agitating debate, the two sections stood arrayed against each other; the South in favor of the bill without amendment, and the North opposed to it without it. . . . A Compromise (as it was called) was offered, based on the terms, that the North should cease to oppose the admission of Missouri on the grounds for which the South contended, and that the provisions of the Ordinance of 1787, for the government of the Northwestern Territory, should be applied to all the territory acquired by the United States from France under the treaty of Louisiana lying North of 36° 30′ except the portion lying in the State of Missouri. The Northern members embraced it; and although not originating with them, adopted it as their own. It was forced through Congress by the almost united votes of the North, against a minority consisting almost entirely of members from the Southern States.

Such was the termination of this, the first conflict, under the Constitution between the two sections, in reference to slavery in connection with the territories. Many hailed it as a permanent and final adjustment that would prevent the recurrence of similar conflicts; but others, less sanguine, took the opposite and more gloomy view, regarding it as the precursor as a train of events which might rend the Union asunder, and prostrate our political system. . . .

For many years the subject of slavery in reference to the territories ceased to agitate the country. Indications, however, connected with the question of annexing Texas, showed clearly that it was ready to break out again, with redoubled violence, on some future occasion. The difference in the case of Texas was adjusted by extending the Missouri compromise line of 36° 30′, from its terminus, on the western boundary of the Louisiana purchase, to the western boundary of Texas. The agitation again ceased for a short period.

The war with Mexico soon followed, and that terminated in the acquisition of New Mexico and Upper California, embracing an area equal to about one half of the entire valley of the Mississippi. If to this we add the portion of Oregon acknowledged to be ours by the recent treaty with England, our whole territory on the Pacific and west of the Rocky Mountains will be found to be in extent but little less than that vast valley. The near prospect of so great an addition rekindled the excitement between the North and South in reference to slavery in its connection with the territories, which has become, since those on the Pacific were acquired, more universal and intense than ever.

The effects have been to widen the difference between the two sections, and give a more determined and hostile character to their conflict. The North no longer respects the Missouri compromise line, although adopted by their almost unanimous vote. Instead of compromise, they avow that their determination is to exclude slavery from all the territories of the United States, acquired, or to be acquired; and, of course, to prevent the citizens of the Southern States from emigrating with their property in slaves into any of them. Their object, they allege, is to prevent the extension of slavery, and ours to extend it, thus making the issue between them and us to be the naked question, shall slavery be extended or not?... What we propose in this connection is, to make a few remarks on what the North alleges, erroneously, to be the issue between us and them.

So far from maintaining the doctrine, which the issue implies, we hold that the Federal Government has no right to extend or restrict slavery, no more than to establish or abolish it; nor has it any right whatever to distinguish between the domestic institutions of one State, or section, and another, in order to favor one and discourage the other. As the federal representative of each and all the States, it is bound to deal out, within the sphere of its powers, equal and exact justice and favor to all. To act otherwise, to undertake to discriminate between the domestic institutions of one and another, would be to act in total subversion of the end for which it was established – to be the common protection and guardian of all. Entertaining these opinions, we ask not, as the North alleges we do, for the extension of slavery. That would make a discrimination in our favor, as unjust and unconstitutional as the discrimination they ask against us in their favor. It is not for them, nor for the Federal Government to determine, whether our domestic institution is good or bad; or whether it should be repressed or preserved. It belongs to us, and us only, to decide such questions. What then we do insist on, is, not to extend slavery, but that we shall not be prohibited from immigrating with our property, into the Territories of the United States, because we are slaveholders....

We rest our claim, not only on the high grounds above stated, but also on the solid foundation of right, justice, and equality. The territories immediately in controversy – New Mexico and California – were acquired by the common sacrifice and efforts of all the States, towards which the South contributed far more than her full share of men, to say nothing of money, and is, of course, on every principle of right, justice, fairness and equality, entitled to participate fully in the benefits to be derived from their acquisition.... To deprive, then, the Southern States and their citizens of their full share in territories declared to belong to them, in common with the other States, would be in derogation of the equality belonging to them as members of a Federal Union, and sink them, from being equals, into a subordinate and dependent condition. Such are the solid and impregnable grounds on which we rest our demand to an equal participation in the territories.

But as solid and impregnable as they are in the eyes of justice and reason, they oppose a feeble resistance to a majority, determined to engross the whole. . . .

Although Congress has been in session but little more than one month, a greater number of measures of an aggressive character have been introduced, and they are more aggravated and dangerous, than have been for years before. And what clearly discloses whence they take their origin, is the fact, that they all relate to the territorial aspect of the subject of slavery, or some other of a nature and character intimately connected with it.

The first of this series of aggressions is a resolution introduced by a member from Massachusetts, the object of which is to repeal all acts which recognize the existence of slavery, or authorize the selling or disposing of slaves in this District. On the question of leave to bring in a bill, the votes stood 69 for and 82 against leave. The next was a resolution offered by a member from Ohio, instructing the Committee on Territories to report forthwith bills for excluding slavery from California and New Mexico. It passed by a vote of 107 to 80. That was followed by a bill introduced by another member from Ohio, to take the votes of the inhabitants of this District, on the question whether slavery within its limits should be abolished.

The bill provided, according to the admission of the mover, that free negroes and slaves should vote. On the question to lay the bill on the table, the votes stood, for 106, against 79. To this succeeded the resolution of a member from New York, in the following words: "Whereas the traffic now prosecuted in this metropolis of the Republic in human beings, as chattels, is contrary to natural justice and the fundamental principles of our political system, and is notoriously a reproach to our country, throughout Christendom, and a serious hindrance to the progress of republican liberty among the nations of the earth. Therefore,

"*Resolved*, That the Committee for the District of Columbia be instructed to report a bill, as soon as practicable, prohibiting the slave trade in said District."

On the question of adopting the resolution, the votes stood 98 for, and 88 against. He was followed by a member from Illinois, who offered a resolution for abolishing slavery in the Territories, and all places where Congress has exclusive powers of legislation, that is, in all forts, magazines, arsenals, dockyards, and other needful buildings, purchased by Congress with the consent of the Legislature of the State.

This resolution was passed over under the rules of the House without being put to vote. The votes in favor of all these measures were confined to the members from the Northern States. True, there are some patriotic members from that section who voted against all of them, and whose high sense of justice is duly appreciated; who in the progress of the aggressions upon the South have, by their votes, sustained the guarantees of the Constitution, and of whom we regret to say many have been sacrificed at home by their patriotic course.

We have now brought to a close a narrative of the series of acts of aggression and encroachment, connected with the subject of this address, including those that are consummated and those still in progress. . . . It may even be made a serious question, whether the encroachments already made, without the aid of any other, would not, if permitted to operate unchecked, end in emancipation, and that at no distant day. But be that as it may, it hardly admits of a doubt that, if the aggressions already commenced in the House, and now in progress, should be consummated, such in the end would certainly be the consequence.

[. . .]

But be that as it may, it is certain, if emancipation did not follow, as a matter of course, the final act in the States would not be long delayed. The want of constitutional power would oppose a feeble resistance. The great body of the North is united against our peculiar institution. Many believe it to be sinful, and the residue, with inconsiderable exceptions, believe it to be wrong. Such being the case, it would indicate a very superficial knowledge of human nature, to think that, after aiming at abolition, systematically, for so many years, and pursuing it with such unscrupulous disregard of law and Constitution, that the fanatics who have led the way and forced the great body of the North to follow them, would, when the finishing stroke only remained to be given, voluntarily suspend it, or permit any constitutional scruples or considerations of justice to arrest it.

[. . .]

To destroy the existing relation between the free and servile races at the South would lead to consequences unparalleled in history. They cannot be separated, and cannot live together in peace, or harmony, or to their mutual advantage, except in their present relation. Under any other, wretchedness, and misery, and desolation would overspread the whole South. . . .

Emancipation would take place with us.... through the agency of the Federal Government, controlled by the dominant power of the Northern States of the Confederacy, against the resistance and struggle of the Southern. It can then only be effected by the prostration of the white race; and that would necessarily engender the bitterest feelings of hostility between them and the North. But the reverse would be the case between the blacks of the South and the people of the North. Owing their emancipation to them, they would regard them as friends, guardians, and patrons, and centre, accordingly, all their sympathy in them. The people of the North would not fail to reciprocate and to favor them, instead of the whites. Under the influence of such feelings, and impelled by fanaticism and love of power, they would not stop at emancipation. Another step would be taken – to raise them to a political and social equality with their former owners, by giving them the right of voting and holding public offices under the Federal Government. We see the first step toward it in the bill already alluded to – to vest the free blacks and slaves with the right to vote on the question of emancipation in this District. But when once raised to an equality, they would become the fast political associates of the North, acting and voting with them on all questions, and by this political union between them, holding the white race at the South in complete subjection. The blacks, and the profligate whites that might unite with them, would become the principal recipients of federal offices and patronage, and would, in consequence, be raised above the whites of the South in the political and social scale. We would, in a word, change conditions with them – a degradation greater than has ever yet fallen to the lot of a free and enlightened people, and one from which we could not escape, should emancipation take place (which it certainly will if not prevented), but by fleeing the homes of ourselves and ancestors, and by abandoning our country to our former slaves, to become the permanent abode of disorder, anarchy, poverty, misery, and wretchedness.

With such a prospect before us, the gravest and most solemn question that ever claimed the attention of a people is presented for your consideration: What is to be done to prevent it? It is a question belonging to you to decide. All we propose is, to give you our opinion.

... If you become united, and prove yourselves in earnest, the North will be brought to a pause, and to a calculation of consequences; and that may lead to a change of measures, and the adoption of a course of policy that may quietly and peaceably terminate this long conflict between the two sections. If it should not, nothing would remain for you but to stand up immovably in defense of rights, involving your all – your property, prosperity, equality, liberty, and safety.

As the assailed, you would stand justified by all laws, human and divine, in repelling a blow so dangerous, without looking to consequences, and to resort to all means necessary for that purpose. Your assailants, and not you, would be responsible for consequences. . . .

Source: Richard K. Cralle, ed. *The Works of John C. Calhoun*, 6 vols. (New York: D. Appleton, 1874–88), 6:290–313.

4. William H. Seward
Irrepressible Conflict, October 25, 1858

The sectional crisis, to which Calhoun and his southern colleagues contributed, ended when more moderate congressmen succeeded in passing the Compromise of 1850. It banned slavery in the new state of California, allowed settlers to decide whether or not slavery would be permitted in New Mexico and Utah territories, upheld slavery in the District of Columbia, and initiated a stronger fugitive slave law. Nevertheless the controversy between the North and South over slavery reopened with greater intensity in May 1854 when Congress passed the Kansas–Nebraska Act. This act repealed the Missouri Compromise and allowed settlers in territories north of the 30° 30' to decide the issue of slavery. As a result, in 1855 a civil war between slave-state and free-state settlers broke out in Kansas Territory. That same year the Republican Party, a sectional northern party opposed to the extension of slavery into the territories and to southern control of the United States government, organized. William H. Seward (1801–72), a United States Senator from New York, emerged as a leading spokesman for the new party. His "irrepressible conflict speech," delivered before an enthusiastic audience in Rochester, New York, in November 1858, provides a mirror image to Calhoun's interpretation of the sectional conflict. Seward emphasizes the inherent incompatibility of wage and slave labor. Compromise, Seward asserts, was impossible between slavery and freedom, because aggressive slaveholders threatened the North. He favors peaceful political action through the Republican Party to end slavery.

. . . Our country is a theatre, which exhibits, in full operation, two radically different political systems; the one resting on the basis of servile or slave labor, the other on the basis of voluntary labor of freemen. The laborers who are enslaved are all negroes, or persons more or less purely of African derivation. But this is only accidental. The principle of the system is, that labor in every society, by whomsoever performed, is necessarily unintellectual, groveling and base; and that the laborer, equally for his own good and for the welfare of the state, ought to be enslaved. The white laboring man, whether native or foreigner, is not enslaved, only because he cannot, as yet, be reduced to bondage.

... This African slave system is one which, in its origin and in its growth, has been altogether foreign from the habits of the races which colonized these states, and established civilization here. It was introduced on this new continent as an engine of conquest, and for the establishment of monarchical power, by the Portuguese and the Spaniards, and was rapidly extended by them all over South America, Central America, Louisiana and Mexico. Its legitimate fruits are seen in the poverty, imbecility, and anarchy, which now pervade all Portuguese and Spanish America. The free-labor system is of German extraction, and it was established in our country by emigrants from Sweden, Holland, Germany, Great Britain and Ireland.

We justly ascribe to its influences the strength, wealth, greatness, intelligence, and freedom, which the whole American people now enjoy. One of the chief elements of the value of human life is freedom in the pursuit of happiness. The slave system is not only intolerable, unjust, and inhuman, towards the laborer, whom, only because he is a laborer, it loads down with chains and converts into merchandise, but is scarcely less severe upon the freeman, to whom, only because he is a laborer from necessity, it denies facilities for employment, and whom it expels from the community because it cannot enslave and convert him into merchandise also. It is necessarily improvident and ruinous, because, as a general truth, communities prosper and flourish or droop and decline in just the degree that they practice or neglect to practice the primary duties of justice and humanity. The free-labor system conforms to the divine law of equality, which is written in the hearts and consciences of man, and therefore is always and everywhere beneficent.

The slave system is one of constant danger, distrust, suspicion, and watchfulness. It debases those whose toil alone can produce wealth and resources for defense, to the lowest degree of which human nature is capable, to guard against mutiny and insurrection, and thus wastes energies which otherwise might be employed in national development and aggrandizement.

The free-labor system educates all alike, and by opening all the fields of industrial employment, and all the departments of authority, to the unchecked and equal rivalry of all classes of men, at once secures universal contentment, and brings into the highest possible activity all the physical, moral and social energies of the whole state. In states where the slave system prevails, the masters, directly or indirectly, secure all political power, and constitute a ruling aristocracy. In states where the free-labor system prevails, universal suffrage necessarily obtains, and the state inevitably becomes, sooner or later, a republic or democracy.

. . . The two systems are at once perceived to be incongruous. But they are more than incongruous – they are incompatible. They never have permanently existed together in one country, and they never can. . . . Slavery . . . existed in every state in Europe. Free labor has supplanted it everywhere except in Russia and Turkey. State necessities developed in modern times, are now obliging even those two nations to encourage and employ free labor; and already, despotic as they are, we find them engaged in abolishing slavery. In the United States, slavery came into collision with free labor at the close of the last century, and fell before it in New England, New York, New Jersey and Pennsylvania, but triumphed over it effectually, and excluded it for a period yet undetermined, from Virginia, the Carolinas and Georgia. Indeed, so incompatible are the two systems, that every new state which is organized within our ever extending domain makes its first political act a choice of the one and the exclusion of the other, even at the cost of civil war, if necessary. . . .

Hitherto, the two systems have existed in different states, but side by side within the American Union. This has happened because the Union is a confederation of states. But in another aspect the United States constitute only one nation. Increase of population, which is filling the states out to their very borders, together with a new and extended network of railroads and other avenues, and an internal commerce which daily becomes more intimate, is rapidly bringing the states into a higher and more perfect social unity or consolidation. Thus, these antagonistic systems are continually coming into closer contact, and collision results.

Shall I tell you what this collision means? They who think that it is accidental, unnecessary, the work of interested or fanatical agitators, and therefore ephemeral, mistake the case altogether. It is an irrepressible conflict between opposing and enduring forces, and it means that the United States must and will, sooner or later, become either entirely a slaveholding nation, or entirely a free-labor nation. Either the cotton and rice-fields of South Carolina and the sugar plantations of Louisiana will ultimately be tilled by free labor, and Charleston and New Orleans become marts for legitimate merchandise alone, or else the rye-fields and wheat-fields of Massachusetts and New York must again be surrendered by their farmers to slave culture and to the production of slaves, and Boston and New York become once more markets for trade in the bodies and souls of men. It is the failure to apprehend this great truth that induces so many unsuccessful attempts at final compromise between the slave and free states, and it is the existence of this great fact that renders all such pretended compromises, when made, vain and ephemeral. Startling as this saying may appear to you, fellow citizens, it is by no means an original . . . one. Our forefathers knew it to be true, and unanimously acted upon it when they framed the constitution of the United

States. They regarded the existence of the servile system in so many of the states with sorrow and shame, which they openly confessed, and they looked upon the collision between them, which was then just revealing itself, and which we are now accustomed to deplore, with favor and hope. They knew that either the one or the other system must exclusively prevail.

Unlike too many of those who in modern time invoke their authority, they had a choice between the two. They preferred the system of free labor, and they determined to organize the government, and so to direct its activity, that that system should surely and certainly prevail. For this purpose, and no other, they based the whole structure of government broadly on the principle that all men are created equal, and therefore free – little dreaming that, within the short period of one hundred years, their descendants would bear to be told by any orator, however popular, that the utterance of that principle was merely a rhetorical rhapsody; or by any judge, however venerated, that it was attended by mental reservations, which rendered it hypocritical and false, By the ordinance of 1787, they dedicated all of the national domain not yet polluted by slavery to free labor immediately, thenceforth and forever; while by the new constitution and laws they invited foreign free labor from all lands under the sun, and interdicted the import-ation of African slave labor, at all times, in all places, and under all circumstances whatsoever. It is true that they necessarily and wisely modi-fied this policy of freedom, by leaving it to the several states, affected as they were by differing circumstances, to abolish slavery in their own way and at their own pleasure, instead of confiding that duty to congress; and that they secured to the slave states, while yet retaining the system of slavery, a three-fifths representation of slaves in the federal government, until they should find themselves able to relinquish it with safety. But the very nature of these modifications fortifies my position that the fathers knew that the two systems could not endure within the Union, and expected that within a short period slavery would disappear forever. Moreover, in order that these modifications might not altogether defeat their grand design of a republic maintaining universal equality, they provided that two-thirds of the states might amend the constitution.

It remains to say on this point only one word, to guard against misap-prehension. . . . While I do confidently believe and hope that my country will yet become a land of universal freedom, I do not expect that it will be made so otherwise than through the action of the several states cooperating with the federal government, and all acting in strict conformity with their respective constitutions.

The strife and contentions concerning slavery, which gently-disposed persons so habitually deprecate, are nothing more than the ripening of the conflict which the fathers themselves not only thus regarded with favor, but which they may be said to have instituted.

It is not to be denied, however, that thus far the course of that contest has not been according to their humane anticipations and wishes. In the field of federal politics, slavery, deriving unlooked-for advantages from commercial changes, and energies unforeseen from the facilities of combination between members of the slaveholding class and between that class and other property classes, early rallied, and has at length made a stand, not merely to retain its original defensive position, but to extend its sway throughout the whole Union.... The plan of operation is this: By continued appliances of patronage and threats of disunion, they will keep a majority favorable to these designs in the senate, where each state has an equal representation. Through that majority they will defeat, as they best can, the admission of free states and secure the admission of slave states. Under the protection of the judiciary, they will...carry slavery into all the territories of the United States now existing and hereafter to be organized. By the action of the president and the senate, using the treaty-making power, they will annex foreign slaveholding states. In a favorable conjecture they will induce congress to repeal the act of 1808, which prohibits the foreign slave trade, and so they will import from Africa, at the cost of only twenty dollars a head, slaves enough to fill up the interior of the continent. Thus relatively increasing the number of slave states, they will allow no amendment to the constitution prejudicial to their interest.... When the free states shall be sufficiently demoralized to tolerate these designs, they reasonably conclude that slavery will be accepted by those states themselves....

Source: William H. Seward, Speech in Rochester, New York, October 25, 1858, in George Baker, ed., *The Works of William H. Seward*, 5 vols. (New York: Redfield, 1853–84), 4:289–302.

5. *Ballou's Pictorial Drawing-Room Companion*
Slaves Picking Cotton, 1858

In the Old South enslaved African Americans performed many tasks. Not only did major crops vary from region to region, slaves worked in mining, manufacturing, forestry, and other nonagricultural pursuits. Yet most slaves cultivated and harvested cotton on large plantations in the Deep South. This 1858 wood engraving, published in Boston by Ballou's Pictorial Drawing-Room Companion, portrays black men, women, and children harvesting cotton on a Georgia Plantation. Maturin M. Ballou, who edited the Companion from 1854 to 1859, was an inveterate traveler and may have observed this scene. It testifies to the large size of cotton fields, to the labor required of slaves from childhood onward, and the type of clothing slaves wore. In its rendition of black men, the drawing reflects and appeals to a popular fantasy among white Americans, holding that African Americans were content and physically unthreatening. Nevertheless all Americans knew that slaves escaped and at times revolted. Moreover northward slave escape and fear among white southerners that abolitionists encouraged slave revolt, helped lead to secession.

PICKING COTTON ON A GEORGIA PLANTATION.

Figure 1   Ballou's Pictorial Drawing-Room Companion, Slaves Picking Cotton, 1858
Source: *Ballou's Pictorial* 14 (1858): 49. Courtesy of Library of Congress.

6. John Brown
Last Speech, November 2, 1859

From the time of Henry Highland Garnet's Address to the Slaves in 1843, abolitionists grew increasingly willing to advocate violence, especially in regard to the right of slaves to escape and revolt. John Brown (1800–59) had, since his boyhood in Connecticut, helped fugitive slaves. He continued to do so in eastern Ohio and western Pennsylvania. Intensely religious, sympathetic to African Americans, and the patriarch of a large family, Brown became the best known of the free-state captains battling in Kansas Territory against the proslavery

"Border Ruffians" from Missouri. At Potawatomi Creek in May 1856, he and two of his sons executed five proslavery men. Brown had long contemplated leading an armed band into the South to spark a slave revolt. He shocked the nation when on October 16, 1859 he and an interracial band of twenty-one men captured the United States arsenal at Harpers Ferry, Virginia. Overwhelmed, wounded, captured, and convicted of treason, Brown displayed profound eloquence prior to his execution on December 2. His actions helped push the South toward secession. His words in his brief address to the court that had just sentenced him to death helped inspire northerners to fight against slavery.

I have, may it please the Court, a few words to say.

In the first place, I deny everything but what I have all along admitted – the design on my part to free the slaves. I intended certainly to have made a clean thing of that matter, as I did last winter, when I went into Missouri and there took slaves without the snapping of a gun on either side, moved them through the country, and finally left them in Canada. I designed to have done the same thing again, on a larger scale. That was all I intended. I never did intend murder, or treason, or the destruction of property, or to excite or incite slaves to rebellion, or to make insurrection.

I have another objection; and that is, it is unjust that I should suffer such a penalty. Had I interfered in the manner which I admit, and which I admit has been fairly proved (for I admire the truthfulness and candor of the greater portion of the witnesses who have testified in this case), – had I so interfered in behalf of the rich, the powerful, the intelligent, the so-called great, or in behalf of any of their friends, – either father, mother, brother, sister, wife, or children, or any of that class – and suffered and sacrificed what I have in this interference, it would have been all right; and every man in this court would have deemed it an act worthy of reward rather than punishment.

This court acknowledges, as I suppose, the validity of the law of God. I see a book kissed here which I suppose to be the Bible, or at least the New Testament. That teaches me that all things whatsoever I would that men should do to me, I should do even so to them. It teaches me, further, to "remember them that are in bonds, as bound with them," I endeavored to act up to that instruction. I say, I am yet too young to understand that God is any respecter of persons. I believe that to have interfered as I have done – as I have always freely admitted I have done – in behalf of His despised poor, was not wrong but right. Now, if it is deemed necessary that I should forfeit my life for the furtherance of the ends of justice, and mingle my blood further with the blood of my children and with the blood of millions in this slave country whose rights are disregarded by wicked, cruel, and unjust enactments – I submit; so let it be done!

Let me say one word further.

I feel entirely satisfied with the treatment I have received in my trial. Considering all the circumstances, it has been more generous than I expected. But I feel no consciousness of my guilt. I have stated from the first what was my intention, and what was not. I never had any design against the life of any person, nor any disposition to commit treason, or excite slaves to rebel, or make any general insurrection. I never encouraged any man to do so, but always discouraged any idea of that kind.

Let me say, also, a word in regard to the statements made by some of those connected with me. I hear it has been stated by some of them that I induced them to join me. But the contrary is true. I do not say this to injure them, but as regretting their weakness. There is not one of them but joined me of his own accord, and the greater part of them at their own expense. A number of them I never saw, and never had a word of conversation with, till the day they came to me; and that was for the purpose I have stated.

Now I have done.

Source: John Davison Lawson, ed., *American State Trials: A Collection of the Important and Interesting Criminal Trials, which have taken place in the United States from the Beginning of our Government to the Present Day*, 17 vols. (St. Louis: Thomas Law Book Co., 1914–36), 6:800–2.

Discussion Questions

1   The American Anti-Slavery Society, Henry Highland Garnet, and John Brown all criticized slavery and called for action against it. In what ways were their views similar? In what ways did they differ?
2   The woodcut published in *Ballou's Pictorial Drawing-Room Companion* provides an idyllic view of slaves picking cotton. In what respects is this a misleading portrait?
3   How do John C. Calhoun and William H. Seward differ in their interpretation of the sectional conflict between the North and South?
4   Based on your reading of the documents in this chapter, do you believe that the Civil War could have been avoided?

Chapter 2   Disunion to War

1. South Carolina

*Declaration of the Immediate Causes which Induce and Justify the Secession
of South Carolina from the Federal Union, December 20, 1860*

> *The great majority of white South Carolinians took pride in their state's
> leadership in the proslavery cause. Although the center of cotton production
> had moved westward, slaveholders still dominated the state economically,
> culturally, and politically. South Carolina also had a black majority, which
> led all white residents to insist that the restrictions imposed on African
> Americans by slavery remain in place. South Carolina had threatened to
> secede from the Union in 1850 and in 1856. In 1860 it warned that if a
> Republican president were elected it would carry out these threats in order
> to protect its security, interests, and rights. As soon as news of Abraham
> Lincoln's election reached South Carolina, its legislature called a secession
> convention, which on December 20, 1860 repealed the state's ratification
> of the US Constitution and declared it to be an independent republic. By
> February 1, 1861, the six other states of the Deep South had joined South
> Carolina in leaving the Union. By February 9, they had formed the
> Confederate States of America.*

The people of the State of South Carolina, in Convention assembled, on
the 26th day of April, AD, 1852, declared that the frequent violations of the
Constitution of the United States, by the Federal Government, and its
encroachments upon the reserved rights of the States, fully justified this
State in then withdrawing from the Federal Union; but in deference to the
opinions and wishes of the other slaveholding States, she forbore at that

time to exercise this right. Since that time, these encroachments have continued to increase, and further forbearance ceases to be a virtue.

And now the State of South Carolina having resumed her separate and equal place among nations, deems it due to herself, to the remaining United States of America, and to the nations of the world, that she should declare the immediate causes which have led to this act.

[...]

By [the United States] Constitution, certain duties were imposed upon the several States, and the exercise of certain of their powers was restrained, which necessarily implied their continued existence as sovereign States. But to remove all doubt, an amendment was added, which declared that the powers not delegated to the United States by the Constitution, nor prohibited by it to the States, are reserved to the States, respectively, or to the people. On the 23d May, 1788, South Carolina, by a Convention of her People, passed an Ordinance assenting to this Constitution, and afterwards altered her own Constitution, to conform herself to the obligations she had undertaken.

Thus was established, by compact between the States, a Government with refined objects and powers, limited to the express words of the grant. This limitation left the whole remaining mass of power subject to the clause reserving it to the States or to the people, and rendered unnecessary any specification of reserved rights.

We hold that the Government thus established is subject to the two great principles asserted in the Declaration of Independence; and we hold further, that the mode of its formation subjects it to a third fundamental principle, namely: the law of compact. We maintain that in every compact between two or more parties, the obligation is mutual; that the failure of one of the contracting parties to perform a material part of the agreement, entirely releases the obligation of the other; and that where no arbiter is provided, each party is remitted to his own judgment to determine the fact of failure, with all its consequences.

In the present case, that fact is established with certainty. We assert that fourteen of the States have deliberately refused, for years past, to fulfill their constitutional obligations, and we refer to their own Statutes for the proof.

The Constitution of the United States, in its fourth Article, provides as follows:

> "No person held to service or labor in one State, under the laws thereof, escaping into another, shall, in consequence of any law or regulation therein, be discharged from such service or labor, but shall he delivered up, on claim of the party to whom such service or labor may be due."

This stipulation was so material to the compact, that without it that compact would not have been made. The greater number of the contracting parties held slaves, and they had previously evinced their estimate of the value of such a stipulation by making it a condition in the Ordinance for the government of the territory ceded by Virginia, which now composes the States north of the Ohio River.

The same article of the Constitution stipulates also for rendition by the several States of fugitives from justice from the other States.

The General Government, as the common agent, passed laws to carry into effect these stipulations of the States. For many years these laws were executed. But an increasing hostility on the part of the non-slaveholding States to the institution of slavery, has led to a disregard of their obligations, and the laws of the General Government have ceased to effect the objects of the Constitution. The States of Maine, New Hampshire, Vermont, Massachusetts, Connecticut, Rhode Island, New York, Pennsylvania, Illinois, Indiana, Michigan, Wisconsin and Iowa, have enacted laws which either nullify the Acts of Congress or render useless any attempt to execute them. In many of these States the fugitive is discharged from service or labor claimed, and in none of them has the State Government complied with the stipulation made in the Constitution. The State of New Jersey, at an early day, passed a law in conformity with her constitutional obligation; but the current of anti-slavery feeling has led her more recently to enact laws which render inoperative the remedies provided by her own law and by the laws of Congress. In the State of New York even the right of transit for a slave has been denied by her tribunals; and the States of Ohio and Iowa have refused to surrender to justice fugitives charged with murder, and with inciting servile insurrection in the State of Virginia. Thus the constituted compact has been deliberately broken and disregarded by the non-slaveholding States, and the consequence follows that South Carolina is released from her obligation.

The ends for which this Constitution was framed are declared by itself to be "to form a more perfect union, establish justice, insure domestic tranquility, provide for the common defence, promote the general welfare, and secure the blessings of liberty to ourselves and our posterity."

These ends it endeavored to accomplish by a Federal Government, in which each State was recognized as an equal, and had separate control over its own institutions. The right of property in slaves was recognized by giving to free persons distinct political rights, by giving them the right to represent, and burthening them with direct taxes for three-fifths of their slaves; by authorizing the importation of slaves for twenty years; and by stipulating for the rendition of fugitives from labor.

We affirm that these ends for which this Government was instituted have been defeated, and the Government itself has been made destructive of them by the action of the non-slaveholding States. Those States have assumed the right of deciding upon the propriety of our domestic institutions; and have denied the rights of property established in fifteen of the States and recognized by the Constitution; they have denounced as sinful the institution of slavery; they have permitted open establishment among them of societies, whose avowed object is to disturb the peace and to eloign [carry away] property of the citizens of other States. They have encouraged and assisted thousands of our slaves to leave their homes; and those who remain, have been incited by emissaries, books and pictures to servile insurrection.

For twenty-five years this agitation has been steadily increasing, until it has now secured to its aid the power of the common Government. Observing the forms of the Constitution, a sectional party has found within that Article establishing the Executive Department, the means of subverting the Constitution itself. A geographical line has been drawn across the Union, and all the States north of that line have united in the election of a man to the high office of President of the United States, whose opinions and purposes are hostile to slavery. He is to be entrusted with the administration of the common Government, because he has declared that "Government cannot endure permanently half slave, half free," and that the public mind must rest in the belief that slavery is in the course of ultimate extinction.

This sectional combination for the subversion of the Constitution, has been aided in some of the States by elevating to citizenship, persons who, by the supreme law of the land, are incapable of becoming citizens; and their votes have been used to inaugurate a new policy, hostile to the South, and destructive of its peace and safety.

On the 4th of March next, this party will take possession of the Government. It has announced that the South shall be excluded from the common territory, that the judicial tribunals shall be made sectional, and that a war must be waged against slavery until it shall cease throughout the United States.

The guaranties of the Constitution will then no longer exist; the equal rights of the States will be lost. The slaveholding States will no longer have the power of self-government, or self-protection, and the Federal Government will have become their enemy.

Sectional interest and animosity will deepen the irritation, and all hope of remedy is rendered vain, by the fact that public opinion at the North has invested a great political error with the sanctions of a more erroneous religious belief.

We, therefore, the People of South Carolina, by our delegates in Convention assembled, appealing to the Supreme Judge of the world for the rectitude of our intentions, have solemnly declared that the Union heretofore existing between this State and the other States of North America, is dissolved, and that the State of South Carolina has resumed her position among the nations of the world, as a separate and independent State; with full power to levy war, conclude peace, contract alliances, establish commerce, and to do all other acts and things which independent States may of right do.

Source: Frank H. Moore, ed., *The Rebellion Record*, 8 vols. (New York: G. P. Putnam, 1861–8), 1:3–4.

2. John J. Crittenden
Crittenden Compromise Proposal, December 19, 1860

Between the election of Abraham Lincoln to the presidency in November 1860 and the formation of the Confederacy in February 1861, considerable support existed in the North and Upper South for compromise measures designed to placate the Deep South and save the Union. On the eve of South Carolina's secession, Senator John J. Crittenden of Kentucky (1787–1863) presented the most comprehensive compromise proposal. Crittenden represented the interests of the border slave states, whose citizens feared they would be on the frontline of battle in a war between the North and South. Initially Crittenden's proposals attracted support among conservative Republicans as well as Democrats. But Republicans soon recognized that the measures Crittenden presented were not so much a sectional compromise as a capitulation to southern demands. The key measure applying the Missouri Compromise Line to all new territories acquired by the United States would have opened all of Latin America to proslavery aggression. In addition, President-elect Lincoln warned members of his party that it would be political suicide for them to repudiate their opposition to slavery expansion. On January 16, 1861 the US Senate defeated the Crittenden Comprise by a vote of 25 to 23, with 6 departing southern senators abstaining.

A joint resolution (S. No. 50) proposing certain amendments
to the Constitution of the United States.
Whereas serious and alarming dissensions have arisen between the northern and southern states, concerning the rights and security of the rights of the slaveholding States, and especially their rights in the common territory of the United States; and whereas it is eminently desirable and proper that these dissensions, which now threaten the very existence of this Union, should be permanently quieted and settled by constitutional provisions, which shall do equal justice to all sections, and thereby restore to all the

people that peace and good-will which ought to prevail between all the citizens of the United States: Therefore,

Resolved by the Senate and House of Representatives of the United States of America in Congress assembled, (two thirds of both Houses concurring,) That the following articles be, and are hereby, proposed and submitted as amendments to the Constitution of the United States, which shall be valid to all intents and purposes, as part of said Constitution, when ratified by conventions of three-fourths of the several States:

ARTICLE 1. In all the territory of the United States now held, or hereafter acquired, situated north of 36 degrees 30 minutes, slavery or involuntary servitude, except as a punishment for crime, is prohibited while such territory shall remain under territorial government. In all the territory south of said line of latitude, slavery of the African race is hereby recognized as existing, and shall not be interfered with by Congress, but shall be protected as property by all the departments of the territorial government during its continuance. And when any territory, north or south of said line, within such boundaries as Congress may prescribe, shall contain the population requisite for a member of Congress according to the then Federal ratio of representation of the people of the United States, it shall, if its form of government be republican, be admitted into the Union, on an equal footing with the original States, with or without slavery, as the constitution of such new States may provide.

ART. 2. Congress shall have no power to abolish slavery in places under its exclusive jurisdiction, and situate within the limits of States that permit the holding of slaves.

ART. 3. Congress shall have no power to abolish slavery within the District of Columbia, so long as it exists in the adjoining States of Virginia and Maryland, or either, nor without the consent of the inhabitants, nor without just compensation first made to such owners of slaves as do not consent to such abolishment. Nor shall Congress at any time prohibit officers of the Federal Government, or members of Congress, whose duties require them to be in said District, from bringing with them their slaves, and holding them as such during the time their duties may require them to remain there, and afterwards taking them from the District.

ART. 4. Congress shall have no power to prohibit or hinder the transportation of slaves from one State to another, or to a Territory, in which slaves are by law permitted to be held, whether that transportation be by land, navigable river, or by the sea.

ART. 5. That in addition to the provisions of the third paragraph of the second section of the fourth article of the Constitution of the United States, Congress shall have power to provide by law, and it shall be its duty so to provide, that the United States shall pay to the owner who shall apply for it, the full value of his fugitive slave in all cases where the marshal or other officer whose duty it was to arrest said fugitive was prevented from so doing by violence or intimidation, or when, after arrest, said fugitive was rescued by force, and the owner thereby prevented and obstructed in the pursuit of his remedy for the recovery of his fugitive slave under the said clause of the Constitution and the laws made in pursuance thereof. And in all such cases, when the United States shall pay for such fugitive, they shall have the right, in their own name, to sue the county in which said violence, intimidation, or rescue was committed, and to recover from it, with interest and damages, the amount paid by them for said fugitive slave. And the said county, after it has paid said amount to the United States, may, for its indemnity, sue and recover from the wrong-doers or rescuers by whom the owner was prevented from the recovery of his fugitive slave, in like manner as the owner himself might have sued and recovered.

ART. 6. No future amendment of the Constitution shall affect the five preceding articles; nor the third paragraph of the second section of the first article of the Constitution; nor the third paragraph of the second section of the fourth article of said Constitution; and no amendment will be made to the Constitution which shall authorize or give to Congress any power to abolish or interfere with slavery in any of the States by whose laws it is, or may be, allowed or permitted.

And whereas, also, besides those causes of dissension embraced in the foregoing Amendments proposed to the Constitution of the United States, there are others which come within the jurisdiction of Congress, and may be remedied by its legislative power; and whereas it is the desire of Congress, so far as its power will extend, to remove all just cause for the popular discontent and agitation which now disturb the peace of the country, and threaten the stability of its institutions; Therefore,

1. *Resolved by the Senate and House of Representatives of the United States of America, in Congress assembled*, That the laws now in force for the recovery of fugitive slaves are in strict pursuance of the plain and mandatory provisions of the Constitution, and have been sanctioned as valid and constitutional by the judgment of the Supreme Court of the United States; that the slaveholding States are entitled to the faithful observance and execution of those laws, and that they ought not to be repealed, or so modified or changed as to impair their efficiency; and that laws ought to be made for the punishment of those who attempt by rescue of the slave, or other illegal means, to hinder or defeat the due execution of said laws.

2. That all State laws which conflict with the fugitive slave acts of Congress, or any other constitutional acts of Congress, or which, in their operation, impede, hinder, or delay the free course and due execution of any of said acts, are null and void by the plain provisions of the Constitution of the United States; yet those State laws, void as they are, have given color to practices, and led to consequences, which have obstructed the due administration and execution of acts of Congress, and especially the acts for the delivery of fugitive slaves, and have thereby contributed much to the discord and commotion now prevailing. Congress, therefore, in the present perilous juncture, does not deem it improper, respectfully and earnestly to recommend the repeal of those laws to the several States which have enacted them, or such legislative corrections or explanations of them as may prevent their being used or perverted to such mischievous purposes.

3. That the act of the 18th of September, 1850, commonly called the fugitive slave law, ought to be so amended as to make the fee of the commissioner, mentioned in the eighth section of the act, equal in amount in the cases decided by him, whether his decision be in favor of or against the claimant. And to avoid misconstruction, the last clause of the fifth section of said act, which authorizes the person holding a warrant for the arrest or detention of a fugitive slave, to summon to his aid the posse comitatus, and which declares it to be the duty of all good citizens to assist him in its execution, ought to be so amended as to expressly limit the authority and duty to cases in which there shall be resistance or danger of resistance or rescue.

4. That the laws for the suppression of the African slave trade, and especially those prohibiting the importation of slaves in the United States, ought to be made effectual, and ought to be thoroughly executed; and all further enactments necessary to those ends ought to be promptly made.

Source: *Congressional Globe*, 36th Cong., 2d sess. (December 18, 1860): 114.

3. *Frank Leslie's Illustrated Newspaper*
Jefferson Davis about to become Provisional President of the Confederacy, February 16, 1861

> *In early 1861 the Deep South states established a central government called the Confederate States of America. Several weeks before the inauguration of Abraham Lincoln in Washington, they wrote a constitution patterned on the US Constitution and elected Jefferson Davis of Mississippi, a former US Senator and Secretary of War, as provisional president. Davis recognized that*

he faced a difficult task. Shortly after his election, he wrote, "We are without machinery, without means, and threatened by powerful opposition." But amid pomp and circumstance, as he arrived in Montgomery, Alabama (the original Confederate capital), for his inauguration, he exuded confidence. A "special artist" working for Frank Leslie's Illustrated Newspaper *sketched Davis as he addressed citizens of Montgomery from the balcony of the city's Exchange Hotel, two nights before his official induction into office on February 18. This woodcut, produced from the sketch by a team of engravers, captures the exuberance of the event.*

Figure 2   Frank Leslie's Illustrated Newspaper, Jefferson Davis about to become Provisional President of the Confederacy, 1861
Source: *Frank Leslie's Illustrated Newspaper,* March 16 (1861).

4. Daniel Decatur Emmett
"I Wish I Was in Dixie's Land," 1860

Songs were an important part of the Civil War era. There was, of course, only live music. Professional musicians of all varieties presented public concerts, musicals dominated the theater, and the sheet music industry provided thousands of tunes for family pianos. Soldiers and civilians sang a wide variety of songs for their own entertainment. Several songs, including "The Bonnie Blue Flag" and "Maryland! My Maryland!," are identified with the Confederacy. But none surpassed "Dixie" in popularity. The song has long been attributed to Daniel Decatur Emmett (1815–1904), a white northern black-face minstrel, who introduced it to a New York City audience on April 4, 1859, during a performance of the popular comedy Pocahontas. *It is likely, however, that the song originated with Thomas and Ellen Snowden, a black couple living in Knox County, Ohio. A performance of* Pocahontas *in Montgomery, Alabama, during late 1860 made "Dixie" very popular in the city. When those attending Jefferson Davis's inauguration in that city on February 18, 1861 sang the song, it became the unofficial Confederate anthem. There are many versions of its lyrics. Emmett published this dialect version in 1860.*

I wish I was in de land ob cotton,
Old times dar am not forgotten;
Look away! look away!
Look away! Dixie Land.
In Dixie Land whar I was born in,
Early on one frosty mornin
Look away! look away!
Look away! Dixie Land.

Chorus:
Den I wish I was in Dixie, Hooray! Hooray!
In Dixie Land I'll take my Stand, to lib an die in Dixie,
Away, away, away down south in Dixie,
Away, away, away down south in Dixie.

Ole Missus marry "Will-de-weaber,"
William was a gay deceaber;
   Look away! &c–
But when he put his arm around 'er
He smiled as fierce as a forty-pounder.
   Look away! &c–
      Chorus – Den I wish I was in Dixie, &c–

His face was sharp as a butchers cleaber,
But dat did not seem to greab 'er;
   Look away! &c–
Ole Missus acted de foolish part,
And died for a man dat broke her heart.
   Look away! &c–
      Chorus – Den I wish I was in Dixie, &c–

Now here's a health to the next old Missus,
An all de gals dat want to kiss us;
   Look away! &c–
But if you want to drive 'way sorrow,
Come and hear dis song tomorrow,
   Look away! &c–
      Chorus – Den I wish I was in Dixie, &c–

Dar's buck-wheat cakes and "Ingen" batter,
Makes you fat or a little fatter;
   Look away! &c–
Den hoe it down an scratch your grabble,
To Dixie's Land I'm bound to trabble.
   Look away! &c–
      Chorus – Den I wish I was in Dixie, &c–

Source: Dan D. Emmett, *I Wish I Was in Dixie's Land* (New York: Firth, Pond, and Co., 1860).

5. Abraham Lincoln
First Inaugural Address, March 4, 1861

Abraham Lincoln (1809–65) was elected president in November 1860. But, because Lincoln did not take office until March 4, 1861, outgoing Democratic president James Buchanan dealt with the early stages of the secession crisis. Prior to his inaugural address, Lincoln privately opposed any compromise that would permit the expansion of slavery, while insisting that his administration would not threaten slavery in the southern states. His inaugural address provided the first public indication of his intentions. Although Lincoln in this address promises to enforce the Fugitive Slave Law and not violate constitutional rights, he brands secession illegal and anarchical. He interprets American constitutional history in sharp contrast to the interpretation endorsed by the seceding states. Although he rejects coercing or using force against those states, he pledges to enforce United States laws and to defend United States property within their bounds. Each of these latter policies was incompatible with the Deep South states' claim to independence and could only be achieved through military action. Lincoln informs the secessionist leaders that the choice between peace and war rests with them. They regarded his words as a "declaration of war."

Fellow-Citizens of the United States:

In compliance with a custom as old as the Government itself, I appear before you to address you briefly and to take in your presence the oath prescribed by the Constitution of the United States to be taken by the President "before he enters on the execution of this office." ...

Apprehension seems to exist among the people of the Southern States that by the accession of a Republican Administration their property and their peace and personal security are to be endangered. There has never been any reasonable cause for such apprehension. Indeed, the most ample evidence to the contrary has all the while existed and been open to their inspection. It is found in nearly all the published speeches of him who now addresses you. I do but quote from one of those speeches when I declare that –

I have no purpose directly or indirectly, to interfere with the institution of slavery in the States where it exists. I believe I have no lawful right to do so, and I have no inclination to do so.

Those who nominated and elected me did so with full knowledge that I had made this and many similar declarations and had never recanted them; and more than this, they placed in the platform for my acceptance, and as a law to themselves and to me the dear and emphatic resolution which I now read:

Resolved, That the maintenance inviolate of the rights of the States, and especially the right of each State to order and control its own domestic institutions according to its own judgment exclusively, is essential to that balance of power on which the perfection and endurance of our political fabric depend; and we denounce the lawless invasion by armed force of the soil of any State or Territory, no matter under what pretext, as among the gravest of crimes.

I now reiterate these sentiments, and in doing so I only press upon the public attention the most conclusive evidence of which the case is suscep-tible that the property, peace, and security of no section are to be in any wise endangered by the now incoming Administration. I add, too, that all the protection which, consistently with the Constitution and the laws, can be given will be cheerfully given to all the States when lawfully demanded, for whatever cause – as cheerfully to one section as to another. There is much controversy about the delivering up of fugitives from service or labor. The clause I now read is as plainly written in the Constitution as any other of its provisions:

> No person held to service or labor in one State, under the laws thereof, escaping into another, shall in consequence of any law or regulation therein be discharged from such service or labor, but shall be delivered up on claim of the party to whom such service or labor may be due.

It is scarcely questioned that this provision was intended by those who made it for the reclaiming of what we call fugitive slaves; and the intention of the lawgiver is the law. All members of Congress swear their support to the whole Constitution – to this provision as much as to any other. To the proposition, then, that slaves whose cases come within the terms of this clause "shall be delivered up" their oaths are unanimous. Now, if they would make the effort in good temper, could they not with nearly equal unanimity frame and pass a law by means of which to keep good that unanimous oath?

There is some difference of opinion whether this clause should be enforced by national or by State authority, but surely that difference is not a very material one. If the slave is to be surrendered, it can be of but little consequence to him or to others by which authority it is done. And should anyone in any case be content that his oath shall go unkept on a merely unsubstantial controversy as to how it shall be kept?

Again: In any law upon this subject ought not all the safeguards of liberty known in civilized and humane jurisprudence to be introduced, so that a free man be not in any case surrendered as a slave? And might it not be well at the same time to provide by law for the enforcement of that clause in the Constitution which guarantees that "the citizens of each State shall be entitled to all privileges and immunities of citizens in the several States"? [. . .]

I hold that in contemplation of universal law and of the Constitution the Union of these States is perpetual. Perpetuity is implied, if not expressed, in the fundamental law of all national governments. It is safe to assert that no government proper ever had a provision in its organic law for its own termination. . . .

Again: If the United States be not a government proper, but an association of States in the nature of contract merely, can it, as a contract, he peaceably unmade by less than all the parties who made it? One party to a contract may violate it – break it, so to speak – but does it not require all to lawfully rescind it?

Descending from these general principles, we find the proposition that in legal contemplation the Union is perpetual confirmed by the history of the Union itself. The Union is much older than the Constitution. It was formed, in fact, by the Articles of Association in 1774. It was matured and continued by the Declaration of Independence in 1776. It was further matured, and the faith of all the then thirteen States expressly plighted and engaged that it should be perpetual, by the Articles of Confederation in 1778. And finally, in 1787, one of the declared objects for ordaining and establishing the Constitution was *"to form a more perfect Union."* But if destruction of the Union by one or by a part only of the States be lawfully possible, the Union is less perfect than before the Constitution, having lost the vital element of perpetuity.

It follows from these views that no State upon its own mere motion can lawfully get out of the Union; that *resolves* and *ordinances* to that effect are legally void, and that acts of violence within any State or States against the authority of the United States are insurrectionary or revolutionary, according to circumstances.

I therefore consider that in view of the Constitution and the laws the Union is unbroken, and to the extent of my ability, I shall take care, as the Constitution itself expressly enjoins upon me, that the laws of the Union be faithfully executed in all the States. Doing this I deem to be only a simple duty on my part, and I shall perform it so far as practicable unless my rightful masters, the American people, shall withhold the requisite means or in some authoritative manner direct the contrary. I trust this will not be regarded as a menace, but only as the declared purpose of the Union that it *will* constitutionally defend and maintain itself.

In doing this there needs to be no bloodshed or violence, and there shall be none unless it be forced upon the national authority. The power confided to me will be used to hold, occupy, and possess the property and places belonging to the Government and to collect the duties and imposts; but beyond what may be necessary for these objects, there will be no invasion, no using of force against or among the people anywhere. Where hostility to the United States in any interior locality shall be so great and universal as to prevent competent resident citizens from holding the Federal offices, there will be no attempt to force obnoxious strangers among the people for that object. While the strict legal right may exist in the Government to enforce the exercise of these offices, the attempt to do so would be so irritating and so nearly impracticable withal that I deem it better to forego for the time the uses of such offices.

The mails, unless repelled, will continue to be furnished in all parts of the Union. So far as possible the people everywhere shall have that sense of perfect security which is most favorable to calm thought and reflection. The course here indicated will be followed unless current events and experience shall show a modification or change to be proper, and in every case and exigency my best discretion will be exercised, according to circumstances actually existing and with a view and a hope of a peaceful solution of the national troubles and the restoration of fraternal sympathies and affections.

That there are persons in one section or another who seek to destroy the Union at all events and are glad of any pretext to do it I will neither affirm nor deny; but if there be such, I need address no word to them. To those, however, who really love the Union may I not speak?

Before entering upon so grave a matter as the destruction of our national fabric, with all its benefits, its memories, and its hopes, would it not be wise to ascertain precisely why we do it? Will you hazard so desperate a step while there is any possibility that any portion of the ills you fly from have no real existence? Will you, while the certain ills you fly to are greater than all the real ones you fly from, will you risk the commission of so fearful a mistake?

All profess to be content in the Union if all constitutional rights can be maintained. Is it true, then, that any right plainly written in the Constitution has been denied? I think not. Happily, the human mind is so constituted that no party can reach to the audacity of doing this. Think, if you can, of a single instance in which a plainly written provision of the Constitution has ever been denied. If by the mere force of numbers a majority should deprive a minority of any clearly written constitutional right, it might in a moral point of view justify revolution; certainly would if such right were a vital one. But such is not our case. All the vital rights of minorities and of individuals are so plainly assured to them by affirmations and negations, guaranties and prohibitions, in the Constitution that controversies never arise concerning them. But no organic law can ever be framed with a provision specifically applicable to every question which may occur in practical administration. No foresight can anticipate nor any document of reasonable length contain express provisions for all possible questions. Shall fugitives from labor be surrendered by national or by State authority? The Constitution does not expressly say. *May* Congress prohibit slavery in the Territories? The Constitution does not expressly say. *Must* Congress protect slavery in the Territories? The Constitution does not expressly say.

From questions of this class spring all our constitutional controversies, and we divide upon them into majorities and minorities. If the minority will not acquiesce, the majority must, or the Government must cease. There is no other alternative, for continuing the Government is acquiescence on one side or the other. If a minority in such case will secede rather than acquiesce, they make a precedent which in turn will divide and ruin them, for a minority of their own will secede from them whenever a majority refuses to be controlled by such minority. For instance, why may not any portion of a new confederacy a year or two hence arbitrarily secede again, precisely as portions of the present Union now claim to secede from it? All who cherish disunion sentiments are now being educated to the exact temper of doing this.

[...]

Plainly the central idea of secession is the essence of anarchy. A majority held in restraint by constitutional checks and limitations, and always changing easily with deliberate changes of popular opinions and sentiments, is the only true sovereign of a free people. Whoever rejects it does of necessity fly to anarchy or to despotism. Unanimity is impossible. The rule of a minority, as a permanent arrangement, is wholly inadmissible; so that, rejecting the majority principle, anarchy or despotism in some form is all that is left.

[...]

One section of our country believes slavery is *right* and ought to be extended, while the other believes it is wrong and ought not to be extended. This is the only substantial dispute. The fugitive–slave clause of the Constitution and the law for the suppression of the foreign slave trade are each as well enforced, perhaps, as any law can ever be in a community where the moral sense of the people imperfectly supports the law itself. The great body of the people abide by the dry legal obligation in both cases, and a few break over in each. This, I think, can not be perfectly cured, and it would be worse in both cases after the separation of the sections than before. The foreign slave trade, now imperfectly suppressed, would be ultimately revived without restriction in one section, while fugitive slaves, now only partially surrendered, would not he surrendered at all by the other.

Physically speaking, we can not separate. We can not remove our respective sections from each other nor build an impassable wall between them. A husband and wife may he divorced and go out of the presence and beyond the reach of each other, but the different parts of our country can not do this. They can not but remain face to face, and intercourse, either amicable or hostile, must continue between them. Is it possible, then, to make that intercourse more advantageous or more satisfactory after separation than before? Can aliens make treaties easier than friends can make laws? Can treaties he more faithfully enforced between aliens than laws can among friends? Suppose you go to war, you can not fight always; and when, after much loss on both sides and no gain on either, you cease fighting, the identical old questions, as to terms of intercourse, are again upon you.

This country, with its institutions, belongs to the people who inhabit it. Whenever they shall grow weary of the existing Government, they can exercise their *constitutional* right of amending it or their *revolutionary* right to dismember or overthrow it. I can not be ignorant of the fact that many worthy and patriotic citizens are desirous of having the National Constitution amended. While I make no recommendation of amendments, I fully recognize the rightful authority of the people over the whole subject, to be exercised in either of the modes prescribed in the instrument itself; and I should, under existing circumstances, favor rather than oppose a fair opportunity being afforded the people to act upon it.... I understand a proposed amendment to the Constitution – which amendment, however, I have not seen – has passed Congress, to the effect that the Federal Government shall never interfere with the domestic institutions of the States, including that of persons held to service. To avoid misconstruction of what I have said, I depart from my purpose not to speak of particular amendments so far as to say that, holding such a provision to now be implied constitutional law, I have no objection to its being made express and irrevocable.

The Chief Magistrate derives all his authority from the people, and they have referred none upon him to fix terms for the separation of the States. The people themselves can do this if also they choose, but the Executive as such has nothing to do with it. His duty is to administer the present Government as it came to his hands and to transmit it unimpaired by him to his successor.

Why should there not be a patient confidence in the ultimate justice of the people? Is there any better or equal hope in the world? In our present differences, is either party without faith of being in the right? If the Almighty Ruler of Nations, with His eternal truth and justice, be on your side of the North, or on yours of the South, that truth and that justice will surely prevail by the judgment of this great tribunal of the American people.

By the frame of the Government under which we live this same people have wisely given their public servants but little power for mischief, and have with equal wisdom provided for the return of that little to their own hands at very short intervals. While the people retain their virtue and vigilance no Administration by any extreme of wickedness or folly can very seriously injure the Government in the short space of four years.

My countrymen, one and all, think calmly and *well* upon this whole subject. Nothing valuable can be lost by taking time. If there be an object to *hurry* any of you in hot haste to a step which you would never take *deliberately*, that object will be frustrated by taking time; but no good object can be frustrated by it. Such of you as are now dissatisfied still have the old Constitution unimpaired, and, on the sensitive point, the laws of your own framing under it; while the new Administration will have no immediate power, if it would, to change either. If it were admitted that you who are dissatisfied hold the right side in the dispute, there still is no single good reason for precipitate action. Intelligence, patriotism, Christianity, and a firm reliance on Him who has never yet forsaken this favored land are still competent to adjust in the best way all our present difficulty.

In *your* hands, my dissatisfied fellow-countrymen, and not in *mine*, is the momentous issue of civil war. The Government will not assail *you*. You can have no conflict without being yourselves the aggressors. *You* have no oath registered in heaven to destroy the Government, while I shall have the most solemn one to "preserve, protect, and defend it."

I am loath to close. We are not enemies, but friends. We must not be enemies. Though passion may have strained it must not break our bonds of affection. The mystic chords of memory, stretching from every battlefield and patriot grave to every living heart and hearthstone all over this broad land, will yet swell the chorus of the Union, when again touched, as surely they will be, by the better angels of our nature.

Source: James D. Richardson, ed., *A Compilation of the Messages and Papers of the President*, 10 vols. (Washington, DC: Government Printing Office, 1897), 6:5–12.

6. Alexander H. Stephens
Cornerstone Speech, March 21, 1861

*Several weeks after Lincoln refused to recognize secession, Alexander
H. Stephens (1812–83), a former US Senator from Georgia and the recently
chosen vice-president of the Confederacy, celebrated the resolve of white
southerners and the distinctiveness of southern civilization. Although he was
a fervent advocate of state sovereignty, Stephens had opposed secession until
early 1861. In the impromptu speech he delivered before an enthusiastic
audience in Savannah on March 21, 1861, he argues that the "cornerstone"
of southern greatness lay in slavery and white supremacy. Portraying African
Americans as members of an inherently inferior race who benefited from
enslavement, Stephens asserts unequivocally that white southerners had the
resources and will to form a powerful new nation. Science and experience,
he claims, had proved wrong the principle asserted in the Declaration of
Independence that all men were created equal.*

... We are in the midst of one of the greatest epochs in our history. The last ninety days will mark one of the most memorable eras in the history of modern civilization.... Seven States have within the last three months thrown off an old government and formed a new. This revolution has been signally marked, up to this time, by the fact of its having been accomplished without the loss of a single drop of blood.

This new constitution, or form of government, constitutes the subject to which your attention will be partly invited. In reference to it, I make this first general remark.... All the essentials of the old constitution, which have endeared it to the hearts of the American people, have been preserved and perpetuated. Some changes have been made....

Allow me briefly to allude to some of these improvements. The question of building up class interests, or fostering one branch of industry to the prejudice of another under the exercise of the revenue power, which gave us so much trouble under the old constitution, is put at rest.... This old thorn of the tariff, which was the cause of so much irritation in the old body politic, is removed forever from the new.

Again, the subject of internal improvements, under the power of Congress to regulate commerce, is put at rest under our system. The power claimed by construction under the old constitution, was at least a doubtful one – it rested solely upon construction. We of the South, generally apart from considerations of constitutional principles, opposed its exercise upon rounds of its inexpediency and injustice....

Another feature to which I will allude, is that the new constitution provides that cabinet ministers and heads of departments may have the privilege of seats upon the floor of the Senate and House of Representatives – may have the right to participate in the debates and discussions upon the various subjects of administration....

Another change in the constitution relates to the length of the tenure of the presidential office. In the new constitution it is six years instead of four, and the President rendered ineligible for a re-election. This is certainly a decidedly conservative change. It will remove from the incumbent all temptation to use his office or exert the powers confided to him for any objects of personal ambition....

But not to be tedious in enumerating the numerous changes for the better, allow me to allude to one other – though last, not least. The new constitution has put at rest, forever, all the agitating questions relating to our peculiar institution – African slavery as it exists amongst us – the proper status of the negro in our form of civilization. This was the immediate cause of the late rupture and present revolution. Jefferson in his forecast, had anticipated this, as the "rock upon which the old Union would split." He was right. What was conjecture with him, is now a realized fact. But whether he fully comprehended the great truth upon which that rock stood and stands, may be doubted. The prevailing ideas entertained by him and most of the leading statesmen at the time of the formation of the old constitution, were that the enslavement of the African was in violation of the laws of nature; that it was wrong in principle, socially, morally, and politically. It was an evil they knew not well how to deal with, but the general opinion of the men of that day was that, somehow or other in the order of Providence, the institution would be evanescent and pass away. This idea, though not incorporated in the constitution, was the prevailing idea at that time. The constitution, it is true, secured every essential guarantee to the institution while it should last, and hence no argument can be justly urged against the constitutional guarantees thus secured, because of the common sentiment of the day. Those ideas, however, were fundamentally wrong. They rested upon the assumption of the equality of races. This was an error. It was a sandy foundation, and the government built upon it fell when the "storm came and the wind blew."

Our new government is founded upon exactly the opposite idea; its foundations are laid, its corner-stone rests upon the great truth, that the negro is not equal to the white man; that slavery – subordination to the superior race – is his natural and normal condition. . . . This, our new government, is the first, in the history of the world, based upon this great physical, philosophical, and moral truth. This truth has been slow in the process of its development, like all other truths in the various departments of science. It has been so even amongst us. Many who hear me, perhaps, can recollect well, that this truth was not generally admitted, even within their day. The errors of the past generation still clung to many as late as twenty years ago. Those at the North, who still cling to these errors, with a zeal above knowledge, we justly denominate as fanatics. All fanaticism springs from an aberration of the mind – from a defect in reasoning. It is a species of insanity. One of the most striking characteristics of insanity, in many instances, is forming correct conclusions from fancied or erroneous premises; so with the anti-slavery fanatics; their conclusions are right if their premises were. They assume that the negro is equal, and hence conclude that he is entitled to equal privileges and rights with the white man. If their premises were correct, their conclusions would be logical and just – but their premise being wrong, their whole argument fails. I recollect once of having heard a gentleman from one of the northern States, of great power and ability, announce in the House of Representatives, with imposing effect, that we of the South would be compelled, ultimately, to yield upon this subject of slavery, that it was as impossible to war successfully against a principle in politics, as it was in physics or mechanics. That the principle would ultimately prevail. That we, in maintaining slavery as it exists with us, were warring against a principle, a principle founded in nature, the principle of the equality of men. The reply I made to him was, that upon his own grounds, we should, ultimately, succeed, and that he and his associates, in this crusade against our institutions, would ultimately fail. The truth announced, that it was as impossible to war successfully against a principle in politics as it was in physics and mechanics, I admitted; but told him that it was he, and those acting with him, who were warring against a principle. They were attempting to make things equal which the Creator had made unequal.

In the conflict thus far, success has been on our side, complete throughout the length and breadth of the Confederate States. It is upon this, as I have stated, our social fabric is firmly planted; and I cannot permit myself to doubt the ultimate success of a full recognition of this principle throughout the civilized and enlightened world.

As I have stated, the truth of this principle may be slow in development, as all truths are and ever have been, in the various branches of science. It was so with the principles announced by Galileo – it was so with Adam Smith and his principles of political economy. It was so with Harvey, and his theory of the circulation of the blood. It is stated that not a single one of the medical profession, living at the time of the announcement of the truths made by him, admitted them. Now, they are universally acknowledged.

May we not, therefore, look with confidence to the ultimate universal acknowledgment of the truths upon which our system rests? It is the first government ever instituted upon the principles in strict conformity to nature, and the ordination of Providence, in furnishing the materials of human society. Many governments have been founded upon the principle of the subordination and serfdom of certain classes of the same race; such were and are in violation of the laws of nature. Our system commits no such violation of nature's laws. With us, all of the white race, however high or low, rich or poor, are equal in the eye of the law. Not so with the negro. Subordination is his place. He, by nature, or by the curse against Canaan, is fitted for that condition which he occupies in our system. The architect, in the construction of buildings, lays the foundation with the proper material – the granite; then comes the brick or the marble. The substratum of our society is made of the material fitted by nature for it, and by experience we know that it is best, not only for the superior, but for the inferior race, that it should be so. It is, indeed, in conformity with the ordinance of the Creator. It is not for us to inquire into the wisdom of his ordinances, or to question them. For his own purposes, he has made one race to differ from another, as he has made "one star to differ from another star in glory."

The great objects of humanity are best attained when there is conformity to his laws and decrees, in the formation of governments as well as in all things else. Our confederacy is founded upon principles in strict conformity with these laws. This stone which was rejected by the first builders "is become the chief of the corner" – the real "corner-stone" – in our new edifice. . . .

I have been asked, what of the future? It has been apprehended by some that we would have arrayed against us the civilized world. I care not who or how many they may be against us, when we stand upon the eternal principles of truth, if we are true to ourselves and the principles for which we contend, we are obliged to, and must triumph.

[. . .]

But to pass on: Some have propounded the inquiry whether it is practicable for us to go on with the confederacy without further accessions? Have we the means and ability to maintain nationality among the powers of the earth? On this point I would barely say, that as anxiously as we all have been, and are, for the border States, with institutions similar to ours, to join us, still we are abundantly able to maintain our position, even if they should ultimately make up their minds not to cast their destiny with us. That they ultimately will join us – be compelled to do it – is my confident belief; but we can get on very well without them, even if they should not.

We have all the essential elements of a high national career. The idea has been given out at the North, and even in the border States, that we are too small and too weak to maintain a separate nationality. This is a great mistake. In extent of territory we embrace five hundred and sixty-four thousand square miles and upward. This is upward of two hundred thousand square miles more than was included within the limits of the original thirteen States. It is an area of country more than double the territory of France or the Austrian empire. . . . It is greater than all France, Spain, Portugal, and Great Britain, including England, Ireland, and Scotland, together. In population we have upward of five millions, according to the census of 1860; this includes white and black. The entire population, including white and black, of the original thirteen States, was less than four millions in 1790, and still less in '76, when the independence of our fathers was achieved. If they, with a less population, dared maintain their independence against the greatest power on earth, shall we have any apprehension of maintaining ours now?

In point of material wealth and resources, we are greatly in advance of them. The taxable property of the Confederate States cannot be less than twenty-two hundred millions of dollars! This, I think I venture but little in saying, may be considered as five times more than the colonies possessed at the time they achieved their independence. . . . With such an area of territory as we have – with such an amount of population – with a climate and soil unsurpassed by any on the face of the earth – with such resources already at our command – with productions which control the commerce of the world, who can entertain any apprehensions as to our ability to succeed, whether others join us or not?

It is true, I believe I state but the common sentiment, when I declare my earnest desire that the border States should join us. The differences of opinion that existed among us anterior to secession, related more to the policy in securing that result by co-operation than from any difference upon the ultimate security we all looked to in common. . . .

In this connection I take this occasion to state, that I was not without grave and serious apprehensions that if the worst came to the worst, and cutting loose from the old government should be the only remedy for our safety and security, it would be attended with much more serious ills than it has been as yet. Thus far we have seen none of those incidents which usually attend revolutions. No such material as such convulsions usually throw up has been seen. Wisdom, prudence, and patriotism, have marked every step of our progress thus far. This augurs well for the future, and it is a matter of sincere gratification to me, that I am enabled to make the declaration. Of the men I met in the Congress at Montgomery, I may be pardoned for saying this, an abler, wiser, a more conservative, deliberate, determined, resolute, and patriotic body of men, I never met in my life.

Source: H. Cleveland, *Alexander H. Stephens, in Public and Private: With Letters and Speeches, Before, During, and Since the War* (Philadelphia, PA: National Publishing, 1866), 717–29.

7. Mary Boykin Chesnut
Approaching Conflict at Fort Sumter, March–April 1861

The Civil War began on the morning of April 12, 1861 as Confederate batteries opened fire on Fort Sumter and the United States troops who occupied it. Other Union forts in the Deep South had either gone over to the Confederacy or were offshore, where they could be easily supplied and defended by the US Navy. In contrast, Sumter stood in Charleston Harbor surrounded by Confederate cannon and mortars. Just before Lincoln became president, Major Robert Anderson, who commanded the fort, announced that Sumter was running out of food. Anderson indicated that the fort had either to be re-supplied or surrendered. Lincoln recognized that surrendering the fort would reinforce Confederate claims to independence and an attempt to re-supply the fort would start a war. After a month of indecision, he concluded that, while a re-supply expedition would not succeed, he could strengthen the Union politically by forcing the Confederates to fire the first shots. He informed South Carolina governor Francis W. Pickens that the Union would undertake a peaceful navel expedition to provide food to the fort. Pickens and other Confederate leaders ordered the attack on Sumter because they understood that a successful relief expedition would undercut their claim to independence and strengthen Lincoln's position. Few of these concerns were apparent to Mary Boykin Chesnut (1823–86) and her elite circle in Charleston, even though the circle included prominent Confederate political and military leaders. Although many of them were ready for a fight, Chestnut was by no means naïve about the dangers of war, including the likelihood of slave revolt. Her diary entries reveal how the approaching calamity impinged on everyday life among Charleston's leading families.

APRIL 4th. – ...A ship was fired into yesterday and went back to sea. Is that the first shot? How can one settle down to anything? One's heart is in one's mouth all the time. Any minute, the cannon may open on us, the fleet come in.

APRIL 6th. – The plot thickens, the air is red-hot with rumors. The mystery is to find out where these utterly groundless tales originate.

In spite of all, Tom Huger [commander of the Confederate battery on Morris Island] came for us and we went on the *Planter* to take a look at Morris Island and its present inhabitants. Mrs. [Louis T.] Wigfall and the Cheves girls [daughters of Langdon Cheves Jr.], Maxcy Gregg and Colonel [William H. C.] Whiting, John Rutledge of the Navy, Dan Hamilton and William Haskell....

[Confederate General P. G. T.] Beauregard is a demigod here to most of the natives, but there are always some who say "wait and see." They give you to understand that Whiting has all the brains now in use for our defence. He does the work, Beauregard reaps the glory.

Things seem to draw near a crisis. Colonel Whiting is clever enough for anything; so we made up our minds today, Maxcy Gregg and I. Mr. Gregg told me that my husband [former US Senator James Chesnut] was in a minority in the Convention. So much for cool sense, when the atmosphere is phosphorescent....

APRIL 8th. – ...Mr. Robert Gourdin and Mr. Miles called. [Former] Governor [John] Manning walked in, bowed gravely, seated himself by me, and said, in mock heroic style and with a grand wave of his hand:

"Madame, your country is invaded." When I had breath to speak, I asked: "What does he mean?" "He means this. There are six men-of-war outside the Bar. Talbot and Chew have come to say that hostilities are to begin. Governor Pickens and Beauregard are holding a Council of War." Mr. Chesnut then came in. He confirmed the story. Wigfall next entered in boisterous spirits. He said "there was a sound of revelry by night ... " In any stir or confusion my heart is apt to beat so painfully. Now the agony was so stifling that I could hardly see or hear. The men went off almost immediately, and I crept silently to my room where I sat down to a good cry.

Mrs. Wigfall came in and we had it out, on the subject of civil war. We solaced ourselves with dwelling on all its known horrors, and then we added some remarks about what we had a right to expect with Yankees in front and Negroes in the rear. "The slave owners must expect a servile insurrection, of course," said Mrs. Wigfall, to make sure that we were unhappy enough.

Suddenly loud shouting was heard. We ran out. Cannon after cannon roared. We met Mrs. Allan Green in the passageway with blanched cheeks and streaming eyes. Governor Means rushed out of his room in his dressing gown and begged us to be calm. "Governor Pickens has ordered, in the plenitude of his wisdom, seven cannon to be fired as a signal to the 7th Regiment. Anderson will hear, as well as the 7th Regiment. Now you go back and be quiet. Fighting in the streets has not begun yet." So we retired.... There was no placidity today, no sleep for any-body last night. The streets were alive with soldiers and other men shouting, marching, singing. Wigfall, the "stormy petrel," was in his glory, the only thoroughly happy person I saw. Today things seem to have settled down a little. One can but hope. Lincoln or [William H.] Seward have made such silly advances, and then far sillier drawings back. There may be a chance for peace after all.

Things are happening so fast. My husband has been made an aide-de-camp of General Beauregard. Three hours ago we were quietly packing to go home. The Convention had adjourned. Now he tells me the attack upon Fort Sumter may begin tonight.

It depends upon Anderson and the fleet outside. John Manning came in with his sword and red sash, pleased as a boy to be on Beauregard's staff while the row goes on. He has gone with Wigfall to Captain Hartstein with instructions....

Jack Preston, Willie Allston – "the take-life-easy," as they are called – with John Green, "the big brave," have gone down to the Island and volunteered as privates. Seven hundred men were sent over. Ammunition wagons rumbling along the streets all night. Anderson burning blue lights; signs and signals for the fleet outside, I suppose.

Today at dinner there was no allusion to things as they stand in Charleston Harbor, but there was an undercurrent of intense excitement. There could not have been a more brilliant circle. In addition to our usual quartette (Judge Withers, Langdon Cheves and Trescot), our two Ex-Governors dined with us; [John H.] Means and Manning. These men all talked so delightfully, and for once in my life I listened. That over, business began in earnest. Governor Means had found a sword and a red sash and brought them for Colonel Chesnut, who has gone to demand the surrender of Fort Sumter.

And now, patience! We must wait. Why did that green goose Anderson go into Fort Sumter? Then everything began to go wrong. Now they have intercepted a letter from him urging them to let him surrender. He paints the horrors likely to ensue – they will not. He ought to have thought of all that before he put his head in the hole.

APRIL 12th. – Anderson will not capitulate!

Yesterday was the merriest, maddest dinner we have had yet. Men were more audaciously wise and witty. We had an unspoken foreboding it was to be our last pleasant meeting. Mr. Miles dined with us today. Mrs. Henry King rushed in. "The news? I come for the latest news! All of the men of the King family are on the Island," of which fact she seemed proud.

While she was here, our peace negotiator or our envoy came in; that is, Mr. Chesnut returned. His interview with Colonel Anderson had been deeply interesting but he was not inclined to be communicative, and wanted his dinner. He felt for Anderson. He had telegraphed to President [Jefferson] Davis for instructions as to what answer to give Anderson. He has now gone back to Fort Sumter with additional instructions. When they were about to leave the wharf, A. H. Boykin sprang into the boat in great excitement. He thought himself ill used; a likelihood of fighting and he to be left behind.

I do not pretend to go to sleep. How can I? If Anderson does not accept terms at four o'clock, the orders are he shall be fired upon.

I count four by St. Michael's chimes, and I begin to hope. At half past four, the heavy booming of a cannon! I sprang out of bed and on my knees, prostrate, I prayed as I never prayed before.

There was a sound of stir all over the house, a pattering of feet in the corridor. All seemed hurrying one way. I put on my double-gown and a shawl and went to the house top. The shells were bursting. In the dark I heard a man say: "Waste of ammunition!" I knew my husband was rowing about in a boat somewhere in that dark bay, and that the shells were roofing it over, bursting toward the Fort. If Anderson was obstinate, Mr. Chesnut was to order the Forts on our side to open fire. Certainly fire had begun. The regular roar of the cannon, there it was! And who could tell what each volley accomplished of death and destruction.

The women were wild, there on the house top. Prayers from the women and imprecations from the men; and then a shell would light up the scene. Tonight, they say, the forces are to attempt to land. The *Harriet Lane* had her wheel house smashed and put back to sea.

We watched up there, and everybody wondered why Fort Sumter did not fire a shot. Today Miles and Manning, Colonels now, and aids to Beauregard, dined with us. The latter hoped I would keep the peace. I gave him only good words, for he was to be under fire all day and night, in the bay carrying orders.

Last night – or this morning, truly – up on the house top, I was so weak and weary I sat down on something that looked like a black stool. "Get up, you foolish woman! Your dress is on fire," cried a man; and he put me out. It was a chimney, and the sparks caught my clothes; but my fire had been extinguished before it broke out into a regular blaze.

Do you know, after all that noise, and our tears and prayers, nobody has been hurt. Sound and fury signifying nothing! A delusion and a snare!

Louisa Hamilton comes here now. This is a sort of news center. Jack Hamilton, her handsome young husband, has all the credit of a famous battery which is made of railroad iron. Mr. Petigru calls it The Boomerang, because it throws the balls back the way they came. So Louisa Hamilton tells us. She had no children during her first marriage; hence the value of this lately achieved baby. To divert Louisa from the glories of "the Battery" of which she raves, we asked if the baby could talk yet. "No, not exactly, but he imitates the big gun. When he hears that, he claps his hands and cries 'Boom Boom.' " Her mind is distinctly occupied by three things; Lent Hamilton, whom she calls "Randolph," the baby, and the big gun – and it refuses to hold more. . . .

Somebody came in just now and reported Colonel Chesnut asleep on the sofa in General Beauregard's room. After two such nights he must be so tired as to be able to sleep anywhere.

Just bade farewell to Langdon Cheves. He is forced to go home, to leave this interesting place. He says he feels like the man who was not killed at Thermopylae. I think he said that that unfortunate had to hang himself when he got home for very shame; maybe fell on his sword, which was a strictly classic way of ending matters. . . .

"Richmond and Washington Ablaze," say the papers. Blazing with excitement! Why not? To us these last days' events seem frightfully great. We were all, on that iron balcony, women. Men we only see now at a distance. Stark Means marching under the piazza at the head of his regiment held his cap in his hand all the time he was in sight. Mrs. Means was leaning over, looking with tearful eyes. "Why did he take his hat off?"

said an unknown creature. Mrs. Means stood straight up. "He did that in honor of his mother. He saw me." She is a proud mother, and at the same time most unhappy. Her lovely daughter Emma is dying before her eyes of consumption. At that moment, I am sure Mrs. Means had a spasm of the heart. At least she looked as I sometimes feel. She took my arm and we came in.

APRIL 13th. – Nobody hurt, after all. How gay we were last night. Reaction after the dread of all the slaughter we thought those dreadful cannons were making such a noise in doing. Not even a battery the worse for wear.

Fort Sumter has been on fire. He has not yet silenced any of our guns, or so the aids – still with swords and red sashes by way of uniform – tell us. But the sound of those guns makes regular meals impossible. None of us go to table, but tea trays pervade the corridors going everywhere. Some of the anxious hearts lie on their beds and moan in solitary misery. Mrs. Wigfall and I solace ourselves with tea in my room. These women have all a satisfying faith. "God is on our side," they cry. When we are shut in, we, Mrs. Wigfall and I, ask: "Why?" Answer: "Of course, He hates the Yankees! You'll think that well of Him."

Not by one word or look can we detect any change in the demeanor of these Negro servants. Lawrence sits at our door, as sleepy and as respectful and as profoundly indifferent. So are they all. They carry it too far. You could not tell that they even hear the awful noise that is going on in the bay, though it is dinning in their ears night and day. And people talk before them as if they were chairs and tables, and they make no sign. Are they stolidly stupid, or wiser than we are, silent and strong, biding their time....

APRIL 15th. – I did not know that one could live such days of excitement. They called: "Come out! There is a crowd coming." A mob, indeed; but it was headed by Colonels Chesnut and Manning. The crowd was shouting and showing these two as messengers of good news whom they were escorting to Beauregard's Headquarters. Fort Sumter had surrendered! Those up on the housetop shouted to us: "The Fort is on fire." That had been the story once or twice before.

When we had calmed down, Colonel Chesnut, who had taken it all quietly enough, if anything more unruffled than usual in his serenity, told us how the surrender came about.

Wigfall was with them on Morris Island when he saw the fire in the Fort, jumped in a little boat, and with his handkerchief as a white flag, rowed over to Fort Sumter. Wigfall went in through a porthole. When Colonel Chesnut arrived shortly after, and was received by the regular entrance, Colonel Anderson told him he had need to pick his way warily, for it was all mined. As far as I can make out, the Fort surrendered to Wigfall. But it is all confusion. Our flag is flying there. Fire engines have been sent to put out the fire. Everybody tells you half of something and then rushes off to tell someone else, or to hear the last news.

In the afternoon Mrs. Preston, Mrs. Joe Heyward and I drove around the Battery. We were in an open carriage. What a changed scene! The very liveliest crowd I think I ever saw. Everybody talking at once, all glasses still turned on the grim old Fort. [William Howard] Russell, the English reporter for the Times, was there. They took him everywhere. One man studied up his Thackeray to converse with him on equal terms. Poor Russell was awfully bored, they say. He only wanted to see the Forts and get news that was suitable to make an interesting article. Thackeray was stale news over the water.

Mrs. Frank Hampton and I went to see the camp of the Richland troops. South Carolina College had volunteered to a boy. Professor [Charles Scott] Venable (The Mathematical) intends to raise a company from among them for the war, a permanent company. This is a grand frolic, no more – for the students at least!

Even the staid and severe-of-aspect [former US Senator Thomas L.] Clingman is here. He says Virginia and North Carolina are arming to come to our rescue; for now the United States will swoop down on us. Of that we may be sure. We have burned our ships. We are obliged to go on now. He calls us a poor little hot-blooded, headlong, rash and troublesome sister state. . . .

Preston Hampton in all the flush of his youth and beauty – he is six feet in stature, and after all only in his teens – appeared in lemon-colored kid gloves to grace the scene. The camp in a fit of horse play seized him and rubbed them in the mud. He fought manfully but took it all, naturally, as a good joke.

Mrs. Frank Hampton knows already what civil war means. Her brother was in the New York Seventh Regiment so roughly received in Baltimore. Frank will be in the opposite camp.

Source: Mary Boykin Chesnut, *A Diary from Dixie*, ed. Ben Ames Williams (Boston: Houghton Mifflin, 1949), 47–54.

Discussion Questions

1   According to the South Carolina secession convention and Alexander H. Stephens, why did white southerners believe their states had to leave the Union?
2   In what respects was it appropriate to play "Dixie" at Jefferson Davis's inauguration as Confederate president? In what respects was it not appropriate?

3 What do the Crittenden Compromise proposals and Lincoln's First Inaugural
   Address have in common? How do they differ?
4 How should Mary Boykin Chesnut's observations concerning the approaching
   conflict over Fort Sumter inform interpretations of the political documents in
   this chapter?

Chapter 3   Battles

1. William Howard Russell
First Battle of Bull Run, July 20, 1861

> *When Virginia seceded following the initiation of warfare at Fort Sumter, the*
> *Confederacy moved its capital from Montgomery to Richmond. This made*
> *the 100 miles between that city and Washington the major battleground*
> *of the war, as capturing the Confederate capital became a major Union*
> *objective. Although Union General-in-Chief Winfield Scott recognized that*
> *an army had to be trained before it advanced, Republican newspapers and*
> *politicians during the early summer of 1861 demanded action to prevent the*
> *Confederate Congress from meeting in Richmond. In response, Lincoln*
> *ordered General Irvin McDowell, commander of the 35,000-man Army*
> *of the Potomac, to attack the 20,000 Confederate troops, commanded by*
> *General P. G. T. Beauregard, who blocked the path to Richmond. Beauregard*
> *had positioned his army on the southern bank of Bull Run at the town of*
> *Manassas Junction. Despite great confusion among officers and men at Bull*
> *Run, the Union army appeared to be on the verge of victory until 10,000*
> *Confederate reinforcements arrived by train. Then Union troops gave way in*
> *a disastrous rout. British journalist William Howard Russell (1820–1907), of*
> *the* London Times, *was caught up in the retreat. His depiction of the Union*
> *debacle led to death threats. Within a year, the US Department of War revoked*
> *his press pass.*

July 20th, 1861 – The great battle which is to arrest rebellion or to make it a
power in the land is no longer distant or doubtful. McDowell has completed
his reconnaissance of the country in front of the enemy, and General Scott
anticipates that he will be in possession of Manassas tomorrow night.

All statements of officers concur in describing the Confederates as strongly intrenched along the line of Bull Run covering the railroad. . . .

[. . .]

Some senators and many congressmen have already gone to join McDowell's army or to follow in its wake in the hope of seeing the Lord deliver the Philistines into his hands. . . . Every carriage, gig, wagon, and hack has been engaged by people going out to see the fight. The price is enhanced by mysterious communications respecting the horrible slaughter in the skirmishes at Bull Run. The French cooks and hotel keepers, by some occult process of reasoning, have arrived at the conclusion that they must treble the prices of their wines and of the hampers of provisions which the Washington [DC] people are ordering to comfort themselves at their bloody Derby. . . .

[. . .]

. . . The sounds which came upon the breeze and the sights which met our eyes were in terrible variance with the tranquil character of the landscape. The woods far and near echoed to the roar of cannon, and thin, frayed lines of blue smoke marked the spots whence came the muttering sound of rolling musketry; the white puffs of smoke burst high above the treetops, and the gunners' rings from shell and howitzer marked the fire of the artillery.

[. . .]

On the hill beside me there was a crowd of Civilians on horseback and in all sorts of vehicles, with a few of the fairer, if not gentler, sex. A few officers and some soldiers, who had straggled from the regiments in reserve, moved about among the Spectators and pretended to explain the movements of the troops below of which they were profoundly ignorant. . . .

[. . .]

The spectators were all excited, and a lady with an Opera glass who was near me was quite beside herself when an unusually heavy discharge roused the current of her blood – "That is splendid. Oh, my! Is not that first-rate! I guess we will be in Richmond this time tomorrow." These, mingled with coarser exclamations, burst from the politicians who had come out to see the triumph of the Union arms. . . .

[. . .]

Loud cheers suddenly burst from the spectators as a man dressed in the uniform of an officer, whom I had seen riding violently across the plain in an open space below, galloped along the front, waving his cap and shouting at the top of his voice. He was brought up, by the press of people round his horse, close to where I stood. "We've whipped them on all points," he cried. "We have taken all their batteries. They are retreating as fast as they can, and we are after them." Such cheers as rent the welkin! The congressmen shook hands with each other and cried out; "Bully for us! Bravo! Didn't I tell you so?" The Germans uttered their martial cheers, and the Irish hurrahed wildly. At this moment my horse was brought up the hill and I mounted and turned toward the road to the front. . . .

[. . .]

I had ridden between three and a half and four miles, as well as I could judge, when I was obliged to turn for the third and fourth time into the road by a considerable stream which was spanned by a bridge, toward which I was threading my way, when my attention was attracted by loud shouts in advance and I perceived several wagons coming from the direction of the battlefield, the drivers of which were endeavoring to force their horses past the ammunition carts going in the contrary direction near the bridge; a thick cloud of dust rose behind them, and running by the side of the wagons were a number of men in uniform whom I supposed to be the guard. My first impression was that the wagons were returning for fresh supplies of ammunition. But every moment the crowd increased; drivers and men cried out with the most vehement gestures: 'Turn back! Turn back! We are whipped." They seized the heads of the horses and swore at the opposing drivers. Emerging from the crowd, a breathless man in the uniform of an officer, with an empty scabbard dangling by his side, was cut off by getting between my horse and a cart for a moment. "What is the matter, sir? What is all this about?" "Why, it means we are pretty badly whipped, that's the truth," he gasped, and continued.

By this time the confusion had been communicating itself through the line of wagons toward the rear, and the drivers endeavored to turn round their vehicles in the narrow road, which caused the usual amount of imprecations from the men and plunging and kicking from the horses.

[. . .]

A few shells could be heard bursting not far off, but there was nothing to account for such an extraordinary scene. . . . In a few seconds a crowd of men rushed out of the wood down toward the guns, and the artillery-men near me seized the trail of a piece and were wheeling it round to fire when an officer or sergeant called out: "Stop! stop! They are our own men"; and in two or three minutes the whole battalion came sweeping past the guns at the double and in the utmost disorder. Some of the artillery-men dragged the horses out of the tumbrils, and for a moment the confusion was so great I could not understand what had taken place; but a soldier whom I stopped said, "We are pursued by their cavalry; they have cut us all to pieces."

. . . It could not be doubted that some thing serious was taking place; and at that moment a shell burst in front of the house, scattering the soldiers near it, which was followed by another that bounded along the road; and in a few minutes more out came another regiment from the wood, almost as broken as the first. The scene on the road had now assumed an aspect which has not a parallel in any description I have ever read. Infantry soldiers on mules and draft horses with the harness clinging to their heels, as much frightened as their riders; Negro servants on their masters' chargers; ambulances crowded with unwounded soldiers; wagons swarming with men who threw out the contents in the road to make room, grinding through a shouting, screaming mass of men on foot who were literally yelling with rage at every halt and shrieking out: "Here are the cavalry! Will you get on?" This portion of the force was evidently in discord.

There was nothing left for it but to go with the current one could not stem. I turned round my horse.... I was unwillingly approaching Centerville [five miles northeast of Mansassas Junction] in the midst of heat, dust, confusion, imprecations inconceivable. On arriving at the place where a small rivulet crossed the road the throng increased still more. The ground over which I had passed going out was now covered with arms, clothing of all kinds, accouterments thrown off and left to be trampled in the dust under the hoofs of men and horses. The runaways ran along side the wagons, striving to force themselves in among the occupants, who resisted tooth and nail. The drivers spurred and whipped and urged the horses to the utmost of their bent. I felt an inclination to laugh which was overcome by disgust and by that vague sense of something extraordinary taking place which is experienced when a man sees a number of people acting as if driven by some unknown terror. As I rode in the crowd, with men clinging to the stirrup leathers or holding on by anything they could lay hands on, so that I had some apprehension of being pulled off, I spoke to the men and asked them over and over again not to be in such a hurry. "There's no enemy to pursue you. All the cavalry in the world could not get at you." But I might as well have talked to the stones....

[...]

It never occurred to me that this was a grand debacle. All along I believed the mass of the army was not broken and that all I saw around was the result of confusion created in a crude organization by a forced retreat, and knowing the reserves were at Centerville and beyond, I said to myself, "Let us see how this will be when we get to the hill."...

[...]

I was trotting quietly down the hill road beyond Centerville when suddenly the guns on the other side or from a battery very near opened fire, and a fresh outburst of artillery sounded through the woods. In an instant the mass of vehicles and retreating soldiers, teamsters, and civilians, as if agonized by an electric shock, quivered throughout the tortuous line. With dreadful shouts and cursings the drivers lashed their maddened horses and, leaping from the carts, left them to their fate and ran on foot. Artillerymen and foot soldiers and Negroes, mounted on gun horses with the chain traces and loose trappings trailing in the dust, spurred and flogged their steeds down the road or by the side paths. The firing continued and seemed to approach the hill, and at every report the agitated body of horsemen and waggons was seized, as it were, with a fresh convulsion.

Once more the dreaded cry: "The cavalry! cavalry are coming!" rang through the crowd, and looking back to Centerville, I perceived coming down the hill, between me and the sky, a number of mounted men who might at a hasty glance be taken for horsemen in the act of sabering the fugitives. In reality they were soldiers and civilians, with, I regret to say, some officers among them, who were whipping and striking their horses with sticks or whatever else they could lay hands on. I called out to the men who were frantic with terror beside me, "They are not cavalry at all; they're your Own men" – but they did not heed me.... When I was passing by the line of the bivouacs a battalion of men came tumbling down the bank from the field into the road with fixed bayonets, and as some fell in the road and others tumbled on top of them, there must have been a few ingloriously wounded....

[...]

22d. – I awoke [in Washington] from a deep sleep this morning about six o'clock. The rain was falling in torrents and beat with a dull, thudding sound on the leads outside my window; but louder than all came a strange sound as if of the tread of men, a confused tramp and splashing and a murmuring of voices. I got up and ran to the front room, the windows of which looked on the street, and there, to my intense surprise, I saw a steady stream of men covered with mud, soaked through with rain, who were pouring irregularly, without any semblance of order, up Pennsylvania Avenue toward the Capitol. A dense stream of vapor rose from the multitude, but looking closely at the men, I perceived they belonged to different regiments, New Yorkers, Michiganders, Rhode Islanders, Massachusetters, Minnesotans, mingled pellmell together. Many of them were without knapsacks, crossbelts, and fire-locks. Some had neither greatcoats nor shoes; others were covered with blankets. Hastily putting on my clothes, I ran downstairs and asked an officer who was passing by, a pale young man who looked exhausted to death and who had lost his sword, for the empty sheath dangled at his side, where the men were coming from. "Where from? Well, sir, I guess we're all coming out of Virginny as far as we can, and pretty well whipped too." "What! the whole army, sir?" "That's more than I know....I know I'm going home. I've had enough of fighting to last my lifetime."

The news seemed incredible. But there before my eyes were the jaded, dispirited, broken remnants of regiments passing onward, where and for what I knew not, and it was evident enough that the mass of the grand army of the Potomac was placing that river between it and the enemy as rapidly as possible. "Is there any pursuit?" I asked of several men. Some were too surly to reply; others said, "They're coining as fast as they can after us"; others, "I guess they've stopped it now – the rain is too much for them." A few said they did not know and looked as if they did not care....

[...]

The rain has abated a little, and the pavements are densely packed with men in uniforms, some with, others without, arms, on whom the shopkeepers are looking with evident alarm. They seem to be in possession of all the spirit houses [taverns]. Now and then shots are heard down the street or in the distance, and cries and shouting, as if a scuffle or a difficulty were occurring. Willard's [Hotel] is turned into a barrack for officers and presents such a scene in the hall as could only be witnessed in a city occupied by a demoralized army. There is no provost guard, no patrol, no authority visible in the streets. General Scott is quite overwhelmed by the affair and is unable to stir. General McDowell has not yet arrived. The Secretary of War [Simon Cameron] knows not what to do, Mr. [Abraham] Lincoln is equally helpless, and Mr. [William H.] Seward, who retains some calmness, is, notwithstanding his military rank and militia experience, without resource or expedient. There are a good many troops hanging on about the camps and forts on the other side of the river, it is said; but they are thoroughly disorganized and will run away if the enemy comes in sight without a shot, and then the capital must fall at once. Why [P. G. T.] Beauregard does not come I know not, nor can I well guess. I have been expecting every hour since noon to hear his cannon. Here is a golden opportunity. If the Confederates do not grasp that which will never come again on such terms, it stamps them with mediocrity.

Source: William Howard Russell, *My Diary North and South* (Boston: T. O. H. P. Burnam, 1863), 434–79.

2. Walt Whitman
"1861"

> *Walt Whitman (1819–92) is counted among America's great poets. He had little formal education and liked to present himself as a member of the working class – one of "the roughs." But before the Civil War he worked as a journalist in Brooklyn, New York, and knew the major philosophical*

*and literary currents of his time. During the war, Whitman volunteered as
a nurse in military hospitals in Washington, DC. He was especially sensitive
to what the war meant to northern farmers and working men. In "1861,"
which Atlantic editor James Russell Lowell refused to publish that year,
Whitman explores the tension between the danger of war and its masculine
appeal.*

ARM'D year! year of the struggle!
No dainty rhymes or sentimental love verses for you
  terrible year!
Not you as some pale poetling seated at a desk, lisping
  cadenzas piano;
But as a strong man, erect, clothed in blue clothes,
  advancing, carrying a rifle on your shoulder,
With well-gristled body and sunburnt face and hands –
  with a knife in the belt at your side,
As I heard you shouting loud – your sonorous voice
  ringing across the continent;
Your masculine voice, O year, as rising amid the great
  cities,
Amid the men of Manhattan I saw you, as one of the
  workmen, the dwellers in Manhattan;
Or with large steps crossing the prairies out of Illinois
  and Indiana,
Rapidly crossing the West with springy gait and
  descending the Alleghenies;
Or down from the great lakes, or in Pennsylvania, or on
  deck along the Ohio river,
Or southward along the Tennessee or Cumberland
  rivers, or at Chattanooga on the mountain top,
Saw I your gait and saw I your sinewy limbs clothed in
  blue, bearing weapons, robust year;
Heard your determin'd voice launch'd forth again and
  again;
Year that suddenly sang by the mouths of the round
  lipp'd cannon,
I repeat you, hurrying, crashing, sad, distracted year.

Source: Walt Whitman, *Drum Taps* (New York: privately printed, 1865), 17.

3. William Monks
Battle of Wilson Creek and Guerilla War in Missouri, 1861–62

Confederate irregulars waged guerilla war in Missouri, West Virginia,
Virginia, and Tennessee. As James M. McPherson points out, historians
disagree concerning the effectiveness of these irregulars. They distracted
Union troops, interfered with supplies and communications, and in some cases
slowed the advance of Union armies. But the guerillas' brutal treatment of
civilians undermined the Confederate cause and invited reprisals. It might
be argued that guerrilla war began in 1855 with the actions of proslavery
Missouri "Border Ruffians" in Kansas Territory. Although the overwhelming
majority of white Missourians – including most slaveholders – supported the
Union, about 3,000 Confederate guerillas, led by such men as William
Quantrill, remained active throughout the war and into Reconstruction.
William Monks (1830–1913), a Union colonel, as well as an irregular on
the Union side, describes the actions of the Confederate guerillas in Missouri
following the disastrous Union defeat at the hands of regular Confederate
troops at the August 10, 1861 Battle of Wilson Creek.

On reaching Springfield [in June 1861], I was conducted directly to the head quarters of Gen. [Nathaniel] Lyon, gave him all the information in my possession and told him I had been entirely stripped, had no means with me for support and I would like to join the army. He remarked to me, "I don't want you to join the army; we intend to move south next spring and you are one of the men that will be in great demand. We have a position for you and the Government will pay you good wages."

... About five days before the Wilson Creek battle it was reported that the Rebels were on Cane creek, west of Springfield, in considerable force. Gen. Lyon moved out with a considerable force ... [and] on seeing the federal forces approaching they [the Rebels] retreated. On the 8th day of August the rebels appeared in large force, being commanded by Gen. [Sterling] Price and Gen. [Ben] McCullough.

Gen. Lyon sent out scouts with glasses for the purpose, if possible, of ascertaining their number. The rebels had gone into camp about ten miles from Springfield, with the avowed purpose of attacking Gen. Lyon the next day at Springfield, and as the scouts were not able with their glasses to see the largest force of rebels, which was encamped around a point out of sight, reported as to what they thought the number was. Lyon and [Franz] Siegel [sic] came to the conclusion that by strategy they could easily whip them, so on the morning of the 10th, about midnight, they broke camp at Springfield, taking all of their available men. The morning being very foggy and misty, they easily surrounded the pickets and took them prisoners without the firing of a gun, then drew up and fired the artillery into them before they knew they were there.

So the memorable fight known as the battle of Wilson Creek was begun. . . . Both the Confederate and Union side were founding all their future hopes upon the result of that battle, as to settling the question in Missouri. The author heard the artillery all day. Late in the evening word came to the Union men that Gen. Lyon had been killed and that the Federal army was retreating in the direction of Rolla, Missouri, and that all the Union men and the home guard would fall in and meet them at once. O! the scene that followed. Men would hurriedly ride around, meet their wives and children, tell them that the battle was lost and they were then retreating and they had only time to come around and bid them good-bye, and to do the best they could; that they didn't know that they would ever be permitted to see them again. We could hear the wife and children crying and sending up the most pitiful petitions to God to have mercy.

Everything on the Union side appeared to be dark, although it was a drawn battle and the rebels commenced retreating at the same time, and retreated about twenty-five miles west, but on learning that the Federal troops were retreating, they faced about, taking possession of the battle-ground and all of the southern and western portion of the state; and then the rebels, being encouraged by the late victory, determined to rid the country of all Union men at once. About that time about 350 [Confederate] men mostly from Oregon county commanded by two very prominent men, made a scout into Ozark county, Missouri. On reaching the North fork of White river they went into camp at what was known as Jesse James' mill. The owner, a man of about 55 or 60 years of age, as good a man as resided in Ozark county, was charged with grinding grain for Union men and their families; at the time he, and a man by the name of Brown, were cutting sawlogs about two miles from home in the pinery. They went out and arrested them, arrested an old man by the name of Russell and several others, carried them to a man's house, who was a Union man, and had fled to prevent arrest. They took Brown and James about 300 yards from the house, procured a rope, hunted a long limb of a tree, rolled a big rock up to the first rope where it was tied to the limb, placed the noose around James' neck, stood him on the rock, rolled the rock from under him and left him swinging, rolled the rock to the next rope, stood Brown on it, placed the noose around his neck, rolled the rock out and left Brown swinging in the air, went to the third rope, placed Russell on the rock, and just as they aimed to adjust the noose, word came that the home guards and Federals were right upon them in considerable force. They fled, leaving Russell standing upon the rock and both Brown and James dangling in the air.

Every Union man now having fled in fear of his life, the next day the wives of Brown and James, with the help of a few other women, buried them as best they could. They dug graves underneath the swinging bodies, laid bed clothing in the graves and cut them loose. The bodies fell into the coffinless graves and the earth was replaced. So the author is satisfied that the bones of these men still remain in the lonely earth underneath where they met their untimely death with no charge against them except that they had been feeding Union men, with no one to bury them but their wives and a few other women who aided. . . .

A short time after this hanging there was a man by the name of Rhodes, who resided on the head of Bennett's Bayou in Howell county. He was about eighty years of age and had been a soldier under General [Andrew] Jackson. His head was perfectly white and he was very feeble. When he heard of the hanging of Brown and James he said openly that there was no civil war in that, and that the men who did it were guilty of murder.

Some two weeks from the date of the hanging of Brown and James, about twenty-five [Confederate] men, hearing of what he had said, organized themselves and commanded by Dr. Nunly and William Sapp, proceeded to the house of Rhodes, where he and his aged wife resided alone, called him out and told him they wanted him to go with them. His aged wife came out, and being acquainted with a part of the men, and knowing that they had participated in the hanging and shooting of a number of Union men, talked with them and asked: "You are not going to hurt my old man?" They said: "We just want him to go a piece with us over here." Ordering the old man to come along, they went over to a point about one quarter from the house and informed him of what he had said. There they shot him, cut his ears off and his heart out. Dr. Nunly remarked that he was going to take the heart home with him, pickle it and keep it so people could see how a black republican's heart looked.

They left him lying on the ground, proceeded directly to Joseph Spears' who resided about six miles west of town on the Yellville road, declaring that they were going to treat him the same way. They reached his house about two hours in the night, all full of whiskey. When they arrived there Spears was sick in bed. They dismounted, came in, ordered their suppers and their horses fed. Spears at that time owned a Negro man, and he ordered him to put up the horses and feed them, and his wife to get them supper. After supper, they concluded to remain until morning. During the night they became sober, and concluded, since Spears owned a "nigger," that it could not be possible that he was a Union man, and the reports that they had heard that he was a Union man might be untrue, and they would let him alone until they could investigate further.

In the meantime, Rhodes not having returned home, and not a single Union man left in the country that Mrs. Rhodes could get to look after him, and having heard when they reached Joseph Spears' that the old man was not with them, although very feeble, she still continued the search; on the second day, about fifty yards from the road and about a quarter of a mile from home, while she was looking for him, she heard hogs squealing and grunting as though they were eating something. She proceeded to the place and found the hogs were just about to commence eating the remains of her husband. The Union men having fled, she notified some of the neighbors, and the women came in and helped dress the body and buried him the best they could; and neither at the taking down or burial of Brown and James and the burial of the old man Rhodes did a single rebel put in an appearance.

There never was a man arrested by the Confederate authorities, or a single word of condemnation uttered, but as far as could be heard there was general approval. It was said that the means used were desperate, but that was the only way to get rid of the men and strike terror to them so they could neither give aid nor countenance to the . . . [Union].

[. . .]

After they had hung, shot, captured and driven from the country all of the Union men [during the weeks following the Battle of Wilson Creek], they called a public meeting for the purpose of taking into consideration what should be done with the families of the Union men, which meeting had a number of preachers in it. After discussing the premises, they arrived at the conclusion that if they let the families of the Union men, who had escaped and gone into the Federal lines, remain, they would return. . . . They didn't believe that both parties could ever live together, and as they now had the country completely rid of the Union men, they would force their families to leave. They at once appointed men, among whom were several preachers, to go to each one of the Union families and notify them that they would not be allowed to remain; because if they let them stay, their men would be trying to come back, and they didn't believe both parties could live together. They stated at the same time that they were really sorry for the women and children, but nobody was to blame but their husbands and sons, who had cast their lot with the . . . [Union]. Also, as they had taken up arms against the Confederate states, all the property they had, both real and personal, was subject to confiscation and belonged to the Confederate authorities; but they would allow them to take enough of the property to carry them inside of the [Union] lines . . . where they supposed their men were and where they then could care for them.

They said they might have a reasonable time to make preparations to leave the country, and if they didn't leave, they would be forced to do so, if they had to arrest them and carry them out.

The wildest excitement then prevailed among the women and children. They had no men to transact their business and make preparations to leave. Little had they thought, while they [the Confederates] were chasing, arresting, hanging and shooting their men, that they, too, would become victims of the rebel hatred and be forced to leave house and home, not knowing where their men were or whether they were dead or alive. All they knew of their whereabouts was, that those who escaped arrest had left their homes, aiming to reach the nearest Federal lines.

Women were at once dispatched to reach the nearest Federal lines, if possible, and inform them of the Confederate order, and procure help to take them out. Their homes and houses were being continually raided by small bands of Confederates roaming over the country, claiming that they were hunting Union men, taking all classes of property that they might see proper to take, without any restraint whatever.

When the Union men heard that an order had been made requiring their families to leave, not thinking that a thing of that kind would ever occur, having left them with comfortable homes and plenty to eat, the wildest consternation reigned amongst them.

The Federal authorities were willing to give them aid, but were placed in such a condition that they needed every man in the field, and for that reason couldn't give them any help in getting out. The women had to speedily fit up as best they could, close their doors and start for the Federal lines, leaving the most of their property in the hands of the rebels. The rebels proceeded at once to take possession of and occupy most of the homes.

The suffering that followed the women and children is indescribable. They had to drive their own teams, take care of the little ones, travel through the storms, exposed to it all without a man to help them, nor could they hear a single word of comfort spoken by husband, son or friend. On reaching the Federal lines, all vacant houses and places of shelter were soon filled, and they were known and styled as refugees. Many of them went into soldier huts, where the soldiers had wintered and covered the tops of their huts with earth. They had to leave home with a small amount of rations, and on the road the rebels would stop them and make them divide up the little they had started with, and reaching the Federal lines they would be almost destitute of food and many of them very scantily clothed.

[...]

Those who did meet their husbands and sons were also disappointed; they had either joined the service or been employed by the government as guides and scouts, and the small amount of pay they received from the government, wouldn't provide food and raiment for their families. They were compelled to still be absent from their families, although they were suffering greatly for all of the necessaries of life and for clothing and shelter. The women's task of caring for and looking after the family and the little ones was just as great after they had reached the Federal lines as before. The government ordered that wherever aid could be given, rations should be issued to the families, and while the government did all it could in this way, it was not able to furnish shelter and houses for their comfort. Winter came on and they underwent untold suffering; disease set in from exposure, besides the contagious diseases of smallpox and measles, and hundreds of them died for want of proper attention, while their men were in the lines of the service of the government.

Source: William Monks, *A History of Southern Missouri and Northern Arkansas* (West Plains, MO: West Plains Journal Co., 1907), 79–91.

4. S. Dana Greene
The Monitor *Battles the* Virginia *(Merrimac), August 9, 1862*

> *The naval engagement between the Union ironclad* Monitor *and its Confederate counterpart, the* Virginia *(a.k.a. the* Merrimac*) illustrates the importance of coastal warfare as well as technological advancement in the Civil War. The Union enjoyed naval superiority throughout the war and used it to blockade Confederate ports. But the transformation early in 1862 of the former USS* Merrimac *into the ironclad CSS* Virginia *threatened that strategy in Chesapeake Bay, where on March 8, 1862 the* Virginia *attacked a Union fleet. Although slow and unwieldy, the* Virginia *was impervious to the Union ships' cannon. In less than five hours, it sank two wooden Union warships, forced three others aground, and fired on Union shore batteries. Warned in advance, the technologically innovative but unseaworthy* Monitor *barely managed to reach the battle site. Its distinguishing characteristics included a shallow draft, a deck just one foot above the water line, and a single revolving turret with two 11-inch cannon. On March 9 it engaged the* Virginia *in a momentous though indecisive struggle. This account by S. Dana Greene (c.1840–84), the* Monitor's *young executive officer, exaggerates the success of the* Monitor, *but suggests the impact of new technology in a battle that made wooden warships obsolete. The* Monitor *became the model for a new fleet of Union ironclads.*

U. S. STEAMER MONITOR, Hampton Roads,
March 14th, 1864.

MY DEAR MOTHER AND FATHER – I commence this now, but don't know when I shall finish, as I have to write it at odd moments, when I can find leisure.... At eleven A.M., Thursday [March 6] we started down [New York] harbor, in company with the gun-boats Sachem and Currituck. About noon [Friday] the wind freshened, and the sea was quite rough. In the afternoon the sea was breaking over our decks at a great rate, and coming in our hawse-pipe forward in perfect floods.... At four P.M. the water had gone down our smoke-stacks and blowers to such an extent that the blowers gave out, and the engine-room was filled with gas.... Fortunately the wind was off shore, so we hailed the tug-boat and told them to steer directly for the shore, in order to get into smooth water. After five hours of hard steaming we got near the land and in smooth water. At eight P.M. we succeeded in getting the engines to work, and everything apparently quiet....

The first watch passed away nicely; smooth sea, clear sky, the moon out, and the old tank going along at the rate of six knots.... At twelve o'clock...I was startled by the most infernal noise I ever heard. The Merrimac's firing on Sunday last was music [compared] to it. We were just passing a shoal, when the sea suddenly became very rough, and right ahead. It came up with tremendous force through our anchor-well, and forced the air through our hawse-pipe, where the chain comes, and then the water would come through in a perfect stream.... From 4 A.M. [Saturday, March 8] until daylight was the longest hour and a half I ever spent.... At last, however, we... made the tug-boat understand to go nearer in shore, and get in smooth water, which we did at about 8 A.M.... At 4 P.M. we passed Cape Henry, and heard heavy firing in the direction of Fortress Monroe. As we approached it increased, and we immediately cleared the ship for action. When about half way between Fortress Monroe and Cape Henry, we spoke the pilot-boat. He told us the Cumberland was sunk, and the Congress was on fire, and had surrendered to the Merrimac. We could not credit it at first, but as we approached Hampton Roads, we could see the fine old Congress burning brightly, and we then knew it must be true. Sadly, indeed, did we feel to think those two fine old vessels had gone to their last homes with so many of their brave crews. Our hearts were very full, and we vowed vengeance on the Merrimac.... At 9 P.M. we anchored near the frigate Roanoke, the flag-ship... Captain [John L.] Worden [of the Monitor] immediately went on board, and received orders to proceed to Newport News, and protect the Minnesota (then aground) from the Merrimac.

We got under way and arrived at the Minnesota at 11 P.M. I went on board in our cutter, and asked the captain what his prospects were of getting off. He said he should try to get afloat at 2 A.M., when it was high water.... I then told him we should do all in our power to protect him from the Merrimac. He thanked me kindly and wished us success. Just as I arrived back to the Monitor, the Congress blew up, and certainly a grander sight was never seen; but it went straight to the marrow of our bones. Not a word was said, but deep did each man think, and wish we were by the side of the Merrimac. At 1 A.M. we anchored near the Minnesota.... At daylight we discovered the Merrimac at anchor, with several vessels, under Sewall's Point. We immediately made every preparation for battle. At 8 A.M. on Sunday, the Merrimac got under way, accompanied by several steamers, and started direct for the Minnesota. When a mile distant she fired two guns at her. By this time our anchor was up, the men at quarters, the guns loaded, and every thing ready for action. As the Merrimac came close, the captain passed the word to commence firing. I triced up the port, ran out the gun, and fired the *first* gun, and thus commenced the great battle between the Monitor and the Merrimac.

Now mark the condition our men and officers were in. Since Friday morning, forty-eight hours, they had had no rest, and very little food, as we could not conveniently cook. They had been hard at work all night, and nothing to eat for breakfast, except hard bread, and were thoroughly worn out.... But after the first gun was fired we forgot all fatigues, hard work, and every thing else, and fought as hard as men ever fought. We loaded and fired as fast as we could. I pointed and fired the guns myself. Every shot I would ask the captain the effect, and the majority of them were encouraging. The captain was in the pilot-house, directing the movements of the vessel.... The speaking-trumpet from the tower to the pilot-house was broken, so we passed the word from the captain to myself on the berth-deck by Paymaster Keeler and Captain's Clerk Toffey. Five times during the engagement we touched each other, and each time I fired a gun at her, and I will vouch the 168 pounds penetrated her sides. Once she tried to run us down with her iron prow, but did no damage whatever. After fighting for two hours we hauled off for half an hour to hoist shot in the tower. At it we went again as hard as we could, the shot, shell, grape, canister, musket and rifle-balls flying in every direction, but doing no damage. Our tower was struck several times, and though the noise was pretty loud it did not affect us any.... At about 11.30 A.M. the captain sent for me. I went forward, and there stood as noble a man as lives, at the foot of the ladder to the pilot-house, his face perfectly black with powder and iron, and apparently perfectly blind. I asked him what was the matter. He said a shot had struck the pilot-house exactly opposite his eyes and blinded him, and he thought the pilot-house was damaged. He told me to take charge of the ship and use my own discretion. I led him to his room, laid him on the sofa, and then took his position. On examining the pilot-house, I found the iron hatch on top, on the forward side, was completely cracked through. We still continued firing, the tower being under the direction of [A. C.] Steiners. We were between two fires – the Minnesota on one side, and the Merrimac on the other. The latter was retreating to Sewall's Point, and the Minnesota had struck us twice on the tower. I knew if another shot should strike our pilot-house in the same place, our steering apparatus would be disabled, and we should be at the mercy of the batteries on Sewall's Point. We had *strict* orders to act on the defensive, and protect the Minnesota.

We had evidently finished the Merrimac as far as the Minnesota was concerned. Our pilot-house was damaged, and we had orders *not* to follow the Merrimac up; therefore, after the Merrimac had retreated, I went to the Minnesota and remained by her until she was afloat. General [John E.] Wool and Secretary [Gustavus V.] Fox both commended me for acting as I did, and said it was the strict military plan to follow. This is the reason we did not sink the Merrimac; and every one here, capable of judging, says we acted perfectly right.

The fight was over now, and we were victorious. My men and myself were perfectly black with smoke and powder. As we ran alongside the Minnesota, Secretary Fox hailed us, and told us we had fought the greatest naval battle on record, and behaved as gallantly as men could. He saw the whole fight. I felt proud and happy, then, mother, and was fully repaid for all I had suffered. . . .

[. . .]

We literally hold all the property ashore and afloat in these regions, as the wooden vessels are useless against the Merrimac. At no time during the war, either in the army or navy, has any position been so important as this vessel. You may think I am exaggerating somewhat, because I am in the Monitor, but the President, General Wool, Secretary Fox, all think so, and have telegraphed to that effect. . . .

Your affectionate son,

S. D. GREENE.

Source: Lydia Minturn Post, *Soldiers' Letters from Camp, Battle-field and Prison* (New York: Bunce & Huntington, 1865), 106–15.

5. David H. Strother
Battle of Antietam, September 17, 1862

> *After a series of Confederate victories in Virginia, General Robert E. Lee led the 45,000-man Army of Northern Virginia into Maryland. Lee hoped to "liberate" that slave state from "foreign" control, threaten Washington, DC, and – in the process – gain British and French recognition of the Confederacy.*

Union commanding general, George B. McClellan, moved cautiously with the 78,000-man Army of the Potomac to force a battle. It occurred along Antietam Creek at Sharpsburg. It was the biggest battle in American history up to that time, and the bloodiest of the Civil War, with combined Confederate and Union casualties reaching 22,000 in dead and wounded. McClellan held the field, and Lee retreated to Virginia. But, when McClellan failed to pursue and destroy Lee's army, President Lincoln removed him from command. Nevertheless the outcome at Antietam encouraged Lincoln, who did not want to make abolition a Union war aim while the Confederacy seemed to be winning the war, to issue his Preliminary Emancipation Proclamation five days later. Union colonel, David H. Strother (1816–88), a Virginia-born professional illustrator, describes the battle from the vantage point of McClellan's command center.

September 17, Wednesday.... I found the Commander-in-Chief [General George B. McClellan] surrounded by a number of subordinate generals, planning and receiving orders. Thus far the great argument had been opened and conducted solely by those stately and bombastic orators – the cannon. The dispute presently assumed a closer and more conversational tone as the angry chattering of the musketry prevailed. About half past seven o'clock this had swelled to an ominous roar, accompanied by repeated and triumphant cheers. The General-in-Chief, followed by all his attendants, hurried to a bluff just behind the house, whence they had a splendid view of [General Joseph] Hooker's advance driving the enemy before them in rapid and disordered flight.

Horses were forthwith ordered, and we rode rapidly across to a commanding knoll on the eastern side of the Sharpsburg turnpike, about the centre of our line of battle, and nearly opposite the town of Sharpsburg, whose locality was indicated by the belfry of a small church which peered above the opposite hill. This was the same point from which the General reconnoitred the enemy on Monday afternoon, and afforded the most comprehensive view of the field that could be had from any single point.

Our order of battle, as detailed to me by McClellan on yesterday afternoon, was as follows: Our right wing under [General Edwin] Sumner was established across the Antietam, and would swing round, closing in upon the enemy's left and forcing it back upon the centre, thus cutting off the roads to Hagerstown and Williamsport. Our left, under [General Ambrose E.] Burnside, was ordered to force the passage of the Antietam at a stone bridge a mile below the central turnpike, and driving the enemy's right back on Sharpsburg, would bar his retreat toward Antietam Ford on the Potomac and Harper's Ferry, thus (to use the General's own words) pinching him up in a vice. Our centre was refused, and lay behind the stream ready to act as circumstances might require. . . .

The enemy's lines, occupying the ridge which conceals Sharpsburg from us, and thence westward along the Hagerstown pike and the wood behind the Dunker church, are only indicated by the smoke of his guns and an occasional horse man showing himself over the summit to reconnoitre. Meanwhile Sumner had crossed and taken full possession of the position in front of the Dunker church, driving the enemy back into the wood. Several brigades, which I understood to be [General Israel B.] Richardson's Division, advanced to a position still nearer the centre, confronting the enemy between the Dunker church and the town. To meet them the enemy's lines moved out into the open ground and opened fire, when a portion of our troops broke in confusion and ran down the road toward the central bridge. In a few moments, however, they were rallied, and returned to their positions, showing great steadiness for the rest of the day. The rebel line also stood as straight and firm as a stone-wall, although under a heavy fire both of artillery and musketry. I saw the shells strike them frequently, and when there appeared symptoms of wavering I could see the officers collaring the men and forcing them back to their places.

Our troops fought splendidly, and made several advances at a run, but the force seemed entirely too light and too much isolated to effect any decisive purpose. They did their part, however. . . A portion of Sumner's advance had pushed forward nearly to the line of fence in front of the Dunker church; but they seemed to be so cut up and reduced in numbers that they took shelter behind a slope in the field, and only kept up a light skirmishing against the wood.

During these operations the clamor of the artillery along the whole line of battle (several miles in extent) was incessant. We could hear the distant muttering of musketry from the flanks, but Sumner's movement had evidently come to a stand. This produced a lull in the battle within our sight, and I had leisure to remark upon the head-quarters group immediately about me. In the midst was a small redoubt built of fence-rails, behind which sat General Fitz John Porter, who, with a telescope resting on the top rail, studied the field with unremitting attention, scarcely leaving his post during the whole day. His observations he communicated to the commander by nods, signs, or in words so low-toned and brief that the nearest by-standers had but little benefit from them. When not engaged with Porter, McClellan stood in a soldierly attitude intently watching the battle and smoking with the utmost apparent calmness; conversing with surrounding officers and giving his orders in the most quiet under-tones. General [Randolph B.] Marcy, his Chief of Staff, was always near him, and through him orders were usually given to the aides-de-camp to be transmitted to distant points of the field. Several foreign officers of the French, Prussian, and Sardinian service were present. Every thing was as quiet and punctilious as a drawing-room ceremony.

While the activity of the infantry within sight seemed to have been temporarily suspended, the thunder of between two and three hundred pieces of artillery still kept up the continuity of the battle. The shells had set fire to several barns, which were in full blaze, while at intervals I recognized from among the enemy's guns the sudden spring of that tall mushroom-shaped cloud which indicates the explosion of a caisson or ammunition-wagon, showing that our artillery was doing good work.

[General William B.] Franklin's Corps having arrived on the field he is ordered to fill a gap between Sumner and Hooker, occasioned by the rapid advance of the latter doubling back the enemy's left. Shortly after this order was sent I observed a sudden movement from the line of wood behind the Dunker church, and in a moment, as it appeared, the whole field in front was covered with masses of the enemy, formed in columns of grand divisions, advancing at a run, with arms at right shoulder shift, and yelling like demons. I could see the heads of four columns, which seemed to be composed of a brigade each; but the extreme left of the movement was masked by a wood and the smoke of a burning farm-house. The attack was evidently made to recover the wood and position from which they had been driven by Hooker at the commencement of the fight.

The rush of this fiery avalanche swept away the feeble remnant of Sumner's command as the flame of a torch scatters the swarms of blue flies from the shambles. As these, in their disordered and more rapid flight, unmasked the front of the rebel advance there was a swell in the chorus of the battle so vast and voluminous that it seemed as if heaven and earth vibrated with the stunning roar. Cannon and musketry mingled in a tonic outpouring that exceeded in grandeur all sounds I ever heard, except, perhaps, Niagara. The check of pulsation produced by this sudden apparition was relieved by an officer, who whispered: "That's Franklin. Hear him!"

The rebel columns had swept on, disappearing entirely in the dust raised by their own movement through the trampled field, the rolling smoke of the burning houses, and the sulphurous cloud which rose like a snowy mountain over the assailed position. We could distinctly see Sumner's debris rallying behind the wood, forming in line, and returning to the combat. Higher and higher rolled the white clouds, steady and unbroken; the roar of ordnance continued for twenty minutes or more, when, emerging from the smoke, flying in the wildest disorder, thinned and scattered, we saw the enemy returning to the wood from which he had advanced. Shot and shell followed with vengeful rapidity, and anon our ordered lines were seen sweeping over the disputed field to resume their position in front of the Dunker church. As the smoke and dust disappeared I was astonished to observe our troops moving along the front and passing over what appeared to be a long, heavy column of the enemy without paying and discovered this to be actually a column of enemy's dead and wounded lying along a hollow road – afterward known as Bloody Lane. Among the prostrate mass I could easily distinguish the movements of those endeavoring to crawl away from the ground; hands waving as if calling for assistance, and others struggling as if in the agonies of death.

I was standing beside General McClellan during the progress and conclusion of this attack. The studied calmness of his manner scarcely concealed the underlying excitement, and when it was over he exclaimed: "By George, this is a magnificent field, and if we win this fight it will cover all our errors and misfortunes forever!"

"General," I said, "fortune favors the bold; hurl all our power upon them at once, and we will make a glorious finish of the campaign and the war."

"Colonel," said he, "ride forward to [General Alfred] Pleasonton and tell him to throw a couple of squadrons forward on the Sharpsburg road, as far as they can go, to find out what is there."

I Surmise, from this order, the General had suspected the enemy's line immediately in front of our centre was weak. I rode down the turnpike, leaving Potterstown to the left, and near the central bridge. I found General Pleasonton, to whom I delivered the message. He responded promptly by throwing forward two horse-batteries, which took position across the Antietam on either side of the turnpike.

Thus far we had heard nothing and seen no result from Burnside's wing. The General was impatient, and frequently asked: "What is Burnside about? Why do we not hear from him?" During the morning he sent several messengers to hasten his movements; but we only heard vaguely that he had not yet affected a crossing and could not carry the bridge.

Meanwhile the news from the right showed that matters were taking an unfavorable turn there. Hooker was wounded and withdrawn from the field. [General Joseph K. K.] Mansfield was killed, and a number of other valuable general officers *hors de combat*. Our right wing seemed to have spent its aggressive power, and held its ground because the enemy was equally incapable of aggression.

About one o'clock we had news that Burnside had carried the bridge; but there seemed to be a lull in the battle along the whole line from right to left....
[...]

As the afternoon wore away...the fires of death were rekindled along the whole line. Since the overwhelming repulse by Franklin of the enemy's powerful attacking column he seemed to have yielded the contested ground on the right, and to have fallen back to a more sheltered line between the Dunker church and the town. Yet, though his infantry was less demonstrative, his artillery appeared to be stronger and more active than during the forenoon. About this time we witnessed one of the handsomest exhibitions of gallantry which occurred during the day. A battery of ours was seen entering the field in the vicinity of Richardson's Division; moving at a walk and taking position, apparently in advance of our line, it opened fire at short range, and maintained its ground for half an hour under the concentrated fire of at least forty guns of the enemy. As they moved in with the utmost deliberation I saw a number of shells strike and overthrow men and horses, and during the combat the battery sometimes appeared covered with the smoke and dust of the enemy's bursting shells. Unable to sustain the unequal contest they at length withdrew to shelter, and then we saw parties returning to the ground to bring off the wounded in blankets and to remove the limbers of two guns the horses of which had been killed. This, I afterward ascertained, was Graham's Battery United States Artillery, and I was further informed by Lieutenant Elder, who commanded a section in the action, that in half an hour they lost eleven men and seventeen horses. The affair was observed from head-quarters with the greatest interest, and elicited the warmest commendation, especially from the foreign officers on the ground.

At length, about four o'clock in the afternoon, the cumulating thunder on the left announced that Burnside's advance had at last commenced (three hours too late). The advance was distinctly visible from our position, and the movement of the dark columns, with arms and banners glittering in the sun, following the double line of skirmishers, dashing forward at a trot, loading and firing alternately as they moved, was one of the most brilliant and exciting exhibitions of the day. As this splendid advance seemed to be carrying every thing before it our attention was withdrawn to the right by the appearance of large bodies of the enemy with glittering arms and banners moving up the Hagerstown road toward the Dunker church with the apparent intention of renewing the attack in that direction. In a short time, however, this menacing cloud was dispelled by the concentrated fire of forty-two guns which Franklin had in position.

Meanwhile Burnside's attack had carried the height over looking Sharpsburg on the left, having driven the enemy and captured the guns, but a counter attack on his troops, exhausted with their victory, sent them streaming down the hill again, and the last rays of the setting sun shone upon the bayonets of the enemy crowning the hill from which ours had just been driven. At this crisis the General, followed by his whole retinue, rode forward to a bluff nearer the scene of action. It was nearly dark when we reached the point, yet the sullen boom of an occasional gun, and the sparkling lines of musketry on a line about midway between Sharpsburg and the Antietam, showed that ours still held on to a portion of the field they had wrested from the enemy. About this time Burnside's messenger, asking for reinforcements, arrived. It was too late to repair errors or initiate any new movement, and they were not sent.

By eight o'clock the wailing cries of the wounded and the glare of the burning buildings alone interrupted the silence and darkness which reigned over the field of the great battle. The General then led us back to the headquarters camp, established in the rear of Keedysville, where, forgetting the events of the day for the time, we supped heartily and slept profoundly.

Source: D. H. Strother, "Personal Recollections of the War. By a Virginian," *Harper's New Monthly Magazine* 36 (February 1868): 281–4.

6. Frank A. Haskell
Battle of Gettysburg, July 1–3, 1863

> *The Battle of Gettysburg, fought in southeastern Pennsylvania from July 1 to July 3, 1863, is regarded as the "high watermark of the Confederacy." Along with the Union capture of Vicksburg on July 4, 1863, it is considered the turning point of the Civil War. Hoping that by winning a major victory on northern soil he could take pressure off besieged Vicksburg and save the Confederacy's last stronghold on the Mississippi River, Robert E. Lee in June 1863 once again led the Army of Northern Virginia into Union territory. When General Joseph Hooker – commander of the Army of the Potomac – hesitated to engage Lee's army, President Lincoln replaced Hooker with George G. Meade. At the market town of Gettysburg, Meade gave Lee a choice of either attacking an entrenched Union army of 90,000 with Lee's smaller force of 75,000 or retreating. Lee attacked, failed badly on July 2 and 3, and suffered 25,000 casualties – nearly destroying his excellent army. Colonel Frank A. Haskell (1828–64) of Wisconsin's "Iron Brigade," served as aid-de-camp to General John Gibbon, who commanded a division of the Union Second Corps during the battle. Three weeks later Haskell wrote the first comprehensive eyewitness account of the battle. This is an excerpt.*

The enemy...showed a determination and valor worthy of a better cause. Their conduct in this battle even makes me proud of them as Americans. They would have been victorious over any but the best of soldiers. Lee and his generals presumed too much upon some past successes, and did not estimate how much they were due on their part to position, as at Fredericksburg, or on our part to bad generalship, as at the 2d Bull Run and Chancellorsville.

The fight of the 1st of July we do not, of course, claim as a victory; but even that probably would have resulted differently had [General John] Reynolds not been struck. The success of the enemy in the battle ended with the 1st of July. The Rebels were joyous and jubilant – so said our men in their hands, and the citizens of Gettysburg – at their achievements on that day. Fredericksburg and Chancellorsville were remembered by them. They saw victory already won, or only to be snatched from the streaming coat-tails of the 11th corps. or the *"raw Pennsylvania militia"* as they thought they were, when they saw them run; and already the spires of Baltimore and the dome of the National Capitol were forecast upon their glad vision – only two or three days march away through the beautiful valleys of Pennsylvania and *"my"* Maryland. Was there ever anything so fine before? How splendid it would be to enjoy the poultry and the fruit, the meats, the cakes, the beds, the clothing, the *Whiskey*, without price in this rich land of the Yankee! It would, indeed! But on the 2d of July something of a change came over the spirit of these dreams. They were surprised at results and talked less and thought more as they prepared supper that night. After the fight of the 3d they talked only of the means of their own safety from destruction. [George E.] Pickett's splendid division had been almost annihilated, they said, and they talked not of how many were lost, but of who had escaped. They talked of these "Yanks" that had *clubs* on their flags and caps, the trefoils of the 2d corps [which held the Union center on July 3] that are like *clubs* in cards.

The battle of Gettysburg is distinguished in this war, not only as by far the greatest and severest conflict that has occurred, but for some other things that I may mention. The fight of the 2d of July, on the left, which was almost a separate and complete battle, is, so far as I know, alone in the following particulars: the numbers of men actually engaged at one time, and the enormous losses that occurred in killed and wounded in the space of about two hours. . . . Few battles of the war have had so many casualties altogether as those of the two hours on the 2d of July. The 3d of July is distinguished. Then occurred the "great cannonade" – so we call it, and so it would be called in any war, and in almost any battle. And besides this, the main operations that followed have few parallels in history, none in this war, of the magnitude and magnificence of the assault, single and simultan-eous, the disparity of the numbers engaged, and the brilliancy, completeness and overwhelming character of the result in favor of the side numerically the weaker. I think I have not, in giving the results of this encounter, overestimated the numbers or the losses of the enemy. We learned on all hands, by prisoners and by the newspapers, that over two divisions moved up to the assault – Pickett's and [James J.] Pettigrew's – that this was the first engagement of Pickett's in the battle, and the first of Pettigrew's, save a light participation on the 1st of July. The Rebel divisions usually number nine or ten thousand, or did at that time, as we understood. Then I have seen something of troops and think I can estimate their numbers somewhat. The number of the Rebels killed here I have estimated in this way: the 2d and 3d divisions of the 2d corps buried the Rebel dead in their own front, and where they fought upon their own grounds, by count they buried over *one thousand eight hundred*. I think no more than about *two hundred* of these were killed on the 2d of July in front of the 2d division, and the rest must have fallen upon the 3d. My estimates that depend upon this contingency may be erroneous, but to no great extent. The rest of the particulars of the assault, our own losses and our captures, I know are approximately accurate. Yet the whole sounds like romance, a grand stage piece of blood.

Of all the corps d'armie, for hard fighting, severe losses and brilliant results, the palm should be, as by the army it is, awarded to the *"Old Second."* It did more fighting than any other corps, inflicted severer losses upon the enemy in killed and wounded, and sustained a heavier life loss, and captured more flags than all the rest of the army, and almost as many prisoners as the rest of the army. The loss of the 2d corps in killed and wounded in this battle – there is no other test of hard fighting – was almost as great as that of all Gen. Grant's forces in the battle that preceded and in the siege of Vicksburg. Three-eighths of the whole corps were killed and wounded. Why does the Western Army suppose that the Army of the Potomac does not fight? Was ever a more absurd supposition? The Army of the Potomac is grand! Give it good leadership – let it alone – and it will not fail to accomplish all that reasonable men desire.

Source: Frank A. Haskell, "Haskell's Account of the Battle of Gettysburg," in *American Historical Documents, 1000–1904*, The Harvard Classics, vol. 43 (New York: P. F. Collier and Sons, 1910, 400–2.

7. Timothy O'Sullivan
Union Dead on the Gettysburg Battlefield, July 1, 1863

> *The Civil War was the first American war recorded in photographs. Among the more prominent photographers were Mathew Brady and Alexander Gardner. Timothy O'Sullivan (1840–82) worked for both Brady and Gardner, and was employed by Gardner when he took this photograph*

of Union soldiers killed during the Battle of Gettysburg's first day. The photograph later gained the title "Field where General Reynolds Fell," referring to John F. Reynolds, killed by a Confederate sniper as he led his troops in support of General John Buford's cavalry. Americans were accustomed to seeing pictures of dead bodies, because they had deceased family members photographed. They were shocked, however, by the condition, anonymity, and isolation of men whose bodies would never be lovingly prepared for burial by their relatives.

Figure 3   Timothy O'Sullivan, Union Dead on the Gettysburg Battlefield, 1863
Source: Library of Congress.

8. Samuel E. Hope
Black–White Guerilla War in Florida, September 8, 1863

Throughout the Confederacy slaves used the absence of white men and other disruptions caused by the Civil War to seek freedom. In regions invaded from the North, many slaves crossed Union lines and became known as "contrabands." In other areas, black men began to plant food crops rather than cotton. Some escaped into inhospitable terrain and conducted guerilla war against Confederate forces. At times invading Union armies recruited black irregulars. This was the case on the east coast of Florida in early 1863, as black Union troops stationed at Beaufort, South Carolina, raided and encouraged escape. In other regions, however, black guerillas were on their own. Captain Samuel E. Hope (1809–98) of C. Company, 9th Florida Infantry, in this September 1863 letter, reports his company's response to a black raid on a plantation near Crystal River, located southwest of Ocala on Florida's west coast.

Christal river Flor. September 8th 1863

In my report to you of the 1st inst I stated that I had succeeded in capturing the boat and had the negroes cut off so as there would not be much doubt in my getting the Negroes...[who carried out the] raid on Mr. King's plantations. On the morning of the second day I took their trail from where I fired on them the evening previous. They led off towards the mouth of the Withlacoochee River, edging the Coast as near as they could for tide creeks &c. About 4 ock in the evening we discovered one in a cedar tree looking out, on an Island[.] [T]hey discovered us about the same time, we being in the open marsh. [H]ere they seem to have separated only two being together. [A]fter chasing them about two miles through the saw Grass we came up in gun shot of them. [W]e began to fire at them, and they returned the fire very cool and deliberately but we soon got in close range of them and killed them. [O]ne of these negroes was recognized by some of my men as belonging to Mr. Everett, who lives near hear, which ran away from him about nine months ago. [H]e was styled Captain of the party, as I learned from the negroes recaptured of Mr. Kings. [M]yself and men being completely tired down for the want of water, we had to go back and camp until next morning when we took the trail and followed on the third day. [A]bout the same time in the evening of the third day, we came up with two more, and after a Similar chase of the second day, we succeeded in Killing both of them. [F]rom here I never could strike the trail of any more of them, but I am under the impression that we killed or wounded the other three the first day. I could not get any information from either of the four that was killed, as they were all dead.

The only information that I have been able to get is from an old Negro man of Mr. Kings who ran away from them the first day and came back home. [H]e says that [they left] Sea Horse Key at the same time [that] boat did destined for Homasassa, but as yet they have not reached there. [H]e also states that a Gun-boat had gone up the Suwanee River and as soon as it returned it was to come up the river.

Night before last my picket Guard heard several guns down the river in the direction of shell Island. [I]t may be them, but I think if they go up either

River their destiny will be as these has been. I am Captain Very Respectfully Your obt Sevt.

–Samuel E. Hope

Source: Ira Berlin et al., eds., *The Destruction of Slavery* (New York: Cambridge University Press, 1985), 805–6. © 1985 by Cambridge University Press.

9. James Longstreet
Battle of Chickamauga, September 19–20, 1863

> *After Gettysburg and Vicksburg, the Union began to push relentlessly*
> *southward from northeastern Tennessee toward Atlanta. During the late*
> *summer of 1863, Union general William S. Rosecrans, commander of the*
> *Army of the Cumberland, drove southward against the Army of Tennessee,*
> *commanded by General Braxton Bragg. When the Confederate high command*
> *decided to send two divisions westward from Virginia under the command*
> *of James P. Longstreet (1821–1904), Bragg momentarily gained a numerical*
> *advantage of 68,000 troops to Rosecrans's 58,000 and attacked the Union*
> *army at Chickamauga. As Longstreet explains in his official report, his*
> *divisions had a decisive role in this last Confederate offensive victory. But,*
> *because of heavy casualties, Bragg could not follow up. Although the Army*
> *of the Cumberland had suffered similar losses, the Union with its superior*
> *human and material resources soon resumed its southward march with*
> *a victory at Chattanooga on November 25.*

HEADQUARTERS,
Near Chattanooga, October–, 1863

COLONEL: Our train reached Catoosa Platform, near Ringgold [Georgia], about 2 o'clock in the afternoon of September 19. As soon as our horses came up (about 4 o'clock), I started with Colonels Sorrel and Manning, of my staff, to find the headquarters of the commanding general [Braxton Bragg]. We missed our way and did not report till near 11 o'clock at night. Upon my arrival, I was informed that the troops had been engaged during the day in severe skirmishing while endeavoring to get in line for battle. The commanding general gave me a map showing the roads and streams between Lookout Mountain and the Chickamauga River, and a general description of our position, and informed me that the battle was ordered at daylight the next morning, the action to be brought on upon our right and to be taken up successively to the left, the general movement to be a wheel upon my extreme left as a pivot. I was assigned to the command of the Left Wing, composed of [John B.] Hood's and [Thomas C.] Hindman's divisions, an improvised division under Brig. Gen. B[ushrod] R. Johnson, and [Simon B.] Buckner's corps, consisting of [Alexander P.] Stewart's and [William] Preston's divisions. The artillery consisted of the battalions of Majors Williams, Robertson, and Leyden, together with some other batteries attached to brigades.

As soon as the day of the 20th had dawned, I rode to the front to find my troops. The line was arranged from right to left as follows: Stewart's, Johnson's, Hindman's, and Preston's divisions. Hood's division (of which only three brigades were up) was somewhat in the rear of Johnson's. [John B.] Kershaw's and [Benjamin G.] Humphreys' brigades, of [Lafayette] McLaws' division, were ordered forward from Ringgold the night before, but were not yet up. General McLaws had not arrived from Richmond. I set to work to have the line adjusted by closing to the right, in order to occupy some vacant ground between the two wings and to make room for [John B.] Hood in the front line. The divisions were ordered to form with two brigades in the front line, and one supporting where there were but three brigades, and two supporting where there were more than three. General Hood was ordered to take the brigades of Kershaw and Humphreys and use them as supports for his division, thus making his division the main column of attack. Before these arrangements were completed the attack was made by our right wing about 10 o'clock. The battle seemed to rage with considerable fury, but did not progress as had been anticipated. As soon as I was prepared I sent to the commanding general to suggest that I had probably better make my attack. Before the messenger returned I heard that the commanding general had sent orders for the division commanders to move forward and attack. I had no time to find the officer who brought the order, as some of the troops were in motion when I heard of it. Upon this information I at once issued orders to attack to the troops not already in motion, holding one of Buckner's divisions (Preston's) in reserve. As the battle upon our right was not so successful as had been expected in the plan of attack, I was obliged to reverse the order of battle by retaining my right somewhere near the left of the Right Wing. To do this Stewart's division was obliged to halt upon reaching the La Fayette and Chattanooga road.

Hood's column broke the enemy's line near the Brotherton house and made it wheel to the right. In making this movement Major-General Hood fell severely, and it was feared mortally, wounded by a Minnie ball breaking his thigh. He had broken the enemy's line, however, and his own troops and those to his right and left continued to press the enemy with such spirit and force that he could not resist us. Brigadier-General [Evander M.] Law succeeded to the command of Hood's division, and Brigadier-General Kershaw to the command of the two brigades of McLaws' division. General Kershaw, having received no definite orders himself (being under the command of General Hood), was not advised of the wheel to the right, and gained more ground to the front than was intended in the movement of his two brigades. Johnson's division followed the movement made by Hood, and gained the Crawfish Spring and Chattanooga road, having a full share in the conflict. Major-General Hindman, in command of my left division, first met the enemy near the Vineyard house, and drove him back upon his strong position near the Widow Glenn's (or burned) house. By a well-directed front and flank attack, he gained the position after a severe struggle. The enemy's dead at this point mark well his line of battle. Hindman was then ordered to move by his right flank and re-enforce Johnson near the Vidito house, who was pressing forward against great odds.

About 3 o'clock in the afternoon I asked the commanding general for some of the troops of the Right Wing, but was informed by him that they had been beaten back so badly that they could be of no service to me. I had but one division that had not been engaged, and hesitated to venture to put it in, as our distress upon our right seemed to be almost as great as that of the enemy upon his right. I therefore concluded to hold Preston for the time, and urge on to renewed efforts our brave men, who had already been engaged many hours. The heights extending from the Vidito house across to the Snodgrass house gave the enemy strong ground upon which to rally. Here he gathered most of his broken forces and re-enforced them. After a long and bloody struggle, Johnson and Hindman gained the heights near the Crawfish Spring road. Kershaw made a most handsome attack upon the heights at the Snodgrass house simultaneously with Johnson and Hindman, but was not strong enough for the work.

It was evident that with this position gained I should be complete master of the field. I therefore ordered General Buckner to move Preston forward. Before this, however, General Buckner had established a battery of 12 guns, raking down the enemy's line which opposed our Right Wing, and at the same time having fine play upon any force that might attempt to re-enforce the hill that he was about to attack. General Stewart, of his corps, was also ordered to move against any such force in flank. The combination was well-timed and arranged. Preston dashed gallantly at the hill. Stewart flanked a re-enforcing column and captured a large portion of it. At the same time the fire of the battery struck such terror into a heavy force close under it that we took there also a large number of prisoners. Preston's assault, though not a complete success at the onset, taken in connection with the other operations, crippled the enemy so badly that his ranks were badly broken, and by a flank movement and another advance the heights were gained. These re-enforcements were the enemy's last, or reserve, corps, and a part also of the line that had been opposing our Right Wing during the morning. The enemy broke up in great confusion along my front, and about the same time the Right Wing made a gallant dash and gained the line that had been held so long and obstinately against it. A simultaneous and continuous shout from the two wings announced our success complete. The enemy had fought every man that he had, and every one had been in turn beaten. As it was almost dark I ordered my line to remain as it was, ammunition boxes to be refilled, stragglers to be collected, and everything in readiness for the pursuit in the morning.

Early on the 21st, the commanding general stopped at my bivouac and asked my views as to our future movements. I suggested crossing the river above Chattanooga, so as to make ourselves sufficiently felt on the enemy's rear as to force his evacuation of Chattanooga, and, indeed, force him back upon Nashville, and if we should find our transportation inadequate for a continuance of this movement, to follow up the railroad to Knoxville, destroy [Ambrose E.] Burnside, and from there threaten the enemy's rail-road communication in rear of Nashville. This I supposed to be the only practicable flank movement, owing to the scarcity of our transportation, and it seemed to keep us very nearly as close to the railroad as we were at the time. At parting I understood the commanding general to agree that such was probably our best move, and that he was about to give the necessary orders for its execution.

Orders came in the afternoon for the march. The rear of the Right Wing did not move until quite dark. I did not, therefore, put my wing in motion till daylight the following morning.

Before moving on the morning of the 22d, McLaws' division was ordered to follow the enemy on to Chattanooga. The remainder of the command marched for the Red House Ford and halted about noon.

During that night I received orders to march the entire command back to Chattanooga, and moved in pursuance thereof early on the 23d. We reached the Watkins house about 11 a.m., and proceeded to take up a line around the enemy's position at Chattanooga.

[. . .]

The accompanying list of casualties shows a loss by the command (without McNair's brigade, from which no report has been received) of 1,089 killed, 6,506 wounded, and 273 missing. Its strength on going into action on the morning of the 20th was 2,033 officers and 20,849 men.

I have the honor to be, colonel, very respectfully, your most obedient servant,

J. LONGSTREET,
Lieutenant-General.

Source: *War of the Rebellion: A Compilation of the Official Records of the Union and Confederate Armies*, 4 series, 128 vols. (Washington: Government Printing Office, 1890), series 1, vol. 30, pt. 2:287–91.

10. Robert E. Lee
Surrender of the Army of Northern Virginia, April 9, 1865

> *Although General Robert E. Lee's Army of Northern Virginia failed in its invasions of Union territory at Antietam and Gettysburg, it had been nearly invincible in Virginia. President Lincoln sought long to find a Union commander who could defeat Lee (1807–70) in his home state. Lincoln found that commander in Ulysses S. Grant. Grant had won impressive victories in the Western Theater at Forts Henry and Donaldson, Vicksburg, and Chattanooga. In March 1864 Lincoln appointed him supreme Union military commander. Quickly Grant formulated an aggressive strategy in which he would lead the 115,000-man Army of the Potomac into Virginia with the goal of destroying Lee's army. Meanwhile General William Tecumseh Sherman would push south toward Atlanta with an army of 100,000 men. The Army of Northern Virginia continued to fight well, inflicting the greatest Union defeat of the war at Cold Harbor on June 3, 1864. But Grant and the Army of the Potomac were relentless and well-supplied with men and war materials, while accumulated losses steadily weakened the Army of Northern Virginia. Finally, having been driven from his defensive lines at Richmond and Petersburg, Lee reluctantly surrendered at Appomattox Court House on April 9, 1865. Lee describes the end in his report to the President of the Confederacy, Jefferson Davis.*

To His Excellency Jefferson Davis

Near Appomattox Court-House, Va.,
April 12, 1865

Mr. President:

It is with pain that I announce to Your Excellency the surrender of the Army of Northern Virginia. The operations which preceded this result will be reported in full. I will therefore only now state that, upon arriving at

Amelia Court-House on the morning of the 4th with the advance of the army, on the retreat from the lines in front of Richmond and Petersburg, and not finding the supplies ordered to be placed there, nearly twenty-four hours were lost in endeavoring to collect in the country subsistence for men and horses. This delay was fatal, and could not be retrieved. The troops, wearied by continual fighting and marching for several days and nights, obtained neither rest nor refreshment; and on moving, on the 5th, on the Richmond and Danville Railroad, I found at Jetersville the enemy's cavalry, and learned of the approach of his infantry and the general advance of his army toward Burkeville. This deprived us of the use of the railroad, and rendered it impracticable to procure from Danville the supplies ordered to meet us at points of our march. Nothing could be obtained from the adjacent country. Our route to the Roanoke was therefore changed, and the march directed upon Farmville, where supplies were ordered from Lynchburg. The change of route threw the troops over the roads pursued by the artillery and wagon trains west of the railroad, which impeded our advance and embarrassed our movements. On the morning of the 6th General [James] Longstreet's corps reached Rice's Station, on the Lynchburg railroad. It was followed by the commands of Generals R[ichard] H. Anderson, [Richard] Ewell, and [John B.] Gordon, with orders to close upon it as fast as the progress of the trains would permit or as they could be directed on roads farther west. General Anderson, commanding [George] Pickett's and B[ushrod] R. Johnson's divisions, became disconnected with [William] Mahone's division, forming the rear of Longstreet. The enemy's cavalry penetrated the line of march through the interval thus left and attacked the wagon train moving toward Farmville. This caused serious delay in the march of the center and rear of the column, and enabled the enemy to mass upon their flank. After successive attacks Anderson's and Ewell's corps were captured or driven from their position. The latter general, with both of his division commanders, [Joseph B.] Kershaw and Custis Lee, and his brigadiers, were taken prisoners. Gordon, who all the morning, aided by General W. H. F. Lee's cavalry, had checked the advance of the enemy on the road from Amelia Springs and protected the trains, became exposed to his combined assaults, which he bravely resisted and twice repulsed; but the cavalry having been withdrawn to another part of the line of march, and the enemy, massing heavily on his front and both flanks, renewed the attack about 6 p.m., and drove him from the field in much confusion.

The army continued its march during the night, and every effort was made to reorganize the divisions which had been shattered by the day's operations; but the men being depressed by fatigue and hunger, many threw away their arms, while others followed the wagon trains and embarrassed their progress. On the morning of the 7th rations were issued to the troops as they passed Farmville, but the safety of the trains requiring their removal upon the approach of the enemy, all could not be supplied. The army, reduced to two corps, under Longstreet and Gordon, moved steadily on the road to Appomattox Court-House; thence its march was ordered by Campbell Court-House, through Pittsylvania, toward Danville. The roads were wretched and the progress slow. By great efforts the head of the column reached Appomattox Court-House on the evening of the 8th, and the troops were halted for rest. The march was ordered to be resumed at 1 am. on the 9th. Fitz Lee, with the cavalry, supported by Gordon, was ordered to drive the enemy from his front, wheel to the left, and cover the passage of the trains; while Longstreet, who from Rice's Station had formed the rear guard, should close up and hold the position. Two battalions of artillery and the ammunition wagons were directed to accompany the army, the rest of the artillery and wagons to move toward Lynchburg. In the early part of the night the enemy attacked Walker's artillery train near Appomattox Station, on the Lynchburg railroad, and were repelled. Shortly afterward their cavalry dashed toward the Court-House, till halted by our line. During the night there were indications of a large force massing on our left and front. Fitz Lee was directed to ascertain its strength, and to suspend his advance till daylight if necessary. About 5 a.m. on the 9th, with Gordon on his left, he moved forward and opened the way. A heavy force of the enemy was discovered opposite Gordon's right, which, moving in the direction of Appomattox Court-House, drove back the left of the cavalry and threatened to cut off Gordon from Longstreet, his cavalry at the same time threatening to envelop his left flank. Gordon withdrew across the Appomattox River, and the cavalry advanced on the Lynchburg road and became separated from the army.

Learning the condition of affairs on the lines, where I had gone under the expectation of meeting General Grant to learn definitely the terms he proposed in a communication received from him on the 8th, in the event of the surrender of the army, I requested a suspension of hostilities until these terms could be arranged. In the interview which occurred with General Grant in compliance with my request, terms having been agreed on, I surrendered that portion of the Army of Northern Virginia which was on the field, with its arms, artillery, and wagon trains, the officers and men to be paroled, retaining their sidearms and private effects. I deemed this course the best under all the circumstances by which we were surrounded. On the morning of the 9th, according to the reports of the ordnance officers, there were 7,892 organized infantry with arms, with an average of seventy-five rounds of ammunition per man. The artillery, though reduced to sixty-three pieces, with ninety-three rounds of ammunition, was sufficient. These comprised all the supplies of ordnance that could be relied on in the State of Virginia. I have no accurate report of the cavalry, but believe it did not exceed 2,100 effective men. The enemy were more than five times our numbers. If we could have forced our way one day longer it would have been at a great sacrifice of life, and at its end I did not see how a surrender could have been avoided. We had no subsistence for man or horse, and it could not be gathered in the country. The supplies ordered to Pamplin's Station from Lynchburg could not reach us, and the men, deprived of food and sleep for many days, were worn out and exhausted.

With great respect, your obedient servant,

R. E. LEE,

General.

Source: *War of the Rebellion: A Compilation of the Official Records of the Union and Confederate Armies*, 4 series, 128 vols. (Washington, DC: Government Printing Office, 1894), series 1, vol. 46, part 1:1265–7.

11. Ulysses S. Grant
General Report of Operations, March 1864–May 1865

> *That Ulysses S. Grant (1822–85) emerged as the greatest Union general of the Civil War surprised many. In 1843 he graduated low in his West Point class, fought without distinction in the war against Mexico, and – after a bout with alcoholism – left the army in 1854. When the Civil War began he was employed as a clerk in his father's leather goods store in Galena, Illinois. But, starting as a brigadier general, Grant, who lacked charisma, distinguished himself as a trainer of troops, a disciplinarian, administrator, and innovative tactician. As his general report indicates, Grant also excelled as a strategic planner and as a writer. In these excerpts from a much longer report directed to Edwin M. Stanton, Secretary of War, Grant outlines the plan he used to defeat the Confederacy.*

HEADQUARTERS ARMIES OF THE UNITED STATES,
Washington, D.C., July 22, 1865.

SIR: I have the honor to submit the following report of the operations of the armies of the United States from the date of my appointment to command the same:

From an early period in the rebellion I had been impressed with the idea that active and continuous operations of all the troops that could be brought into the field, regardless of season and weather, were necessary to a speedy termination of the war. The resources of the enemy and his numerical strength were far inferior to ours; but as an offset to this, we had a vast territory, with a population hostile to the Government, to garrison, and long lines of river and railroad communications to protect, to enable us to supply the operating armies.

The armies in the East and West acted independently and without concert, like a balky team, no two ever pulling together, enabling the enemy to use to great advantage his interior lines of communication for transporting troops from east to west, re-enforcing the army most vigorously pressed, and to furlough large numbers, during seasons of inactivity on our part, to go to their homes and do the work of producing for the support of their armies. It was a question whether our numerical strength and resources were not more than balanced by these disadvantages and the enemy's superior position.

From the first, I was firm in the conviction that no peace could be had that would be stable and conducive to the happiness of the people, both North and South, until the military power of the rebellion was entirely broken. I therefore determined, first, to use the greatest number of troops practicable against the armed force of the enemy, preventing him from using the same force at different seasons against first one and then another of our armies, and the possibility of repose for refitting and producing necessary supplies for carrying on resistance; second, to hammer continuously against the armed force of the enemy and his resources, until by mere attrition, if in no other way, there should be nothing left to him but an equal submission with the loyal section of our common country to the constitution and laws of the land. These views have been kept constantly in mind, and orders given and campaigns made to carry them out. Whether they might have been better in conception and execution is for the people, who mourn the loss of friends fallen and who have to pay the pecuniary cost, to say. All I can say is, that what I have done has been done conscientiously, to the best of my ability, and in what I conceived to be for the best interests of the whole country.
[...]
There have been severe combats, raids, expeditions, and movements to defeat the designs and purposes of the enemy, most of them reflecting great credit on our arms, and which contributed greatly to our final triumphs, that I have not mentioned. Many of these will be found clearly set forth in the reports herewith submitted; some in the telegrams and brief dispatches announcing them, and others, I regret to say, have not as yet been officially reported. For information touching our Indian difficulties, I would respectfully refer to the reports of the commanders of departments in which they have occurred.

It has been my fortune to see the armies of both the West and the East fight battles, and from what I have seen I know there is no difference in their fighting qualities. All that it was possible for men to do in battle they have done. The Western armies commenced their battles in the Mississippi Valley, and received the final surrender of the remnant of the principal army opposed to them in North Carolina. The armies of the East commenced their battles on the river from which the Army of the Potomac derived its name, and received the final surrender of their old antagonist at Appomattox Court-House, Va. The splendid achievements of each have nationalized our victories, removed all sectional jealousies (of which we have unfortunately experienced too much), and the cause of crimination and recrimination that might have followed had either section failed in its duty. All have a proud record, and all sections can well congratulate themselves and each other for having done their full share in restoring the supremacy of law over every foot of territory belonging to the United States. Let them hope for perpetual peace and harmony with that enemy, whose manhood, however mistaken the cause, drew forth such herculean deeds of valor.

I have the honor to be, very respectfully, your obedient servant,

u. s. grant, Lieutenant-General.

Source: *War of the Rebellion: A Compilation of Official Records of the Union and Confederate Armies*, 4 series, 128 vols. (Washington: Government Printing Office, 1891), series 1, vol. 34, part 1:8–9, 58–9.

Discussion Questions

1   What are some of the common themes that emerge in this chapter's accounts of battles?
2   How well does Walt Whitman's "1861" reflect the actual fighting of the Civil War?
3   How do the accounts of guerilla warfare in Missouri and Florida differ from the accounts of formal warfare at Bull Run, Antietam, Gettysburg, and Chickamauga?
4   How well do Robert E. Lee's description of the surrender of the Army of Northern Virginia and Ulysses S. Grant's General Report indicate why the Civil War ended as it did?

Chapter 4   Soldiers' Experiences

1. Sarah Rosetta Wakeman
A Woman in the New York Volunteers, November 24, 1862–April 14, 1864

The Civil War created new opportunities for women. They became army nurses and clerks in government bureaus. White plantation women assumed the responsibilities of men who went to war. A few women accompanied their husbands into battle zones, and others became camp workers or prostitutes. Fewer yet were the approximately 400 women who disguised themselves as men to enlist in Confederate and Union armies. Like male volunteers, they went to war for a variety of reasons. Among them were patriotism, adventurousness, desire to be near a loved one, and financial gain. Except for frequently futile efforts to hide their sexual identity, the lives of female soldiers were remarkably similar to their male counterparts. This is evident in the letters of Sarah Rosetta Wakeman (1843–64), who in August 1862 enlisted in the 153d Regiment of New York Volunteers. She identified herself as either Lyons or Edwin R. Wakeman, and served until her death at New Orleans from acute diarrhea in June 1864. Her letters reveal a great deal about her motivations, concerns, religious beliefs, and daily life.

Alexandria
Nov. 24, 1862

My Dear Father and mother and sister and brother, one in all,

I receive[d] your letter on Sunday the 23. I was very glad to hear from you und [sic] learn that you were all well. I am well and enjoy good health. Our Regiment is in Camp at Alexandria, Va. We have had no fighting yet.

We have to guard the City and stand on picket. I stood on my post all last night. When I left you I went to Binghamton. I saw you there. I met you coming home from meeting. I left to work with Stephen Saldon the next day. I work[ed] half a month for 4$ in money. I was only 7 miles from Binghamton up the river. I didn't go to the fair. When I got done [with] work I went on the canal to work. I agreed to run 4 trips from Binghamton to Utica for 20$ in money, but this load of coal was going to Canajoharie, Montgomery Co.

When I got there I saw some soldiers. They wanted I should enlist and so I did. I got 100 and 52$ in money. I enlisted for 3 years or soon [as] discharged. All the money I send you I want you should spend it for the family in clothing or something to eat. Don't save it for me for I can get all the money I want. If I ever return I shall have money enough for my self and to divide with you.

If you want to save anything to remember me by, keep that spotted calf and if I ever return I want you to let me have her again. . . . I want you should keep all my things for me for I believe that God will spare my life and that I shall see you all again face to face before I die. Father, if you will send me some postage stamps I will be very thankful for them. I want to drop all old affray and I want you do to do the same and when I come home we will be good friends as ever.
Good-by for the present
Sarah Rosetta Wakeman . . .

Alexandria, Va.
Fairfax Co.
January the 15, 1863

Dear Father,

I receive[d] you[r] letter today. I was much disappointed to hear that you was not agoing to send me that box. What the express office said to you is not so, for the Lieutenant said he did not believe it for there is a box coming in every day to someone or nother [sic] . . . I want you to send me a piece of dried beef. Don't be afraid to send it for it would kill nobody if I shouldn't get it. I Have got faith to believe that it will come right straight through. The express office has no business to open any box and the government is willing that the box should be sent through to the soldiers of the Potomac.

We have had two men die out of our Company. There has died out of our Regiment about 30 as near as I can learn and there is quite a number sick. We have got the measles in our regiment. There was two men taken to Washington that had them out of the next row of tents of ourn. I Hope that

God will Suffer me not to get them again. For your sake I have got faith to believe that I shall come home once more before I die, but if it is God will for me to die here it is my will to die here, his will be done instead of ours on earth as in heaven....

I will see the Captain about them papers and if he will make them out for me I will send them right to you, and then you can go to the town of Afton and get you[r] money. If I do get the papers and you get the money, I want you to divide it with the family and get them some Clothes with the money. I will get it all to you.

I receive the glove and the mittens, yarn, needle and cans. I was very thankfoul [sic] for them. Mother, I will send you and Celestia some money when I draw my pay....
Rosetta Wakeman

...Mother, I use[d] all of the tobacco I want. I think it will keep off from catch[ing] diseases. I wish you all well and I hope that I shall meet you all again, so goodby for the present from you[r]
Affectionate,
Sarah Rosetta Wakeman

Capitol Hill
Washington, D.C.
October the 31/63

Dear Father and Mother,

I received your letter last night. I was glad to hear from you all once more. I am well and I feel thankful to god that he has spared my life and kept me in good health until the present time.... When I get my pay I will send you what money I can spare if it ain't but a little. Tell mother I will send her that ring that I showed to Henry Austin.

Our regiment expect to stay here this winter.... If you are a mind to send me a piece of butter and some cakes, I will be very thankful to you.

...When I think of home it seems like a dream to me, but still I know there is such a place as home that I left one year ago. It is but one chance to ten that I ever shall meet you again in this world. There is a good many temptations in the army. I got led away into this world so bad that I sinned a good deal. But I now believe that God Spirit has been aworking with me, and 'til that I was acoming back to Him again, and I hope and pray that I never shall be led away like it again. I have a hope that if I never meet you again in this world that I shall meet you in paradise where parting will be no more.

...Good-by for this time from,
Rosetta Wakeman...

Capitol Hill
Washington, D.C.
December the 28/63

Dear Father and Mother,

I receive[d] you[r] kind and welcome letter today. I am well and tough as a bear this winter. . . .

As for my coming home on a furlough this winter I don't know whether I can or not. . . . A good many of our men has been home on a furlough. . . . I don't care anything about coming home for I [am] ashamed to come, and I sometimes think that I never will go home in the world. I have enjoyed myself the best since I have been gone away from home than I ever did before in my life. I have had plenty of money to spend and a good time asoldier[ing]. I find just as good friends among strangers as I do at home. . . .

I sometimes think that I will re-enlist for five years and get my eight hundred dollars bounty. I Can do that if I am a mind to. What do you think about that?

I Can't think of any more to write. So good-by from your
Edwin R. Wakeman
or Rosetta Wakeman

Grand Ecore Landing, LA
on the Red River
April the 14/64

Dear Mother and Father, Brothers and Sisters,

I take my time to write a few lines to you. I am well and I in good spirit and I hope those few lines will find you all the same.

Our army made an advance up the river to pleasant hill about 40 miles. There we had a fight. The first day of the fight our army got whip[ped] and we had to retreat back about ten miles. The next day the fight was renewed and the firing took place about eight o-Clock in the morning. There was a heavy Cannonading all day and a Sharp firing of infantry. I was not in the first day's fight but the next day I had to face the enemy bullets with my regiment. I was under fire about four hours and laid on the field of battle all night. There was three wounded in my Co. and one killed.

Albert Weathermax wounded in the head. Ranson Conklin wounded through the hip. Edwin West had one of his fingers shot off. Joseph Blanchard killed. This is all that was hurt in my Co.

I feel thankful to God that he spared my life and I pray to him that he will lead me safe through the field of battle and that I may return safe home. . . .

I can't think of any more to write at present. So good-by from you Affectionate,
Edwin R. Wakeman . . .

Source: Laureen Cook Burgess, *An Uncommon Soldier: The Civil War Letters of Sarah Rosetta Wakeman, alias Pvt. Lyons Wakeman, 153d Regiment, New York State Volunteers, 1862–1864* (Pasadena, MD: The Minerva Center, 1994), 18–19, 22–3, 53, 58, 71–2. © 1994 by Lauren Markland Cook Burgess. Reprinted by permission of The Minerva Center, Inc.

2. Spencer Glasgow Welch
Preserving Discipline in the Army of Northern Virginia, March 5–September 27, 1863

> *When he wrote home to his wife, Spencer Glasgow Welch (1834–?) often mentioned that enlisted men had been punished. The punishments Welch, a surgeon in the 13th South Carolina Infantry, describes were common throughout Confederate and Union armies. During the Civil War each side struggled to enforce discipline on independent and contentious volunteers and conscripts. In addition to desertion, common charges against them included dereliction of duty, drunkenness, fighting among themselves, insubordination, malingering, and theft. Commanding officers often determined punishments for non-capital offenses. Soldiers might be fined, assigned extra guard duty, locked in a guardhouse or subjected to a variety of corporal and/or humiliating punishments. Capital offenses included cowardice, desertion, sleeping while on guard duty, spying, and murder. Courts martial decided these cases. Those convicted might be shot or hanged, although – as Welch indicates – those found guilty of cowardice were not always executed.*

Camp near Rappahannock River, Va.,
March 5, 1863.

. . . A man was shot near our regiment last Sunday for desertion. It was a very solemn scene. The condemned man was seated on his coffin with his hands tied across his breast. A file of twelve soldiers was brought up to within six feet of him, and at the command a volley was fired right into his breast. He was hit by but one ball, because eleven of the guns were loaded with powder only. This was done so that no man can be certain that he killed him. If he was, the thought of it might always be painful to him. I have seen men marched through the camps under guard with boards on their backs which were labeled, "I am a coward," or "I am a thief," or "I am a shirker from battle," and I saw one man tied hand and foot astride the neck of cannon and exposed to view for sixteen hours. These severe punishments seem to preserve discipline....

> Camp near Orange Court House, Va.,
> September 16, 1863.

...Two men will be executed in our division next Saturday for desertion, and the entire division will be ordered out to witness it. I have never cared to witness a military execution, although I have been near enough several times to hear the report of the guns. Two men deserted from our regiment two nights ago, and, if we get them again, and this we are apt to do, they are sure to be shot. There is no other way to put a stop to desertions....

> Camp near Orange Court House, Va.,
> September 27, 1863.

We had nine more military executions in our division yesterday – one man from Thomas' Brigade, one from Scales' and seven from Lane's. Colonel Hunt was a member of the court-martial which sentenced them, and he tells me that one of the men from Lane's Brigade was a brother of your preacher, and that the two looked very much alike. He said he was a very intelligent man and gave as his reason for deserting that the editorials in the Raleigh "Standard" had convinced him that Jeff Davis was a tyrant and that the Confederate cause was wrong. I am surprised that the editor of that miserable little journal is allowed to go at large. It is most unfortunate that this thing of shooting men for desertion was not begun sooner. Many lives would have been saved by it, because a great many men will now have to be shot before the trouble can he stopped....

I must close, as a doctor has just come for me to go with him to assist in dissecting two of the men who were shot yesterday.

Source: Spencer Glasgow Welch, *A Confederate Surgeon's Letters to his Wife – by Spencer Glasgow Welch, Surgeon 13th South Carolina Volunteers, McGowan's Brigade* (New York: Neal Publishing, 1911), 44–5, 78–80.

3. Unattributed photograph
Union Soldiers Recovering from Wounds, May 1864

> *High casualty rates forced the Union and Confederacy to expand and professionalize medical care for wounded soldiers. This 1864 photograph of Union soldiers recovering at Fredricksburg, Virginia after the Battle of the*

Wilderness illustrates the primitive conditions that prevailed in battlefield hospitals. But by then the Union and Confederacy had reorganized their medical services, created ambulance corps, and built modern, sanitary hospitals at locations further removed from the front lines. Especially in Union armies, women replaced men as nurses. The civilian United States Sanitary Commission and similar charitable agencies had a great deal to do with these improvements and changes in Union military medical care. Local agencies served a comparable function in the Confederacy, although less effectively. The woman seated in the doorway is a Sanitary Commission nurse.

Figure 4 Unattributed Photograph, Union Soldiers Recovering from Wounds, 1864
Source: Library of Congress.

4. Frank Holsinger
Union Soldiers under Fire, September 1862–November 1864

Frank Holsinger (1836–1916), a farmer from Bedford County, Pennsylvania, enlisted in the 8th Pennsylvania Reserve Corps on May 8, 1861. Between December 1861 and September 1862, he fought in numerous battles in Virginia and Maryland, including Antietam. In December 1862 he was

wounded at Fredericksburg and sent to a military hospital in Washington, DC.
On recovery he became a captain in the 19th Colored US Infantry. He served
in that capacity until he was wounded at Bermuda Hundred near Petersburg,
Virginia, in November 1864. While official reports strived to describe battles
and casualties dispassionately, Holsinger provides a valuable subjective
interpretation of an individual soldier's battlefield experience.

The influence of a courageous man is most helpful in battle. Thus at
Antietam, when surprised by the Sixth Georgia Regiment, lying immediately behind the fence at the celebrated cornfield, allowing our regiment to
approach within thirty feet, and then pouring in a volley that decimated our
ranks fully one-half; the regiment was demoralized. I was worse – I was
stampeded. I did not expect to stop this side of the Pennsylvania line. I met a
tall, thin young soldier, very boyish in manner, but cool as a cucumber, his
hat off, which he was lustily swinging, who yelled: "Rally, boys, rally! Die
like men; don't run like dogs!" Instantly all fear vanished. "Why can I not
stand and take what this boy can?" I commenced loading and firing, and
from this on. I was as comfortable as I had been in more pleasant places.

How natural it is for a man to suppose that if a gun is discharged, he or
some one is sure to be hit. He soon finds, however, that the only damage
done, in ninety-nine cases out of a hundred, the only thing killed is the
powder! It is not infrequently that a whole line of battle (this among raw
troops) will fire upon an advancing line, and no perceptible damage
ensue.... To undertake to say how many discharges are necessary to the
death of a soldier in battle would be presumptuous but I have frequently
heard the remark that it took a man's weight in lead to kill him.

In presentiments of death I have no confidence.... I have never gone into
battle that I did not expect to he killed. I have seen those who had no
thought of death coming to them killed outright. Thus Corporal George
Horton, wounded at South Mountain [on September 14], wrapped his
handkerchief around his wounded arm and carried the colors of our regiment to Antietam. Being asked why he did not make the best of it and go to
the hospital, that he was liable to be killed, he answered, "The bullet has not
been moulded to kill me." Alas, he was killed the next day.

My sensations at Antietam were a contradiction. When we were in line
"closed *en masse*," passing to the front through the wood at "half distance,"
the boom of cannon and the hurtling shell as it crashed through the trees
or exploding found its lodgment in human flesh; the minies sizzing and
savagely spotting the trees; the deathlike silence save the "steady men" of
our officers, the shock to the nerves were indefinable – one stands, as it

were, on the brink of eternity as he goes into action. One man alone steps from the ranks and cowers behind a large tree, his nerves gone; he could go no farther. General [George] Meade sees him, and, calling a sergeant, says, "Get that man in ranks." The sergeant responds, the man refuses; General Meads rushes up with, "I'll move him!" Whipping out his saber, he deals the man a blow, he falls – who he was, I do not know. The general has no time to tarry or make inquiries. A lesson to those witnessing the scene. . . . I felt at the time the action was cruel and needless on the part of the general. I changed my mind when I became an officer, when with sword and pistol drawn to enforce discipline by keeping my men in place when going into the conflict.

When the nerves are thus unstrung, I have known relief by a silly remark. Thus at Antietam, when in line of battle in front of the wood and exposed to a galling fire from the cornfield, standing waiting expectant with "What next?" the minies zipping by occasionally, one making the awful *thud* as it struck some unfortunate, some one makes an idiotic remark; thus at this time it is Mangle, in a high nasal twang, with "D – d sharp skirmishing in front." There is a laugh, it is infectious, and we are once more called back to life.

The battle when it goes your way is a different proposition. Thus having reached the east wood, each man sought a tree from behind which he not only sought protection, but dealt death to our antagonists. They halt, also seeking protection behind trees. They soon begin to retire, falling back into the cornfield. We now rush forward. We cheer; we are in ecstasies. While shells and canister are still resonant and minies sizzing spitefully, yet I think this one of the supreme moments of my existence. . . .

The worst condition to endure is when you fall wounded upon the field. Now you are helpless. No longer are you filled with the enthusiasm of battle. You are helpless – the bullets still fly over and about you – you no longer are able to shift your position or seek shelter. Every bullet as it strikes near you is a new terror. Perchance you are enabled to take out your handkerchief, which you raise in supplication to the enemy to not fire in your direction and to your friends of your helplessness. This is a trying moment. How slowly times flies! Oh, the agony to the poor wounded man, who alone can ever know its horrors! Thus at Bermuda Hundreds [sic], November 28th [1864], being in charge of the picket-line, we were attacked, which we repulsed and were rejoiced, yet the firing is maintained. I am struck in the left forearm, though not disabled; soon I am struck in the right shoulder by an explosive bullet, which is imbedded in my shoulder strap. We still maintain a spiteful fire. About 12 A.M. I am struck again in my right forearm, which is broken and the main artery cut; soon we improvise a tourniquet by using a canteen-strap and with a bayonet the same is twisted until blood ceases to flow. To retire is impossible, and for nine weary hours, or until late in the night, I remain on the line. I am alone with my thoughts; I think of home, of the seriousness of my condition; I see myself a cripple for life – perchance I may not recover; and all I the time shells are shrieking and minie bullets whistling over and about me. The tongue becomes parched, there is no water to quench it; you cry, "Water! Water!" and pray for night, that you can be carried off the field and to the hospital, and there the surgeons' care – maimed, crippled for life, perchance die. These are your reflections. Who can portray the horrors coming to the wounded?

The experiences of a man under fire differ materially between his first and subsequent engagements. Why? Because of discipline. "Familiarity with death begets contempt" is an old and true saying. . . .

Source: Frank Holsinger, "How Does One Feel Under Fire?," in *War Talks in Kansas . . . Kansas Commandery of the Military Order of the Loyal Legion of the United States* (Kansas City: Franklin Hudson Publishing, 1906), 301–4.

5. Jenkin Lloyd Jones
Religion and the Daily Lives of Union Soldiers in Alabama, January 17–May 10, 1864

> As Abraham Lincoln pointed out, the people of the Union and of the Confederacy prayed to the same god – even though major denominations had split over slavery. Each side interpreted the Civil War in religious terms and regarded battlefield victories and defeats as divine judgments. Although soldiers varied widely in their religious views, they were overwhelmingly Protestant and many were evangelicals. Like other young men away from home for the first time, they found opportunities to engage in behavior that violated the teachings of their parents and religious leaders. But most of them retained strong beliefs, which multitudes of Christian missionaries reinforced. Jenkin Lloyd Jones (1843–1918), who served in the Union army occupying Huntsville, Alabama, was more religious than most. After the war, he became a Unitarian minister, a pacifist, a social reformer, and the editor of a liberal religious journal. His diary entries for the period between January and June 1864 indicate the pervasiveness of religious faith in Civil War armies.

Huntsville [Alabama], Sunday, Jan. 17, 1864. A pleasant day. Meeting was announced to be had at 2 P.M. in the Presbyterian Church. Obtained permission and went down, but found none, it being held at 6 P.M. Walked over town. Visited the waterworks of the city, which is the largest of the kind South, with the exception of one at Columbia, S. C. . . . Returned to camp for supper and evening roll-call, then we walked back again. The church was very neat and filled with soldiers, but one woman in the audience. Chaplain of 18th Wisconsin officiated, of the Calvinistic school, and but ill agreed with my views, but it seemed good to be once more listening to an earnest speaker and hear the old-fashioned tunes swell in the bass voices that filled the room. Returned to camp, if not better, a more thoughtful man. It was the second sermon I have listened to since leaving home, and in common with all soldiers, I have acquired a careless and light way of passing time. [...]

...Sunday, Feb. 7. Rough night for the guard. Rainy and cold. The countersign "Vicksburg" which gave rise to musings which aided in forgetting time. Relieved at 9 A.M. Attended church in company with Gruff, E. W. and D. J. D. Service was held in the Methodist, Presbyterian and Episcopal churches at the same hour (10 A.M.) Curiosity prompted to attend the latter, an elegant furnished church of unique construction, Gothic style, poorly arranged for sound. The civilians were apparently of the aristocratic class, mostly women, equalling the military in numbers. The white-robed minister was a young intelligent Irishman, I should judge. A good choir with the deep-toned organ opened the service with fitting music, after which prayers were read and ceremonies performed for nearly an hour and a half, which to me was mere mockery of religion, reading their desires to God from an established formula, but careful always to omit the prayer for the President of the U. S. A. It was not worship. Ah no! the heart was cold. It was but Phariseeical affectations. A short sermon on charity was read at the close. Very good, the effect of which was tested by passing the plates which were returned well laden with "soldier green backs." The money of that government they will not pray for is very acceptable. I returned to camp, although not pleased with the exercise, yet I trust, benefited. The solemn notes of the organ had awakened feelings that are too apt to lie dormant in the soldier's breast, those that raise the mind above the din of common life, and look to a future of immortality, purity, which all hope to obtain ere long. "Heaven is my home." ...

[...]

...Friday, March 4. Evie Evans and myself went to the city on pass. Visited the Christian Commission rooms. Bought stamps. Also went to the colored school under charge of Chaplain of 17th Colored. Had school-teachers, being volunteers from the ranks, teaching the little woolyheads their "A. B. C's." One class of youngsters was taught by a large negro. A class of young ladies was reading in the *Second* Reader. All seemed attentive and anxious to receive the instruction but poorly imparted to them.....

[...]

... Sunday, March 13. A delightful Sabbath morning. T. J. Hungerford very sick, heavy fever and hard breathing. Afraid he is going to have a fever. Bathed him, towels kept around him, and all we can do for him is done gladly. After inspection 8 A.M. attended Sabbath school and meeting at the Methodist Church.... The minister preached from the 35th and 36th verses of the fourth chapter of St. John, a discourse filled with hell fire and eternal misery, with but little consolation to the many bereaved mothers and sisters present who had lost their all in the Confederate army. Although enemies, I could but feel for their distressing sobs, that were audible all over the room. In the afternoon the day was so cheering that I could not resist the temptation of another walk to town where in a crowded house of soldiers and citizens I listened to an excellent practical sermon on the ten virgins wise and foolish.

[...]

... Tuesday, March 29.... Our camp was visited today by Mother [Mary Ann] Bickerdyke [a major figure in providing for the health of enlisted men] with four mule teams loaded with good things from the North for the soldiers. Left us three barrels of potatoes, turnips, carrots, etc., one barrel of sourkraut with one of dried apples. *Noble woman.* I still remember with gratitude the motherly interest she took in my welfare while lying in the hospital at Corinth. Here again she comes with that which she has gathered by her own labor in the North, not leaving it to be wholly absorbed by surgeons, directors and officers, as is too often the case with sanitary goods.... May God bless her noble, self-sacrificing spirit, is the soldier's prayer.

[...]

Sunday, April 17. A beautiful and holy Sabbath morning. Warmed even the coldest heart to softness and filled the thoughtful mind with piety, though to many imperceptibly. Knapsack inspection at 8 A.M. Afterwards D. J. D. Gruff and myself attended Sabbath school taught by a chaplain. The presiding elder of the Methodist church was sick, and to my astonishment the Yankee chaplain was invited to preach, which he did very fittingly, delivering an excellent sermon from Romans 8th chapter, XV verse. Went down in the afternoon to witness the baptizing at the Methodist church, but we were too late. Visited the new font that is going up, and caught in heavy rain storm before we got back.

[...]

Sunday, April 24. Awoke to hear the rain pattering thick and fast on the pine boards overhead. At first I was dissatisfied with the anticipation of a wet day with mud – very blue, but at the thought of yesterday's dusty ordeal I could but say "blessed be the rain that clears the atmosphere and makes all nature look more pleasing when it ceases." Cleared off into a most delightful day by 9 A.M., and I listened to a thorough scientific sermon from Dr. Ross upon technical points, existence of evil. His arguments were very concise and binding. Although differing in opinion I received many new ideas. He is one of the leading Southern clergy and formerly a rabid secessionist, and to-day he touched upon the war, but so nicely that it could not displease any of his audience which was composed of the two extremes, viz: Yankee soldiers and secesh women. He sat way up, he said, upon his faith in God, "looking down upon the struggle with as much composure as though they were but the convulsions of so many pigmies – God would do it right." Just found it out I suppose....

[...]

Tuesday, May 10.... All the details marched up in line to McBride's head-quarters, where whiskey rations were freely issued to all that wanted, many of the most greedy drinking in several different details. After this issue the Captain mounted a table and read a dispatch from [William Tecumseh] Sherman by telegraph, of glorious news from [Ulysses S.] Grant. Whips [Robert E.] Lee and in full pursuit. [Benjamin F.] Butler in Petersburg within ten miles of Richmond. The news and whiskey brought forth thundering acclamations from the soldiers. After stating the importance of the imme-diate completion of the works, we were dismissed for dinner and started home. Deplorable sight. The intemperate indulgence by those but little used to the poison, caused a large portion of them to be beastly drunk, and our march through town was filled with demoniac yells, tumbling in the mud and mire. I felt ashamed to be seen in the crowd. Such mistaken kindness tends to demoralize the army as well as to increase the hatred of our enemy. Many of the boys had to be carried to their tents, and were unable to return to the work in the afternoon. Rained heavy all the afternoon. Worked hard. After night a terrible thunder storm deluged our camp, water standing in one of the tents eighteen inches deep. Our floor was all afloat, and we had to climb into our bunks to keep dry. Dry land could not be seen. Much noise and fun in order to forget the disagreeable in the humorous.

Source: Jenkin Lloyd Jones, *An Artilleryman's Diary* (Madison: Wisconsin Histori-cal Commission, 1914), 166–208.

6. Charles Minor Blackford

A Confederate Officer Observes the Siege of Petersburg, July 11–August 17, 1864

> By the summer of 1864, fighting between the Union Army of the Potomac, commanded by Ulysses S. Grant, and the Confederate Army of Northern Virginia, commanded by Robert E. Lee, had been transformed into siege

warfare conducted to the east of Petersburg, Virginia. Petersburg stood between Grant's army and the Confederate capital at Richmond. Confederate cavalry officer Captain Charles Minor Blackford (1833–1903) had, since December 1862, been judge advocate for the Army of Northern Virginia's 1st Corps. Although Blackford had considerable combat experience, his judicial position kept him out of battle. It allowed him time to observe and reflect on events near Petersburg. He notes the din of battle, suffering among civilians and soldiers, shortage of food, and diminishing confidence in the Confederate ranks. But he holds true to a belief in the superiority of southern arms and demonstrates a sentimentality common among Confederate and Union soldiers.

The First Corps headquarters, Petersburg, Va., July 11th, 1864.

We are camped just outside of town.... The whole country around here is filled with refugees from Petersburg in any kind of shelter.... Every yard for miles around here is filled with tents and little shelters made of pine boards, in which whole families are packed; many of these people of some means and all of great respectability. There must be much suffering. Thus far, while the shelling [by the Union army] has done much harm to houses and property, only one soldier has been wounded and none killed. Some five or six women have been killed and as many wounded most of whom were negroes.

[...]

July 17th.

No news, and no movement except the incessant shelling and the constant ring of the rifles of the sharpshooters on the lines. Last night, about eleven some five or six mighty siege guns were fired, which made the most terrific sound I ever heard....

I have taken cold and have a headache and fever. I believe the terrible dust has much to do with it and the hard fare. I can get little or nothing to eat, the best is blue-looking beef and the terrible bread cooked in camp. We have no coffee, tea or sugar.... There have been more desertions of late than ever before. I hear that even some Virginians have deserted to the enemy. The hard lives they lead and a certain degree of hopelessness which is stealing over the conviction of the best and bravest will have some effect in inducing demoralization hitherto unknown.

The Richmond papers give me great anxiety. There is a shadow in them of a defeat of [Jubal] Early in the [Shenandoah] Valley. It is only a rumor, but I find bad rumors are always true while good ones are often false. My cold seems touching my vitals. I cannot see, hear or smell, and, but for you [his wife] and Nannie [his daughter], would as soon be dead as alive. Grant is making some move. He is taking troops to the north side of the James River, and as a consequence Kershaw's division moves today. There is a rumor Grant is dead. I do not believe it, but it would make little difference to us. He is a hard fighter but no match for Lee as a commander of an army. [...]

Camp near Drewry's Bluff, July 31st.

...Reports reached us last night of quite a severe attack at Petersburg on yesterday morning. Grant's mining operations culminated there in blowing up one of our batteries, by which twenty-one men and three guns were disabled. An assault on the breach [known as the Battle of the Crater] was at once made with negro troops who, report says, carried the fort in spite of Hayward's South Carolina brigade. This is the story, whether true or not you will know long before this reaches you. We certainly hold our old line, and the enemy took nothing by his attack but a severe repulse. Grant had moved three corps to the north side and General Lee followed with three divisions. Yesterday morning they had all disappeared and the mine exploded at Petersburg, from which we infer that Grant had contemplated a general advance on our lines with his whole force massed at Petersburg. If this is correct he got badly worsted. His strategy was a complete fizzle. The news from Petersburg which has just come in says we captured nine hundred prisoners, thirteen stands of colors, killed about seven hundred and have the same line as before.

Same Camp, August 2d.

My Darling Nannie;
    ...We are camped at a place where there was a battle fought three months ago, and there are some very curious signs now left. Very near us the yankees had their field hospital, and many of them are now buried all around us. In one hole they threw all the arms and legs they cut off, and as they threw only a little dirt over them many of them are sticking out now making a very horrid sight, but one we get used to....
    The most remarkable thing I have seen is a cabin a few hundred yards from here where a dead yankee is lying still unburied. He seems to have been wounded and carried into this cabin and laid on some straw on the floor. There he died, and had, as many bodies do, dried up, for the cabin was

between the two lines and neither side could get to him to aid him or bury him. Right by his side lies the body of a great Newfoundland dog, which the negroes at the house in which we are camped say died of starvation rather than leave his dead master. Master and dog lie there together, strangers in a strange land, unburied and unwept, and perhaps, far away in the North, he has some little girl like you who is still hoping for her father's return and picturing the joy of having him back and romping with the faithful dog. War is a sad thing but if the poor man had stayed home and not come down here to desolate our homes and burn our houses he would have been with his little girl now. . . .

Same Camp, August 1st.

The firing towards Petersburg was very severe yesterday but no harm done. The enemy are digging another mine in the direction of our batteries, and General Lee found it out. He countermined and ran a gallery out under their working party and yesterday evening blew them up so effectively as to stop them. As soon as the explosion took place the enemy anticipated a charge from our lines, and at once commenced a furious cannonade upon them which lasted about an hour, but, though very expensive in the manner of ammunition, was not remunerative in that no harm whatever was done to us. This ends Grant's second great affair. . . .
[. . .]

Chafin's Farm, August 10th.
[. . .]
Our living is now very poor: nothing but corn-bread and poor beef, – blue and tough, – no vegetables, no coffee, sugar, tea or even molasses. I merely eat to live, and live on as little as possible. You would laugh, or cry, when you see me eating my supper, – a pone of corn-bread and a tin cup of water. We have meat only once a day. It is hard to maintain one's patriotism on ashcake and water. . . .

August 17th.

Yesterday was quite an active day along the front. The enemy made an attack on our whole line, and at one point broke through, making a gap in a brigade of Georgians, belonging to the Third Corps, commanded by Brigadier General [Victor J. B.] Girardey, who was promoted a few days since from the position of Captain and assistant adjutant-general. He rushed to the front in an endeavor to rally the men and was shot through the head and was instantly killed. His adjutant was by his side, and, with his pistol fired five shots at the man who killed the general. One ball only took effect. The yankee ran at him, and they closed in a death-grapple and both fell over the breastworks. The adjutant finally succeeded in putting a ball through his adversary's head, but was at once captured. He soon, however, escaped with only a slight wound.

General [Charles W.] Field brought up Anderson's brigade of Georgians and soon drove the enemy back and re-established our line, taking some three hundred prisoners. Captain Mason, of his staff, I am sorry to say, was badly wounded and is a prisoner. Most persons think he was killed. His horse returned with an empty and bloody saddle. The enemy's loss was heavier than ours. . . . We repulsed the enemy all along the whole line with a great loss to him and very little to us.

Source: Charles M. Blackford III, ed., *Letters from Lee's Army or Memoirs of Life In and Out of the Army in Virginia during the War between the States* (New York: Scribner, 1947), 266–73.

7. James S. Brisbin
US Colored Cavalry in Virginia, October 2, 1864

> *Only the Union deployed African Americans as combat troops during the Civil War. Large-scale recruitment of black men began following the Emancipation Proclamation of January 1, 1863, and by war's end as many as 200,000 had served. Black soldiers almost always had white officers. Among them was James S. Brisbin (1838–92), an abolitionist who became a career officer. As Brisbin establishes, prejudice and discrimination marked the lives of black troops. White Union soldiers often disparaged their black comrades. In comparison to white soldiers, black soldiers received low pay, inferior weapons, and poor medical care. They also received unequal and sometimes brutal treatment at the hands of Confederate forces. Brisbin, who describes the experience of the 5th US Colored Cavalry before, during, and after the First Battle of Saltville, Virginia (a Confederate victory) on October 2, 1864, emphasizes the character, resiliency, and bravery of black troops in the face of great difficulty.*

Lexington Ky Oct 20/64

General [Lorenzo Thomas, adjutant general of the army] I have the honor to forward herewith a report of the operations of the 5th U.S. Colored Cavalry during the late operations in Western Virginia against the Salt Works.

After the main body of the forces had moved, Gen'l [Stephen O.] Burbridge Comdg District was informed I had some mounted recruits belonging to the 5th U.S. Colored Cavalry, then organizing at Camp Nelson [Kentucky] and he at once directed me to send them forward.

They were mounted on horses that had been only partly recruited and that had been drawn with the intention of using them only for the purpose of drilling. Six hundred of the best horses were picked out, mounted and Col Jas. F. Wade 6th. U.S.C. Cav'y was ordered to take command of the Detachment.

The Detachment came up with the main body at Prestonburg Ky and was assigned to the Brigade Commanded by Colonel R. W. Ratliff 12th O[hio] V. Cav.

On the march the Colored Soldiers as well as their white Officers were made the subject of much ridicule and many insulting remarks by the White Troops and in some instances petty outrages such as the pulling off the Caps of Colored Soldiers, stealing their horses etc. was practiced by the White Soldiers. These insults as well as the jeers and taunts that they would not fight were borne by the Colored Soldiers patiently or punished with dignity by their Officers but in no instance did I hear Colored soldiers make any reply to insulting language used toward [them] by the White Troops.

On the 2d of October the forces reached the vicinity of the Salt Works and finding the enemy in force preparations were made for battle. Col Ratliffs Brigade was assigned to the left of the line and the Brigade dismounted was disposed as follows. 5th U.S.C. Cav. on the left. 12th [Ohio]. V.C. in the centre and the 11th Mich. Cav. on the right. The point to be attacked was the side of a high mountain, the Rebels being posted about half way up behind rifle pits made of logs and stones to the height of three feet. All being in readiness the Brigade moved to the attack. The Rebels opened upon them a terrible fire but the line pressed steadily forward up the steep side of the mountain until they found themselves within fifty yards of the Enemy. Here Co. Wade ordered his force to charge and the Negroes rushed upon the works with a yell and after a desperate struggle carried the entire line killing and wounding a large number of the enemy and capturing some prisoners. There were four hundred black soldiers engaged in the battle, one hundred having been left behind sick and with broken down horses on the march, and one hundred having been left in the Valley to hold horses. Out of the four hundred engaged, one hundred and fourteen men and four officers fell killed or wounded. Of this fight I can only say that men could not have behaved more bravely. I have seen white troops fight in twenty-seven battles and I never saw any fight better. At dusk the Colored Troops were withdrawn from the enemies works, which they had held for over two hours, with scarcely a round of ammunition in their Cartridge Boxes.

On the return of the forces those who had scoffed at the Colored Troops on the march out were silent.

Nearly all the wounded were brought off though we had not an Ambulance in the command. The negro soldiers preferred present suffering to being murdered at the hands of the cruel enemy. I saw one man riding with his arm off, another shot through the lungs and another shot through both hips.

Such of the Colored Soldiers as fell into the hands of the Enemy during the battle were brutally murdered. The negroes did not retaliate but treated the Rebel wounded with great kindness, carrying them water in their canteens and doing all they could to alleviate the sufferings of those whom the fortunes of war had placed in their hands.

Col. Wade handled his command with skill and bravery and good judgment, evincing his capacity to command a much larger force. I am General Very Respectfully Your Obedt. Servant

–James S. Brisbin

Source: Ira Berlin et al., eds., *Freedom: A Documentary History of Emancipation 1861–1867, Selected from the National Archives of the United States*, Series 2, The Black Military Experience (New York: Cambridge University Press, 1992), 557–8. © 1992 by Cambridge University Press.

8. Unidentified US Sanitary Commission Official
On Soldiers and Prostitutes, City Point, Virginia, late 1864

Civil War soldiers were much more likely to write home about their religious (and drinking) experiences than about their sexual experiences. Rarely did they write about sex in their letters, diaries, or memoirs. But newspaper reports describe the relationship between Confederate and Union armies and prostitution, official records offer glimpses into the sexual proclivities of soldiers, and historian Thomas P. Lowry provides evidence that soldiers had access to a variety of erotic fiction and photographs. Union and Confederate generals had to take extraordinary measures to regulate the prostitutes who followed their armies. Syphilis and gonorrhea reached epidemic proportions. Prostitution was particularly common near military bases. In Washington, DC in 1862 there were 450 registered houses of ill repute, while Nashville, Tennessee, had 352 licensed prostitutes in 1864. City Point, Virginia, which by June 1864 was a Union supply and communications center for the Petersburg and Richmond campaigns, was no exception. In a private letter, an unidentified (and moralistic) Sanitary Commission officer describes the relationship in the town between soldiers and "whores."

But now to the evils of this place. There is a whole city of whores. Yes, father, a whole city. They have laid out a village to the east of where the railroad bends to the docks. Streets, signs and even corduroy sidewalks with drain gutters. Of course, it was all built with Army supplies and by the very men for free that they have extracted their sinful wages from. These whores do pay the Negroes fair wages for whatever work they do, but so much more than we can that the blacks prefer to work for them to us. Our older workers here say that I must accept this evil. They fear it is here yet to the end. I found that my conscience would not let it go unchallenged from me. I determined to see the place for myself, and to protest to General Grant in person. There were three parallel streets about four blocks each long. Each block there are about ten structures on either side. They are for the most part one-storied, northern log or clapboard make. The number of rooms are different. How many, I am not sure, since I have not been in any. For the most part, they do not cook inside but have tents with Negroes behind or on the side of them, with pine or evergreen boughs covering. They, like the rebels, seem to separate the officers from the men. They will not do double duty. To each their own. Most of the officers['] ones have fine horses, saddles, furniture, et cetera, all from our supply houses. The [enlisted] men['s] ones have things in equality from the storehouse. At pay time, the lines before these houses are appalling and men often fight each other for a place. The average charge is three dollars and on paydays some make as much as $250 to $300. Though between pay periods, it is said that they will take their time and do many special things and charge accordingly. Some of these hussies, during their indisposed periods sell their services to the men to write letters for them to their loved ones back home. How foul. A mother, wife or sweetheart receiving a mistle [sic] penned by these soiled hands. I have not yet been able to reach Grant to protest these matters. Though he has ordered our men not to rape the rebel women, under penalty of death, two have been so executed since I have been here. I have talked with Bowers and he tries to defend the village as necessary in view of that order. Think of it, Father, he implies our devoted soldiers would become rapers and satyrs if not for these creatures.

Source: Thomas P. Lowry, *The Story the Soldiers Wouldn't Tell: Sex In the Civil War* (Mechanicsburg, PA: Stackpole Books, 1994), 29. © 1994 by Stackpole Books.

9. Eliza Frances Andrews
A Confederate Woman on Union Prisoners of War at Andersonville, Georgia, January 27, 1865

> *By the summer of 1864 prisoner of war populations had grown to unmanageable proportions in the Union and Confederacy. During the first two years of war the two sides had exchanged prisoners, and military prisons*

had remained small. But, beginning in 1863, the Confederacy's refusal to treat black prisoners the same as white prisoners and its tendency to redeploy exchangees caused the exchange system to break down. Conditions deteriorated in northern and southern prison camps as their populations increased. Poor sanitation, contaminated water, rampant disease, brutal guards, and emotional distress were common. But the men interred in southern camps suffered more as the Confederacy's economy collapsed. The worst conditions existed at the largest Confederate prisons – Andersonville, Georgia, and Belle Isle, Virginia. Eliza Frances Andrews (1840–1931), a loyal member of the slaveholding class and staunch Confederate, describes Andersonville, where 13,000 Union soldiers died.

While going our rounds in the morning we found a very important person in Peter Louis, a paroled Yankee Prisoner, in the employ of Captain Bonham. The captain keeps him out of the stockade, feeds and clothes him, and in return reaps the benefit of his skill. Peter is a French Yankee, a shoemaker by trade, and makes as beautiful shoes as I ever saw imported from France. My heart quite softened toward him when I saw his handiwork, and little Mrs. Sims was so overcome that she gave him a huge slice of her Confederate fruitcake. I talked French with him, which pleased him greatly, and Mett and I engaged him to make us each a pair of shoes. I will feel like a lady once more, with good shoes on my feet. I expect the poor Yank is glad to get away from Anderson on any terms. Although matters have improved somewhat with the cool weather, the tales that are told of the condition of things there last summer are appalling. Mrs. Brisbane heard all about it from Father Hamilton, a Roman Catholic priest from Macon, who has been working like a good Samaritan in those dens of filth and misery. It is a shame to us Protestants that we have let a Roman Catholic get so far ahead of us in this work of charity and mercy. Mrs. Brisbane says Father Hamilton told her that during the summer the wretched prisoners burrowed in the ground like moles to protect themselves from the sun. It was not safe to give them material to build shanties as they might use it for clubs to overcome the guard. These underground huts, he said, were alive with vermin and stank like charnel houses. Many of the prisoners were stark naked, having not so much as a shirt to their backs. He told a pitiful story of a Pole who had no garment but a shirt, and to make it cover him better, he put his legs into the sleeves and tied the tail around his neck. The others guyed him so on his appearance and the poor wretch was so disheartened by suffering that one day he deliberately stepped over the dead line and stood there till the guard was forced to shoot him. But what I can't understand is that a Pole, of all people in the world, should come over here and try to take away our liberty when his own country is in the hands of oppressors. One would think that the Poles, of all nations in the world, ought to sympathize with a people fighting for their liberties. Father Hamilton said that at one time the prisoners died at the rate of 150 a day, and he saw some of them die on the ground without a rag to lie on or a garment to cover them. Dysentery was the most fatal disease, and as they lay on the ground in their own excrements, the smell was so horrible that the good father says he was often obliged to rush from their presence to get a breath of pure air. It is dreadful. My heart aches for the poor wretches, Yankees though they are, and I am afraid God will suffer some terrible retribution to fall upon us for letting such things happen. If the Yankees ever should come to southwest Georgia and go to Anderson and see the graves there, God have mercy on the land! And yet what can we do? The Yankees themselves are really more to blame than we, for they won't exchange these prisoners, and our poor, hard-pressed Confederacy has not the means to provide for them when our own soldiers are starving in the field. Oh, what a horrible thing war is when stripped of all its pomp and circumstance!

Source: Eliza Frances Andrews, *The War-Time Journal of a Georgia Girl 1864–1865* (New York: D. Appleton, 1908), 76–9.

Discussion Questions

1   What do the documents in this chapter indicate about the various ways in which men and women experienced the Civil War?
2   How could religion and prostitution both be major parts of Civil War soldiers' lives?
3   Why were extreme measures required to preserve discipline in Confederate (and Union) ranks?
4   What were the various dangers that Civil War soldiers faced? Were there additional dangers for black soldiers?

Chapter 5   Homefronts

1. Mary A. Ward
Confederate Women Prepare their Men for War, 1861

> *Most Americans, North and South, greeted the start of the Civil War with*
> *excitement and a naïve expectation that their side would triumph after a short*
> *struggle or perhaps only a show of determination. Mary A. Ward (1840–?),*
> *a Confederate patriot from Rome, Georgia, and other women in the*
> *slaveholding elite, shared that excitement and expectation. When in 1885*
> *Ward testified before a US Senate committee on labor conditions in the South,*
> *she recalled the role of women in her town during the winter and spring of*
> *1861. They were, she reports, eager for war and ready to support the local men*
> *who were about to fight. She also recalls the religious sanction the war*
> *received, and a weaker concurrent sense of trepidation that she knows*
> *from hindsight was well justified.*

Well, it was pretty hard for any one in private life, especially for a lady, to
realize or appreciate the imminent danger that existed up to the very
breaking out of the war, up to the time that the troops were ordered out.
Discussions about the state of the country and about the condition of public
affairs and the causes for war were frequent, of course, and I think I may
safely say that in those discussions the women of the South without exception all took the secession side. There were a great many men in the
Southern homes that were disposed to be more conservative and to regret
the threatened disruption of the Union, but the ladies were all enthusiastic-
ally in favor of secession. Their idea was to let war come if it must, but to
have the matter precipitated and get through with it, because this feeling of

apprehension and this political wrangling had been continued for many years previous, and we felt that we in the South were strong in our own resources, and in fact we knew very little of the resources of the North compared with those of the South. My mother was a Northern woman and she always regarded the threat of war with the greatest apprehension and fear, because, as she said, she knew more about the resources of the North than others did, more than I did, for instance, or the other people of my age.... The day that Georgia was declared out of the Union [January 19, 1861] was a day of the wildest excitement in Rome. There was no order or prearrangement about it all, but the people met each other and shook hands and exchanged congratulations over it and manifested the utmost enthusiasm. Of course a great many of the older and wiser heads looked on with a great deal of foreboding at these rejoicings and evidences of delight, but the general feeling was one of excitement and joy. Then we began preparing our soldiers for the war. The ladies were all summoned to public places, to halls and lecture-rooms, and sometimes to churches, and every-body who had sewing-machines were invited to send them; they were never demanded because the mere suggestion was all sufficient. The sewing-machines were sent to these places and ladies that were known to be experts in cutting out garments were engaged in that part of the work, and every lady in town was turned into a seamstress and worked as hard as anybody could work; and the ladies not only worked themselves but they brought colored seamstresses to these places, and these halls and public places would be just filled with busy women all day long. But even while we were doing all these things in this enthusiastic manner, of course there was a great deal of the pathetic manifested in connection with this enthusiasm, because we knew that the war meant the separation of our soldiers from their friends and families and the possibility of their not coming back. Still, while we spoke of these things we really did not think that there was going to be actual war. We had an idea that when our soldiers got upon the ground and showed, unmistakably, that they were really ready and willing to fight – an idea that then, by some sort of hocus pocus, we didn't know what, the whole trouble would be declared at an end. Of course we were not fully conscious of that feeling at the time, but that the feeling existed was beyond doubt from the great disappointment that showed itself afterwards when things turned out differently. We got our soldiers ready for the field, and the Governor of Georgia [Joseph E. Brown] called out the troops and they were ordered out, five companies from Floyd County and three from Rome. They were ordered to Virginia under the command of General Joseph E. Johnston. The young men carried dress suits with them and any quantity of fine linen....

Every soldier, nearly, had a servant with him, and a whole lot of spoons and forks, so as to live comfortably and elegantly in camp, and finally to make a splurge in Washington when they should arrive there, which they expected would be very soon indeed. That is really the way they went off; and their sweethearts gave them embroidered slippers and pin-cushions and needle-books, and all sorts of such little et ceteras, and they finally got off, after having a very eloquent discourse preached to them at the Presbyterian church, by the Presbyterian minister, Rev. John A. Jones. I remember his text very well. It was, "Be strong and [ac]quit yourselves like men." I don't know that I have had occasion to think of that sermon for years, but although this occurred more than twenty years ago, I remember it very distinctly at this moment. Then the choir played music of the most mournful character – "Farewell," and "Good Bye," and all that, and there was just one convulsive sob from one end of the church to the other, for the congregation was composed of the mothers and wives and sisters and daughters of the soldiers who were marching away. The captain of the Light Guards, the most prominent company, a company composed of the *elite* of the town, had been married on the Thursday evening before this night of which I am speaking. He was a young Virginian. His wife came of very patriotic parents, and was a very brave woman herself. She came into the church that day with her husband, and walked up the aisle with him. She had on a brown traveling-dress, and a broad scarf crossed on her dress, and, I think, on it was inscribed, "The Rome Light Guards," and there was pistol on one side and a dagger on the other. This lady went to the war with her husband, and staid there through the whole struggle, and never came home until the war was over.

Source: *Report of the Committee of the Senate upon the Relations between Labor and Capital, and Testimony Taken by the Committee*, 4 vols. (Washington, DC: US Government Printing Office, 1885), 4:331–2.

2. Regis de Trobriand
Corruption in Washington, DC, December 1862

The enormous productive capacity of northern industry contributed greatly to the Union victory in the Civil War. But, as the United States government spent huge amounts on war contracts with private manufacturers to provide war materials ranging from boots and blankets to cannon and warships, the opportunities for corruption multiplied. Although similar tendencies existed in the Confederacy, because the Union could spend much more and because many more businessmen in the North sought government contracts, the corruption became worse there, especially in Washington, DC. During the

1850s, US government spending represented about 2 percent of the gross national product. During the war it rose to 15 percent. Regis de Trobriand (1816–97), who had emigrated from France to the United States in 1841, commanded the largely French–American 55th New York Infantry during the Peninsular Campaign of 1862, and later fought with distinction at Gettysburg. He describes wartime corruption at its worst.

Never … had there been seen such a concourse of people at Washington. The concentration of more than a hundred and fifty thousand men [serving in the Army of the Potomac] around the city developed there an industrial and commercial activity without a precedent. It was like a population quadrupled in a few months, three-quarters of whom consumed without producing anything.

But, besides the army formed to act against the enemy, there was another army – of lobbyists, contractors, speculators, which was continually renewed and never exhausted. These hurried to the assault on the treasury, like a cloud of locusts alighting down upon the capital to devour the substance of the country. They were everywhere; in the streets, in the hotels, in the offices, at the Capitol, and in the White House. They continually besieged the bureaus of administration, the doors of the Senate and House of Representatives, wherever there was a chance to gain something.

Government, obliged to ask the aid of private industry, for every kind of supply that the army and navy must have without delay, was really at the mercy of these hungry spoilers, who combined with one another to make the law for the government. From this arose contracts exceedingly burdensome, which impoverished the treasury, to enrich a few individuals.

As a matter of course, these latter classes, strangers to every patriotic impulse, saw in the war only an extraordinary opportunity of making a fortune. Every means for obtaining it was a good one to them; so that corruption played a great part in the business of contracting. Political protection was purchased by giving an interest in the contracts obtained. Now, as these contracts must be increased or reviewed, according to the duration of the war, its prolongation became a direct advantage to a certain class of people dispensing of large capital and of extended influence. What was the effect on events? It would be difficult to state precisely. But, in any case, this was evidently one of the causes which embarrassed the course of affairs, and delayed, more or less, the reestablishment of the Union.

The government – that is, the people, who, in the end, support the weight of public expenses – was then, fleeced by the more moderate and robbed by the more covetous. The army suffered from it directly, as the supplies, which were furnished at a price which was much above their value if they had been of a good quality, were nearly all of a fraudulent inferiority. For example, instead of heavy woolen blankets, the recruits received, at this time, light, open fabrics, made I do not know of what different substances, which protected them against neither the cold nor the rain. A very short wear changed a large part of the uniform to rags and during the winter spent at Tenallytown the ordinary duration of a pair of shoes was not longer than twenty or thirty days.

This last fact, well attested in my regiment, was followed by energetic remonstrances, on account of which the general commanding the brigade appointed, according to the regulations, a special *Board of Inspection*, with the object of obtaining the condemnation of the defective articles. Amongst the members of the board was an officer expert in these matters, having been employed, before the war, in one of the great shoe factories of Massachusetts. The report was very precise. It showed that the shoes were made of poor leather, not having been properly tanned, that the inside of the soles was filled with gray paper, and that the heels were so poorly fastened that it needed only a little dry weather following a few days of rain to have them drop from the shoes. In fine, the fraud was flagrant in every way.

Source: Regis de Trobriand, *Four Years with the Army of the Potomac* (French edition: 1867; English edition: Boston: Ticknor, 1889), 134–6.

3. Julia A. Wilbur
Contraband Camps in Alexandria, Virginia, March 24, 1863

> *During the Civil War, approximately 500,000 slaves escaped from their masters and crossed Union lines. Soon after the war began, Union General Benjamin F. Butler called these escapees "contraband of war" and put some of them to work at Fortress Monroe, Virginia. As the war progressed refugees from slavery became known as contrabands, and the US government placed them in contraband camps. As young men among the contrabands enlisted in Union armies or found other work, women, children, the elderly, and the infirm populated the camps. The camps were crowded, poorly maintained, and unhealthy. Some of the largest were in Washington, DC and its vicinity. Julia A. Wilbur (1815–95) – a white abolitionist sent by the Rochester, New York Ladies Anti-Slavery Society to Alexandria, Virginia, to help the contrabands – describes conditions in the city's camps. It is important to note that the military commander of the camps, Lieutenant Colonel H. H. Wells, denied Wilbur's charges.*

Alexandria Mar 24th '/63

Hon. E[dwin] M. Stanton
[Secretary of War]

I presume you have entirely forgotten the person who at Gen. [James S.] Wadsworth's suggestion, called at your office in Nov. last & informed you of the condition & wants of the Contrabands in Alexandria. You very kindly assured me that "their wants should be attended to," & soon after a physician was appointed & medical stores provided for these people[.] And I shall never cease to feel grateful to yourself & President Lincoln for ordering comfortable habitations to be built for these people, & I am sure it was no fault of either of you that the buildings progressed so slowly, that it is only about three weeks since that they were ready to be occupied[.]

There are three buildings each 150 ft. in length, containing together 35 living rooms with the same number of sleeping rooms & one large school room, the whole intended to accommodate 500 persons. The former Pro[vost]. Mar[shall] took pleasure in carrying out your orders & through his kindness I obtained some little conveniences for the rooms. I watched the progress of these buildings with great interest & was allowed to plan some of the interior arrangements. I am here to aid these people in this their transition state, & have some plans for their improvement[.]

I supposed that these Barracks were intended for those who could not get comfortable shelter elsewhere & they were to be temporary homes for such persons; & that in these buildings the sick, the old, the widows & children would find a shelter & not be asked to pay for it. Among the 500 deaths from smallpox during the winter there was a large proportion of men & this has added materially to the number of widows & orphans. I have not thought for a moment that either yourself or the President intended to extort from the Contrabands in Alex. $17.00 a year as rent for these rude barracks[.] But such seems to be the present policy, but perhaps not exactly on the part of the present Pro. Mar, for he says "the poorest ones may live in them without paying rent." He has had but little experience here & there is a person at his elbow who gives him any thing but a correct impression of things. It is with extreme reluctance that I say this & no personal considerations would induce me to do it. But I think that what is done for these 1500 or 2000 contrabands in Alex. is something done for the entire race. I believe in their supporting themselves as fast & as far as possible, but I do not like to see advantage taken of these poor creatures.

Some of these people have taken care of themselves entirely since they came here; others w[oul]d, have done so had they been paid regularly for their work. But there is a large proportion of needy helpless ones who must be cared for at present. Their condition on the whole is very much improved, & I wish to add what is much to their credit that in this city where arrests are so frequent it is very seldom that a colored man is arrested. At one time rations were issued to about 1300. But some of these have not drawn rations lately, & others draw only half rations. There is a want of system & order here that hinders the accomplishment of much good that might otherwise be done, & with all proper deference I would say that an efficient & capable superintendent is very much needed here. He should be in the first place a *humane* man; he should be large-minded & thoroughly conscientious; one who believes that these people can be elevated & improved; not one who habitually speaks of them as "thievish, deceitful, ungrateful dishonest"; a people "whom you cannot teach any more than you can horses." Mr. [Albert] Gladwin who wants to be superintendent here has been active in various ways & has helped these people in some things & I do not wish to detract a particle from his merit. But I am not alone in the opinion that he is altogether unfit for Superintendent of these people[.]

The Freedmen's Association in Washington perhaps knows of some person who is suitable for such a position....

I am not asking for any personal favors, although a month ago I did think of asking for the position of *Assistant Superintendent*. There is much that I do that does not come within a man's province, & perhaps it is quite as necessary & important as any work that is done, & I could do still more were I invested with a little more authority. Although a *woman* I would like an appointment with a fair salary attached to it, & I would expect to deserve a salary. But if there is anything in this wish that would operate against the appointment of a good & efficient superintendent I would not indulge it for a moment.

The government has in my humble opinion, done generously by the Contrabands in Alex. & I wish them to reap the benefit of this generosity & I trust they will not become the prey of selfish & designing men. With suitable instruction & proper protection I am sure they will not disappoint the hopes of their friends.

A thousands pardons for trespassing so far on your time, it has been done reluctantly. But you have treated these people with much consideration, & I feel that you are & will continue to be their friend & may God bless you for it; & when, if they ever do, get to living in these new buildings like civilized people I am sure it would give you pleasure to see our "Freedman's Home" in Alex. Hoping devoutly for such a consummation & that I have not presumed too much on your time & patience I beg leave to subscribe myself Very gratefully & respectfully Yours

Julia A. Wilbur

Source: Ira Berlin et al., eds., *Freedom: A Documentary History of Emancipation, 1861–1867, Selected from the Holdings of the National Archives of the United States,*

Series 1, 2 vols. (New York: Cambridge University Press, 1985, 1993), 2:280–3. © 1993 by Cambridge University Press.

4. [Dora Miller]
Life in Besieged Vicksburg, March 20–July 4, 1863

From the time of General Ulysses S. Grant's Vicksburg Campaign, which lasted from December 1862 to July 1863, siege warfare became more common in the South. In August 1864 William Tecumseh Sherman captured Atlanta after an extended siege, and Grant besieged Petersburg, Virginia, from June 1864 to April 1865. Therefore Dora Miller's account of life in besieged Vicksburg reveals a significant aspect of the Confederate homefront. George W. Cable (1844–1925) originally published Miller's diary in 1885, without revealing her name. He described her only as a pro-Union woman from New Orleans. In 1969 historian A. A. Hoehling identified Miller as the diarist. She was a native of Saint Croix in the British West Indies and wife of an Arkansas lawyer. She refers to her husband as H__ and as Mr. L__.

March 20th. – The slow shelling of Vicksburg goes on all the time, and we have grown indifferent. It does not at present interrupt or interfere with daily avocations, but I suspect they are only getting the range of different points; and when they have them all complete, showers of shot will rain on us all at once. Non-combatants have been ordered to leave or prepare accordingly. Those who are to stay are having caves built. Cave-digging has become a regular business; prices range from twenty to fifty dollars, according to size of cave. Two diggers worked at ours a week and charged thirty dollars. It is well made in the hill that slopes just in the rear of the house, and well propped with thick posts, as they all are. It has a shelf also, for holding a light or water. When we went in this evening and sat down, the earthy, suffocating feeling, as of a living tomb, was dreadful to me. I fear I shall risk death outside rather than melt in that dark furnace. The hills are so honeycombed with caves that the streets look like avenues in a cemetery. The hill called the Sky-parlor has become quite a fashionable resort for the few upper circle families left there. Some officers are quartered there, and there is a band and a field glass. Last evening we also climbed the hill to watch the shelling, but found the view not so good as on a quiet hill nearer home. Soon a lady began to talk to one of the officers: "It is such folly for them to waste their ammunition like that. How can they ever take a town that has such advantages for defense and protection as this? We'll just burrow into these hills and let them batter away as hard as they please."
... It is strange I have met no one yet who seems to comprehend an honest difference of opinion, and stranger yet that the ordinary rules of good

breeding are now so entirely ignored. As the spring comes one has the craving for fresh, green food that a monotonous diet produces. There was a bed of radishes and onions in the garden that were a real blessing. An onion salad, dressed only with salt, vinegar, and pepper, seemed fit for a king; but last night the soldiers quartered near made a raid on the garden and took them all.

April 2d. – We have had to move, and thus lost our cave. The owner of the house suddenly returned and notified us that he intended to bring his family back; didn't think there'd be any siege. The cost of the cave could go for the rent. That means he has got tired of the Confederacy and means to stay here and thus get out of it....

April 28th. – I never understood before the full force of those questions – What shall we eat? what shall we drink? and wherewithal shall we be clothed? We have no prophet of the Lord at whose prayer the meal and oil will not waste. Such minute attention must be given the wardrobe to preserve it that I have learned to darn like an artist. Making shoes is now another accomplishment. Mine were in tatters. H__ came across a moth-eaten pair that he bought me, giving ten dollars, I think, and they fell into rags when I tried to wear them; but the soles were good, and that has helped me to shoes. A pair of old coat-sleeves saved – nothing is thrown away now – was in my trunk. I cut an exact pattern from my old shoes, laid it on the sleeves, and cut out thus good uppers and sewed them carefully; then soaked the soles and sewed the cloth to them. I am so proud of these home made shoes, think I'll put them in a glass case when the war is over, as an heirloom.... All these curious labors are performed while the shells are leisurely screaming through the air; but as long as we are out of range we don't worry. For many nights we have had but little sleep, because the Federal gunboats have been running past the batteries. The uproar when this is happening is phenomenal. The first night the thundering artillery burst the bars of sleep, we thought it an attack by the river. To get into garments and rush up-stairs was the work of a moment. From the upper gallery we have a fine view of the river, and soon a red glare lit up the scene and showed a small boat, towing two large barges, gliding by. The Confederates had set fire to a house near the bank. Another night, eight boats ran by, throwing a shower of shot, and two burning houses made the river clear as day. One of the batteries has a remarkable gun they call "Whistling Dick," because of the screeching, whistling sound it gives and certainly it does sound like a tortured thing. Added to all this is the indescribable Confederate yell, which is a soul-harrowing sound to hear.... Yesterday the *Cincinnati* attempted to go by in daylight, but was disabled and sunk. It was a pitiful sight; we could not see the finale, though we saw her rendered helpless.

May 1st, 1863. – ... Sitting at work as usual, listening to the distant sound of bursting shells, apparently aimed at the court-house, there suddenly came a nearer explosion; the house shook, and a tearing sound was followed by terrified screams from the kitchen. I rushed thither, but met in the hall the cook's little girl America, bleeding from a wound in the forehead, and fairly dancing with fright and pain, while she uttered fearful yells. I stopped to examine the wound, and her mother bounded in, her black face ashy from terror. "Oh! Miss V__, my child is killed and the kitchen tore up." Seeing America was too lively to be a killed subject, I consoled Martha and hastened to the kitchen. Evidently a shell had exploded just outside, sending three or four pieces through. When order was restored I endeavored to impress on Martha's mind the necessity for calmness and the uselessness of such excitement. Looking round at the close of the lecture, there stood a group of Confederate soldiers laughing heartily at my sermon and the promising audience I had. They chimed in with a parting chorus: "Yes, it's no use hollerin', old lady." ...

May 17th. – Hardly was our scanty breakfast over this morning when a hurried ring drew us both to the door. Mr. J__, one of H__'s assistants, stood there in high excitement. "Well, Mr. L__, they are upon us; the Yankees will be here by this evening."

"What do you mean?"

"That [General John C.] Pemberton has been whipped at Baker's Creek and Big Black, and his army are running back here as fast as they can come, and the Yanks after them, in such numbers nothing can stop them." ...

What struck us both was the absence of that concern to be expected, and a sort of relief or suppressed pleasure. After twelve some worn-out-looking men sat down under the window....

About three o'clock the rush began. I shall never forget that woeful sight of a beaten, demoralized army that came rushing back – humanity in the last throes of endurance. Wan, hollow eyed, ragged, foot-sore, bloody, the men limped along unarmed, but followed by siege-guns, ambulances, guncarriages, and wagons in aimless confusion. At twilight two or three bands on the court-house hill and other points began playing "Dixie," "Bonnie Blue Flag," and so on, and drums began to beat all about; I suppose they were rallying the scattered army.

May 28th. – Since that day the regular siege has continued. We are utterly cut off from the world, surrounded by a circle of fire. Would it be wise like the scorpion to sting our selves to death? The fiery shower of shells goes on day and night. H__'s occupation, of course, is gone; his office closed. Every man has to carry a pass in his pocket. People do nothing but eat what they can get, sleep when they can, and dodge the shells. There are three intervals when the shelling stops, either for the guns to cool or for the gunners' meals, I suppose, – about eight in the morning, the same in the evening, and at noon. In that time we have both to prepare and eat ours. Clothing cannot be washed or anything else done. On the 19th and 22d, when the assaults were made on the lines, I watched the soldiers cooking on the green opposite. The half-spent balls coming all the way from those lines were flying so thick that they were obliged to dodge at every turn. . . . I think all the dogs and cats must be killed or starved: we don't see any more pitiful animals prowling around. . . . The cellar is so damp and musty the bedding has to be carried out and laid in the sun every day, with the forecast that it may be demolished at any moment. The confinement is dreadful. To sit and listen as if waiting for death in a horrible manner would drive me insane. I don't know what others do, but we read when I am not scribbling in this. H__ borrowed somewhere a lot of Dickens's novels, and we reread them by the dim light in the cellar. When the shelling abates, H__ goes to walk about a little or get the "Daily Citizen," which is still issuing a tiny sheet at twenty-five and fifty cents a copy. It is, of course, but a rehash of speculations which amuses a half hour. Today he heard while out that expert swimmers are crossing the Mississippi on logs at night to bring and carry news to [Confederate general Joseph E.] Johnston. I am so tired of corn-bread, which I never liked, that I eat it with tears in my eyes. We are lucky to get a quart of milk daily from a family near who have a cow they hourly expect to be killed. I send five dollars to market each morning, and it buys a small piece of mule-meat. Rice and milk is my main food; I can't eat the mule-meat. We boil the rice and eat it cold with milk for supper. Martha runs the gauntlet to buy the meat and milk once a day in a perfect terror. . . .

Friday, June 5th. . . . It is our custom in the evening to sit in the front room a little while in the dark, with matches and candle held ready in hand, and watch the shells, whose course at night is shown by the fuse. H__ was at the window and suddenly sprang up, crying, "Run!" – "Where ?" – "Back!" I started through the back room, H__ after me. I was just within the door when the crash came that threw me to the floor. It was the most appalling sensation I'd ever known – worse than an earthquake, which I've also experienced. Shaken and deafened, I picked myself up; H__ had struck a light to find me. I lighted mine, and the smoke guided us to the parlor. . . . The candles were useless in the dense smoke, and it was many minutes before we could see. Then we found the entire side of the room torn out. . . .

[. . .]

June 25th. – A horrible day. The most horrible yet to me, because I've lost my nerve. We were all in the cellar, when a shell came tearing through the roof, burst up-stairs, tore up that room, and the pieces coming through both floors down into the cellar, one of them tore open the leg of H__'s pantaloons. This was tangible proof the cellar was no place of protection from them. On the heels of this came Mr. J__ to tell us that young Mrs. P__ had had her thigh-bone crushed. When Martha went for the milk she came back horror-stricken to tell us the black girl there had her arm taken off by a shell. For the first time I quailed. I do not think people who are physically brave deserve much credit for it; it is a matter of nerves. In this way I am constitutionally brave, and seldom think of danger till it is over; and death has not the terrors for me it has for some others. Every night I had lain down expecting death, and every morning rose to the same prospect, without being unnerved. It was for H__ I trembled. But now I first seemed to realize that something worse than death might come: I might be crippled, and not killed. Life, without all one's powers and limbs, was a thought that broke down my courage. I said to H__, "You must get me out of this horrible place; I cannot stay; I know I shall be crippled." Now the regret comes that I lost control, because H__ is worried, and has lost his composure, because my coolness has broken down.

[…]

July 4th. – … About five yesterday afternoon, Mr. J__, H__'s assistant, who, having no wife to keep him in, dodges about at every change and brings us the news, came to H__ and said:

"Mr. L__, you must both come to our cave tonight. I hear that tonight the shelling is to surpass everything yet. An assault will be made in front and rear. You know we have a double cave; there is room for you in mine, and mother and sister will make a place for Mrs. L__. Come right up; the ball will open about seven."

We got ready, shut up the house, told Martha to go to the church again if she preferred it to the cellar, and walked up to Mr. J__'s. When supper was eaten, all secure, and ladies in their cave night toilet, it was just six, and we crossed the street to the cave opposite. As I crossed a mighty shell flew screaming right over my head. It was the last thrown into Vicksburg. We lay on our pallets waiting for the expected roar, but no sound came except the chatter from neighboring caves, and at last we dropped asleep. I woke at dawn stiff. A draft from the funnel-shaped opening had been blowing on me all night. Every one was expressing surprise at the quiet. We started for home and met the editor of the "Daily Citizen." H__ said:

"This is strangely quiet, Mr. J__."

"Ah, sir," shaking his head gloomily, "I'm afraid the last shell has been thrown into Vicksburg."

"Why do you fear so?"

"It is surrender. At six last evening a man went down to the river and blew a truce signal the shelling stopped at once."

Source: George W. Cable, ed., "A Woman's Diary of the Siege of Vicksburg. Under Fire from the Gunboats," *Century Illustrated Magazine* 30 (September 1885): 767–75.

5. Sallie Brock Putnam
Richmond Bread Riot, April 2, 1863

> *By the second year of the Civil War, the Union naval blockade of Confederate ports had begun to weaken the southern economy. A long drought worsened its affects. Shortages of food, sharply rising prices, hoarding by speculators, and the absence of male wage-earners, caused widespread suffering, centered in towns and cities. On April 2, 1863 hundreds of working-class women – later joined by men and children – rioted in Richmond, Virginia, after Governor John Letcher refused to help them provide food for their families. That spring there were similar uprisings led by women in towns and cities in Georgia, North Carolina, and Alabama, as well as in other Virginia locations. Sallie Brock Putnam (c.1828–1911) describes the Richmond riot from the perspective of a member of the slaveholding elite deeply loyal to the Confederacy.*

This species of trade [smuggling] became so objectionable, and added so greatly to the discomfort of our situation, that "running in goods" in that way was made subject to a heavy legal penalty; but it was either impossible to hinder the underground importation, or it was winked at, for these supplies of goods continued to be brought into Richmond, and the temporary check to the trade by legal prohibition only made an excuse for the increase in price of those goods already on the shelves of the merchants.

Whether it was in the power of Congress to correct the evils entailed upon us so singularly, or whether they lacked the moral courage to pass stringent laws against such abuses, it remains for those better informed to speak.

To add to other afflictions, our city was visited by the small pox early in the winter. This disease not only prevailed among the soldiers in and around the city, but many of the inhabitants, exposed to the contagion they could not tell when, nor where, contracted the disease, and all over the city the infected houses were distinguished by the white flag of alarm from the windows. The mortality from small pox was not extensive, and considering all the circumstances of its appearance and prevalence, it existed for a very short time, and its disappearance was sudden.... By the spring it had entirely disappeared from the city, and only existed at the small pox hospital, more than a mile without the limits of the corporation. In connection with the small pox other violent diseases appeared, and there seemed to remain for us to endure only the last of the three great plagues – war, pestilence and famine! Some of our hopeless ones – the miserable croakers who ever look on the dark side of the picture – added to our distress by predicting that famine would certainly follow in the train of evils, and our enemies had engaged to bring it upon us as one of the means of our subjugation.

These precautions had some influence in originating in Richmond in the Spring of this year, (1863,) a most disgraceful riot, to which, in order to conceal the real designs of the lawless mob engaged in it, was given the name of the "bread riot."

The rioters were represented in a heterogeneous crowd of Dutch, Irish, and free negroes – of men, women, and children – armed with pistols, knives, hammers, hatchets, axes, and every other weapon which could be made useful in their defence, or might subserve their designs in breaking into stores for the purpose of thieving. More impudent and defiant robberies were never committed, than disgraced, in the open light of day, on a bright morning in spring, the city of Richmond. The cry for bread with which this violence commenced was soon subdued, and instead of articles of food, the rioters directed their efforts to stores containing dry-goods, shoes, etc. Women were seen bending under loads of sole-leather, or dragging after them heavy cavalry boots, brandishing their huge knives, and swearing, though apparently well fed, that they were dying from starvation.... Men carried immense loads of cotton cloth, woolen goods, and other articles, and but few were seen to attack the stores where flour, groceries, and other provisions were kept.

This disgraceful mob was put to flight by the military. Cannon were planted in the street, and the order to disperse or be fired upon drove the rioters from the commercial portion of the city to the Capitol Square, where they menaced the Governor, until, by the continued threatenings of the State Guards and the efforts of the police in arresting the ringleaders, a stop was put to these lawless and violent proceedings.

It cannot be denied that *want of bread* was at this time too fatally true, but the sufferers for food were not to be found in this mob of vicious men and lawless viragoes who, inhabiting quarters of the city where reigned riot and depravity, when followed to their homes after this demonstration, were discovered to be well supplied with articles of food. Some of them were the keepers of stores, to which they purposed adding the stock stolen in their raid on wholesale houses.

This demonstration was made use of by the disaffected in our midst, and by our enemies abroad, for the misrepresentation and exaggeration of our real condition. In a little while the papers of the North published the most startling and highly colored accounts of the starving situation of the inhabitants of Richmond. By the prompt preventive measures brought into requisition this riot was effectually silenced, and no demonstration of the kind was afterwards made during the war.

The real sufferers were not of the class who would engage in acts of violence to obtain bread, but included the most worthy and highly cultivated of our citizens, who, by the suspension of the ordinary branches of business, and the extreme inflation in the prices of provisions, were often reduced to abject suffering; and helpless refugees, who, driven from comfortable homes, were compelled to seek relief in the crowded city, at the time insufficiently furnished with the means of living for the resident population, and altogether inadequate to the increased numbers thrown daily into it by the progress of events. How great their necessities must have been can be imagined from the fact that many of our women, reared in the utmost ease, delicacy and refinement, were compelled to dispose of all articles of taste and former luxury, and frequently necessary articles of clothing, to meet the everyday demands of life.

[...]

Our churches were stripped of their cushions, which furnished beds for the hospitals. Private houses were denuded of pillows to place under the heads of the sick. Carpets and curtains were cut up for blankets for the soldiers, and many a poor woman yielded up her couch to the invalid and suffering. Many times the dinner was taken from the table and distributed to soldiers in their march through our streets, when perhaps there was nothing in the larder with which to prepare another for the self-sacrificing family which had so generously disposed of the principal meal of the day. The generosity of our people was unstinted, and became more and more beautifully manifest as our poverty increased. A disposition was evinced to withhold nothing of ease or luxury which might in any way benefit a cause that called forth the most earnest devotion of patriotism.

Source: Sallie Brock Putnam, *Richmond during the War: Four Years of Personal Observation by a Richmond Lady* (New York: G. W. Carleton, 1867), 207–11.

6. *Illustrated London News*
New York City Draft Riot, July 13–17, 1863

> *By early 1862 the combined impact of diminishing voluntary enlistment and no prospect of a speedy end to the Civil War led both sides to inaugurate new methods of enrolling troops. In April 1862 the Confederacy initiated the first military draft in American history. Later that year the US Congress authorized President Lincoln to "conscript militia," and in March 1863 it passed a conscription act. Although the act worked in tandem with bonuses to encourage voluntary enlistment, it also allowed wealthy men to avoid the draft by paying*

$300 or hiring a substitute. The act contributed to an impression among poor,
often foreign-born, men that the government treated them unfairly. This
impression, combined with antiblack prejudice and opposition to the war
among Peace Democrats, produced violent antidraft protest across the North.
It reached a crescendo in New York City in July 1863. The New York rioters,
consisting mainly of working class Irish immigrants, burned the city draft office,
the New York Tribune *building, and Protestant churches. They attacked*
abolitionists, Republicans, and the homes of the wealthy. They vented their
greatest fury on African Americans, looting and burning the Colored Orphans
Asylum and hanging black men from lampposts. The rioters ruled the city until
July 15, when militia units from West Point, New York, and Pennsylvania
arrived to restore order. Illustrations published by northern newspapers portray
the rioters as insanely drunken subhumans. This engraving, published in the
pro-Confederate Illustrated London News, *is more sympathetic to the rioters*
who faced advancing militia on First Avenue. But the proximity of a liquor store
and the desperate posture of the women in the scene suggest that even the
News's *artist questioned the motivation and wisdom of the rioters. By any*
standard the draft riot is among the worst outbreaks of urban violence in
American history. At least 119 died and rioters burned about 50 buildings.

Figure 5   Illustrated London News, New York City Draft Riot, 1863

Source: *Illustrated London News,* August 15 (1863). Reproduced courtesy of
Illustrated London News Picture Library.

7. John Greenleaf Whittier
"Barbara Frietchie," 1864

During the Civil War, patriotic poetry became a mainstay of newspapers and periodicals in the Union and Confederacy. Commercial dailies and the political press, religious journals, and reform weeklies all published verse. Amateurs wrote a great deal of it, and it was often very sentimental. Poets, North and South, also produced volumes of poetry. John Greenleaf Whittier (1807–92) is one of the more famous American poets of the nineteenth century, although he was by no means a great poet. As an abolitionist, he often wrote poems in support of that cause. As a Quaker pacifist, he was at first ambivalent about the Civil War. "Barbara Frietchie," however, is designed to further the Union cause. The poem's simple rhymed couplets and martial rhythm made it very popular across the North – especially among school children. When Whittier first heard the Frietchie story, shortly after the Confederate invasion of Maryland in September 1862, he assumed it was true. By the time he published the poem in 1864, he realized that "the story was probably incorrect in some of its details." It is now considered to be apocryphal.

Up from the meadows rich with corn,
Clear in the cool September morn,

The clustered spires of Frederick stand
Green-walled by the hills of Maryland.

Round about them orchards sweep,
Apple- and peach-tree fruited deep,

Fair as the garden of the Lord
To the eyes of the famished rebel horde,

On that pleasant morn of the early fall
When Lee marched over the mountain-wall,–

Over the mountains winding down,
Horse and foot, into Frederick town.

Forty flags with their silver stars,
Forty flags with their crimson bars,

Flapped in the morning wind: the sun
Of noon looked down, and saw not one.

Up rose old Barbara Frietchie then,
Bowed with her fourscore years and ten;

Bravest of all in Frederick town,
She took up the flag the men hauled down;

In her attic-window the staff she set,
To show that one heart was loyal yet.

Up the street came the rebel tread,
Stonewall Jackson riding ahead.

Under his slouched hat left and right
He glanced: the old flag met his sight.

"Halt!" – the dust-brown ranks stood fast.
"Fire!" – out blazed the rifle-blast.

It shivered the window, pane and sash;
It rent the banner with seam and gash.

Quick, as it fell, from the broken staff
Dame Barbara snatched the silken scarf.

She leaned far out on the window-sill,
And shook it forth with a royal will.

"Shoot if you must, this old gray head,
But spare your country's flag," she said.

A shade of sadness, a blush of shame,
Over the face of the leader came;

The nobler nature within him stirred
To life at the woman's deed and word:

"Who touches a hair of yon gray head
Dies like a dog! March on!" he said.

All day long through Frederick street
Sounded the tread of marching feet:

All day long that free flag tost
Over the heads of the rebel host.

Ever its torn folds rose and fell
On the loyal winds that loved it well;

And through the hill-gaps sunset light
Shone over it with a warm good-night.

Barbara Frietchie's work is o'er,
And the Rebel rides on his raids no more.

Honor to her! and let a tear
Fall, for her sake, on Stonewall's bier.

Over Barbara Frietchie's grave,
Flag of Freedom and Union, wave!

Peace and order and beauty draw
Round thy symbol of light and law;

And ever the stars above look down
On thy stars below in Frederick town!

Source: John Greenleaf Whittier, *In War Time and Other Poems* (Boston: Ticknor and Fields, 1864), 58–62.

Discussion Questions

1   What do Mary A. Ward and Sallie Brock Putnam indicate about the changing role of Confederate women during the Civil War?
2   What do the documents in this chapter suggest concerning violence on the homefronts?
3   Were corruption and injustice inevitable consequences of the Civil War?
4   In what ways was life in besieged Vicksburg similar to life in Alexandria's contraband camps? In what ways was it different?

Chapter 6   Political Perspectives

1. Julia Ward Howe
"The Battle Hymn of the Republic," February 1862

> *Few Civil War songs so effectively blended religion, politics, and abolitionism as did "The Battle Hymn of the Republic." Well before emancipation became an official Union war aim, the song asserted a popular belief that the North fought to free the slaves. The song had complex origins. Its melody came from an African-American spiritual later adopted by white Methodists. Shortly after the execution of John Brown in December 1859, his admirers created new lyrics that began "John Brown's body lies a-moundering in the grave . . . But his soul goes marching on." The lyrics included the refrain "Glory, glory, hallelujah!" Early in the war Union soldiers sang "John Brown's Body" as they marched into battle. In October 1861 Julia Ward Howe (1819–1910), an abolitionist from Boston and later a women's rights advocate, heard Massachusetts troops singing the song when she visited their camp in northern Virginia. The following morning she wrote more transcendent lyrics for the song, militantly linking the Union cause to abolitionism and providential justice. It had become a Union anthem by 1864.*

Mine eyes have seen the glory of the coming of the Lord:
He is trampling out the vintage where grapes of wrath are stored;
He hath loosed the fateful lightning of His terrible swift sword:
His truth is marching on.

[*Chorus*:
Glory, Glory, Hallelujah!
Glory, Glory, Hallelujah!
His truth is marching on.]

I have seen Him in the watch-fires of a hundred circling camps,
They have builded Him an altar in the evening dews and damps;
I can read His righteous sentence by the dim and faring lamps:
His day is marching on. [Chorus]

I have read a fiery gospel writ in burnished rows of steel:
"As ye deal with my contemners, so with you my grace shall deal;
Let the Hero, born of woman, crush the serpent with his heel,
Since God is marching on." [Chorus]

He has sounded forth the trumpet that shall never call retreat;
He is sifting out the hearts of men before His judgement-seat:
Oh, be swift, my soul, to answer Him! be jubilant, my feet!
Our God is marching on. [Chorus]

In the beauty of the lilies Christ was born across the sea,
With a glory in his bosom that transfigures you and me:
As he died to make men holy, let us die to make men free,
While God is marching on. [Chorus]

Source: Julia Ward Howe, "The Battle Hymn of the Republic," *Atlantic Monthly* 9 (February 1862): 145.

2. Horace Greeley and Abraham Lincoln
Union War Aims, August 19–22, 1862

The fates of the Union and African Americans constituted the two most momentous issues in the Civil War. As president, Abraham Lincoln's priority was to save the Union. Well into 1862 he believed that to advocate emancipating the slaves would keep him from achieving that goal. Official abolitionism, he feared, would alienate white southerners who might otherwise support the Union. It would also, he expected, weaken the Republican Party in the North. Nevertheless the Republican majority in Congress passed laws to abolish slavery in the District of Columbia and in US territories. Congress also passed the Confiscation Act on August 6, 1861, authorizing the president to seize slaves used in behalf of the Confederacy and, on July 17, 1862, the Second Confiscation Act, providing for the forfeiture of slaves belonging to anyone who supported the rebellion. Horace Greeley (1811–72) refers to the latter act in his August 19, 1862 open letter to Lincoln. Greeley, as editor of the New York Tribune, *was a powerful white northern advocate of emancipation. Under the heading "The Prayer of Twenty Millions," Greeley emphasized that an emancipationist policy would strengthen the Union cause. Lincoln's response is the most succinct and elegant statement of the conservative position in regard to slavery he had maintained since the he became president.*

New-York, August 19, 1862

To ABRAHAM LINCOLN, *President of the United States*:

DEAR SIR: I do not intrude to tell you – for you must know already – that a great proportion of those who triumphed in your election, and of all who desire the unqualified suppression of the Rebellion now desolating our country, are sorely disappointed and deeply pained by the policy you seem to be pursuing with regard to the slaves of the Rebels. I write only to set succinctly and unmistakably before you what we require, what we think we have a right to expect, and of what we complain.

[...]

...We complain that the Union cause has suffered, and is now suffering immensely, from mistaken deference to Rebel Slavery. Had you, Sir, in your Inaugural Address, unmistakably given notice that, in case the Rebellion already commenced, were persisted in, and your efforts to preserve the Union and enforce the laws should be resisted by armed force, *you would recognize no loyal person as rightfully held in Slavery by a traitor,* we believe the Rebellion would therein have received a staggering if not fatal blow....

[...]

On the face of this wide earth, Mr. President, there is not one disinterested, determined, intelligent champion of the Union cause who does not feel that all attempts to put down the Rebellion and at the same time uphold its inciting cause are preposterous and futile – that the Rebellion, if crushed out tomorrow would be renewed within a year if Slavery were left in full vigor – that Army officers who remain to this day devoted to Slavery can at best be but half-way loyal to the Union – and that every hour of deference to Slavery is an hour of added and deepened peril to the Union. I appeal to the testimony of your Embassadors [sic] in Europe. It is freely at your service, not at mine. Ask them to tell you candidly whether the seeming subserviency of your policy to the slaveholding, slavery-upholding interest, is not the perplexity, the despair of statesmen of all parties, and be admonished by the general answer!

...I close as I began with the statement that what an immense majority of the Loyal Millions of your countrymen require of you is a frank, declared, unqualified, ungrudging execution of the laws of the land, more especially of the Confiscation Act. That Act gives freedom to the slaves of rebels coming within our lines, or whom those lines may at any time inclose – we ask you to render it due obedience by publicly requiring all your subordinates to recognize and obey it. The rebels are everywhere using the late anti-negro riots in the North, as they have long used your officers['] treatment of negroes in the South, to convince the slaves that they have nothing to hope from a Union success – that we mean in that case to sell them into a bitter bondage to defray the cost of the war. Let them impress this as a truth on the great mass of their ignorant and credulous bondmen, and the Union will never be restored – never. We cannot conquer Ten Millions of People united in solid phalanx against us, powerfully aided by Northern sympathizers and European allies. We must have scouts, guides, spies, cooks, teamsters, diggers, and choppers from the Blacks of the South, whether we allow them to fight for us or not, or we shall be baffled and repelled. As one of the millions who would gladly have avoided this struggle at any sacrifice but that of Principle and Honor, but who now feel that the triumph of the Union is indispensable not only to the existence of our country but to the well-being of mankind, I entreat you to render a hearty and unequivocal obedience to the law of the land.

Yours,

Horace Greeley.

Executive Mansion,
Washington, August 22, 1862

Hon. Horace Greeley:
Dear Sir:

I have just read yours of the 19th, addressed to myself through the New-York Tribune. If there be in it any statements or assumptions of fact, which I may know to be erroneous, I do not now and here, controvert them. If there be in it any inferences which I may believe to be falsely drawn, I do not now and here argue against them. If there be perceptible [sic] in it an impatient and dictatorial tone, I waive it in deference to an old friend, whose heart I have always supposed to be right.

As to the policy I "seem to be pursuing," as you say, I have not meant to leave any one in doubt.

I would save the Union. I would save it the shortest way under the Constitution. The sooner the national authority can be restored, the nearer the Union will be "the Union as it was." If there be those who would not save the Union unless they could at the same time *save* Slavery, I do not agree with them. If there be those who would not save the Union unless they could at the same time *destroy* Slavery, I do not agree with them. My paramount object in this struggle *is* to save the Union, and is *not* either to save or destroy Slavery. If I could save the Union without freeing *any* slave, I would do it, and if I could save it by freeing *all* the slaves, I would do it; and if I could save it by freeing some and leaving others alone I would also do that. What I do about Slavery and the colored race, I do because I believe it helps to save this Union; and what I forbear, I forbear because I do *not* believe it would help to save the Union. I shall do *less* whenever I shall believe what I am doing hurts the cause, and I shall do *more* whenever I shall believe doing more will help the cause. I shall try to correct errors when shown to be errors; and I shall adopt new views so fast as they shall appear to be true views.

I have here stated my purpose according to my view of *official* duty, and I intend no modification of my oft-expressed *personal* wish that all men, everywhere, could be free.

Yours,

A. Lincoln

Sources: *New York Daily Tribune*, August 20 (1862); Roy P. Basler, ed., *Abraham Lincoln: His Speeches and Writings* (New York: World, 1946), 651–2.

3. Joseph E. Brown
State Sovereignty in the Confederacy, September 1, 1862

> *The thesis that state rights sentiments doomed the Confederacy has declined among historians. Nevertheless the principle of state sovereignty animated powerful southern critics of the Confederate government and President Jefferson Davis. Centered in Georgia and North Carolina, these critics contended that military rule and centralization of political power in Richmond threatened the liberties white southerners had seceded from the Union to protect. Among the critics were Confederate vice-president Alexander H. Stephens, former US Senator Robert Toombs, Governor Zebulon B. Vance of North Carolina, and Governor Joseph E. Brown of Georgia. Brown (1821–94) opposed the February 1862 act, passed by the Confederate Congress, giving Davis power to suspend the writ of habeas corpus. Brown also opposed the Confederate conscription act of April 1862 and kept about 8,000 Georgians from serving in Confederate armies. In this September 1862 letter to Toombs, Brown expresses his fears concerning the increasing power of "military men" in the Confederacy.*

Joseph E. Brown to Alexander H. Stephens (Private)

CANTON [Georgia],
Sept. 1st, 1862.

Dear Sir: I have the pleasure to acknowledge the receipt of your letter of the 26th ult. and am gratified that you take the view which you have expressed about the action of Genl. [Braxton] Bragg in his declaration of martial law over Atlanta and his appoint[ment], as the newspapers say, of a civil governor with aids, etc.

I have viewed this proceeding as I have others of our military authorities of late with painful apprehensiveness for the future. It seems military men are assuming the whole powers of government to themselves and setting at defiance constitutions, laws, state rights, state sovereignty, and every other principle of civil liberty, and that our people engrossed in the struggle with the enemy are disposed to submit to these bold usurpations tending to military despotism without murmur, much less resistance. I should have called this proceeding into question before this time but I was hopeful from the indications which I had noted that Congress would take such action as would check these dangerous usurpations of power, and for the further reasons that I have already come almost into conflict with the Confederate authorities in vindication of what I have considered the rights of the State and people of Georgia, and I was fearful, as no other governor seems to raise these questions, that I might be considered by good and true men in and out of Congress too refractory for the times. I had therefore concluded to take no notice of this matter till the meeting of the legislature when I expect to ask the representatives of the people to define the bounds to which they desire the Governor to go in the defense of the rights and sovereignty of the state. I confess I have apprehensions that our present General Assembly does not properly reflect the sentiments of our people upon this great question, but if the Executive goes beyond the bounds where he is sustained by the representatives of the people he exposes himself to censure without the moral power to do service to the great principles involved. I fear we have much more to apprehend from military despotism than from subjugation by the enemy. I trust our generals will improve well their time while we have the advantage and the enemy are organizing another army. Hoping that your health is good and begging that you will write me when your important duties are not too pressing to permit it, I am – very truly your friend.

Source: Ulrich B. Phillips, ed., "The Correspondence of Robert Toombs, Alexander H. Stephens, and Howell Cobb," *Annual Report of the American Historical Association for the Year of 1911*, 2 vols. (Washington, DC: Government Printing Office, 1913), 2:605–6.

4. Abraham Lincoln
Emancipation Proclamation, January 1, 1863

> *By August 1862, when Abraham Lincoln replied to Horace Greeley's "The Prayer of Twenty Millions," he had already reconsidered his views on the relationship between an emancipationist policy and preserving the Union. He had come to believe that, for several reasons, adopting emancipation as*

a war aim would help the Union war effort. It would discourage such emancipationist European powers as Great Britain and France from recognizing the Confederacy. It would encourage more slaves to escape. It was essential to a new policy promoting black enlistment in Union armies. Lincoln had also tired of placating proslavery sentiment in the border slave states. But Lincoln realized that to declare emancipation to be his goal, at a time when the Union appeared to be losing the war, would appear to be weak and desperate. Therefore he waited until after the Army of the Potomac had turned back Robert E. Lee's invasion of Maryland at Antietam to issue his Preliminary Emancipation Proclamation on September 22. It declared that slaves in those portions of the South still in rebellion on January 1, 1863 would "be then, thenceforward, and forever free." When, by that date, no Confederate state sought to end the conflict, Lincoln, fully supported by the Republican Party, issued his final Emancipation Proclamation. It was a war measure rather than a declaration of human rights, affected slaves only in areas not under Union control, and lacked Lincoln's famous eloquence. Nevertheless it transformed the character of the Civil War and encouraged black men to participate in Union armies.

Whereas on the 22nd day of September, AD 1862, a proclamation was issued by the President of the United States, containing, among other things, the following, to wit:

That on the 1st day of January, AD 1863, all persons held as slaves within any State or designated part of a State, the people whereof shall then be in rebellion against the United States, shall be then, thenceforward, and forever free; and the executive government of the United States, including the military and naval authority thereof, will recognize and maintain the freedom of such persons and will do no act or acts to repress such persons or any of them in any efforts they may make for their actual freedom.

That the Executive will on the 1st day of January aforesaid, by proclamation, designate the States and parts of States, if any, in which the people thereof, respectively, shall then be in rebellion against the United States; and the fact that any State or the people thereof shall on that day be in good faith represented in the Congress of the United States by members chosen thereto at elections wherein a majority of the qualified voters of such States shall have participated shall, in the absence of strong countervailing testimony, be deemed conclusive evidence that such State and the people thereof are not then in rebellion against the United States.

Now, therefore, I, Abraham Lincoln, President of the United States, by virtue of the power in me vested as Commander-In-Chief of the Army and Navy of the United States in time of actual armed rebellion against the authority and government of the United States, and as a fit and necessary war measure for suppressing said rebellion, do, on this 1st day of January, AD 1863, and in accordance with my purpose so to do publicly proclaimed for the full period of one hundred days from the first day above mentioned, order and designate as the States and parts of States wherein the people thereof, respectively, are this day in rebellion against the United States the following to wit

Arkansas, Texas, Louisiana (except the parishes of St. Bernard, Paiquemities, Jefferson, St. John, St. Charles, St. James, Ascension, Assumption, Terrebone, Lafourche, St. Mary, St. Martin, and Orleans, including the city of New Orleans), Mississippi, Alabama, Florida, Georgia, South Carolina, North Carolina, and Virginia (except the forty-eight counties designated as West Virginia, and also the counties of Berkeley, Accomac, Northhampton, Elizabeth City, York, Princess Anne, and Norfolk, including the cities of Norfolk and Portsmouth), and which excepted parts are for the present left precisely as if this proclamation were not issued.

And by virtue of the power and for the purpose aforesaid, I do order and declare that all persons held as slaves within said designated States and parts of States are, and henceforward shall be, free; and that the Executive Government of the United States, including the military and naval authorities thereof, will recognize and maintain the freedom of said persons.

And I hereby enjoin upon the people so declared to be free to abstain from all violence, unless in necessary self-defence; and I recommend to them that, in all cases when allowed, they labor faithfully for reasonable wages.

And I further declare and make known that such persons of suitable condition will be received into the armed service of the United States to garrison forts, positions, stations, and other places, and to man vessels of all sorts in said service.

And upon this act, sincerely believed to be an act of justice, warranted by the Constitution upon military necessity, I invoke the considerate judgment of mankind and the gracious favor of Almighty God.

In witness whereof I have hereunto set my hand and caused the seal of the United States to be affixed.

Done at the city of Washington, this 1st day of January, AD 1863, and of the Independence of the United States of America the eighty-seventh.

ABRAHAM LINCOLN
By the President

Source: James D. Richardson, ed., *A Compilation of the Messages and Papers of the Presidents*, 10 vols. (Washington, DC: Government Printing Office, 1897), 6:157–9.

5. Clement L. Vallandigham
Northern Opposition to the Civil War, January 14, 1863

Defeats suffered by Union armies, combined with opposition in the North to military conscription and the Emancipation Proclamations, strengthened the Civil War's northern opponents. These Democratic politicians and journalists referred to themselves as Peace Democrats, *but Republican and some War Democrats called them* Copperheads. *They advocated compromise with the South, the retention of slavery, a cease-fire, and a negotiated peace. Peace Democrats were strongest in the southern portions of Ohio, Indiana, and Illinois, but also had support in New York City and other parts of the Northeast. They were most influential prior to the Union victories at Gettysburg and Vicksburg in July 1863, but retained considerable influence in the Democratic Party through the national election of 1864. Lame-duck congressman Clement L. Vallandigham (1820–71) of Ohio was the most prominent Peace Democrat when he delivered his "Great Civil War in America" speech in the House of Representatives shortly after Lincoln issued the Emancipation Proclamation. Vallandigham criticizes the Union war effort as unconstitutional, unwise, a threat to civil liberties, unjustly emancipationist, and doomed to failure.*

Mr. Speaker: . . . I propose to consider the STATE OF THE UNION to-day, and to inquire what the duty is of every public man and every citizen in this the very crisis of the Great Revolution.

It is now two years, sir, since Congress assembled soon after the Presidential election. A sectional anti-slavery party had then just succeeded through the forms of the Constitution. For the first time a President had been chosen upon a platform of avowed hostility to an institution peculiar to nearly one half of the States of the Union, and who had himself proclaimed that there was an irrepressible conflict, because of that institution, between the States; and that the Union could not endure "part slave and part free." Congress met, therefore, in the midst of the profoundest agitation, not here only, but throughout the entire South. Revolution glared upon us. Repeated efforts for conciliation and compromise were attempted, in Congress and out of it. All were rejected by the party just coming into power, except only the promise in the lst hours of the session, and that, too, against the consent of a majority of that party both in the Senate and House: that Congress – not the Executive – should never be authorized to abolish or interfere with slavery in the States where it existed. South Carolina seceded; Georgia, Alabama, Florida, Mississippi, Louisiana, and Texas speedily followed. The Confederate Government was established. The other slave

States held back.... But neither in the Senate nor the House were they allowed even a respectful consideration.... On the 4th of March [Abraham Lincoln] was inaugurated, surrounded by soldiery; and swearing to support the Constitution of the United States, announced in the same breath that the platform of his party should be the law unto him. From that moment all hope of peaceable adjustment fled.... Just after the spring elections, and the secret meeting in this city of the Governors of several northern and western States, a fleet carrying a large number of men was sent down ostensibly to provision Fort Sumpter [sic]. The authorities of South Carolina eagerly accepted the challenge, and bombarded the fort into surrender.... It was Sunday, the 14th of April 1861; and that day the President, in fatal haste, and without the advice or consent of Congress, issued his proclamation, dated the next day, calling out seventy-five thousand militia for three months, to repossess the forts, places, and property seized from the United States, and commanding the insurgents to disperse in twenty days. Again the gage [gauntlet] was taken up by the South, and thus the flames of a civil war, the grandest, bloodiest, and saddest in history, lighted up the whole heavens. Virginia forthwith seceded. North Carolina, Tennessee, and Arkansas, followed; Delaware, Maryland, Kentucky, and Missouri were in a blaze of agitation, and within a week ... the line of the confederate states was transferred from the cotton States to the Potomac, and almost to the Ohio and the Missouri, and their population and fighting men doubled.

In the North and West, too, the storm raged with the fury of a hurricane. Never in history was anything equal to it.... The spirit of persecution for opinion's sake, almost extinct in the old world, now by some mysterious transmigration, appeared incarnate in the new. Social relations were dissolved; friendships broken up; the ties of family and kindred snapped asunder. Stripes and hanging were every where threatened, sometimes executed.... The gospel of love perished; hate sat enthroned, and the sacrifices of blood smoked upon every altar.

But the reign of the mob was inaugurated only to be supplanted by the iron domination of arbitrary power. Constitutional limitation was broken down; *habeas corpus* fell; liberty of the press, of speech, of the person, of the mails, of travel, of one's own house, and of religion; the right to bear arms, due process of law, judical [sic] trial, trial by jury, trial at all; every badge and mumiment [sic] of freedom in republican government or kingly government – all went down at a blow; ... Midnight and arbitrary arrests commenced; travel was interdicted; trade embargoed; passports demanded; bastilles were introduced; strange oaths invented; a secret police organized.... The right to declare war, to raise and support armies, and to provide and maintain a navy, was usurped by the Executive; and in a little more than two months a land and naval force of over three hundred thousand men was in the field or upon the sea. An army of public plunderers followed, and curruption [sic] struggled with power in friendly strife for the mastery at home.

On the 4th of July Congress met ... to register and ratify the edicts of the Executive; and ... to invoke a universal baptism of fire and blood amid the roar of cannon and the din of battle.... Five hundred thousand men, an immense navy, and two hundred and fifty millions of money were speedily granted. In twenty, at most sixty days, the rebellion was to be crushed out.... Abject submission was demanded. Lay down your arms, sue for peace, surrender your leaders – forfeiture, death – this was the only language heard on this floor....

Thus was CIVIL WAR inaugurated in America. Can any man today see the end of it?

[...]

I did not support the war; and to-day I bless God, that not the smell of so much as one drop of its blood is upon my garments. Sir, I censure no brave man who rushed patriotically into this war; neither will I quarrel with any one, here or elsewhere, who gave to it an honest support. Had their convictions been mine, I, too, would doubtless have done as they did. With my convictions I could not....

I can comprehend a war to compel a people to accept a master; to change a form of government; to give up territory; to abolish a domestic institution – in short, a war of conquest and subjugation; but a war for union! Was the Union thus made? Was it ever thus preserved? Sir, history will record that, after six thousand years of folly and wickedness in every form and administration of government ... it was reserved to American statesmanship, in the nineteenth century of the Christian era, to try the grand experiment, on a scale the most costly and gigantic in its proportions, of creating love by force, and developing fraternal affection by war! And history will record, too, on the same page, the utter, disastrous, and most bloody failure of the experiment.

[...]

And now, sir, I recur to the state of the Union to-day. What is it? Sir, twenty months have elapsed, but the rebellion is not crushed out; its military power has not been broken; the insurgents have not dispersed. The Union is not restored; nor the Constitution maintained; nor the laws enforced.... A thousand millions [have] been expended; and three hundred thousand lives lost or bodies mangled; and to-day the Confederate flag is still near the Potomac and the Ohio, and the Confederate Government stronger, many times, than at the beginning. Not a State has been restored, not any party of any State has voluntarily returned to the Union....

[...]

And now, sir, I come to the great and controlling question within which the whole issue of union or disunion is bound up: Is there "an irrepressible conflict" between the slaveholding and non-slaveholding States? Must "the cotton and rice fields of South Carolina, and the sugar plantations of Louisiana," in the language of Mr. Seward, "be ultimately tilled by free labor, and Charleston and New Orleans become marts for legitimate merchandise alone, or else the rye fields and wheat fields of Massachusetts and New York again be surrendered by their farmers to slave culture and the production of slaves, and Boston and New York become, once more markets for trade in the bodies and souls of men?" If so, then there is an end of all union, and forever. You can not abolish slavery by the sword; still lest by proclamations, though the President were to "proclaim" every month. Of what possible avail was his [Preliminary Emancipation] proclamation of September [1862]? Did the South submit? Was she even alarmed? And yet he has now fulmined [sic] another "bull against the comet" . . . and, threatening servile insurrection with all its horrors, has yet coolly appealed to the judgment of mankind, and invoked the blessing of the God of peace and love! But declaring it a military necessity, an essential measure of war to subdue the rebels, yet, with admirable wisdom, he expressly exempts from its operation the only States, and parts of States, in the South, where he has the military power to execute it.

Neither, sir, can you abolish slavery by argument. As well attempt to abolish marriage, or the relation of paternity. The South is resolved to maintain it at every hazard, and by every sacrifice; and if "this Union can not endure, part slave and part free," then it is already and finally dissolved. . . .
[. . .]
Sir, I repeat it, we are in the midst of the very crisis of this revolution. If, to-day, we secure peace, and begin the work of reunion, we shall yet escape; if not, I see nothing before us but universal political and social revolution, anarchy, and bloodshed, compared with which the Reign of Terror in France was a merciful visitation.

Source: Clement L. Vallandigham, *The Record of Hon. C. L. Vallandigham on Abolition, the Union, and the Civil War* (Columbus, Ohio: J. Walter, 1863), 173–204.

6. Frederick Douglass
"Men of Color to Arms!" March 2, 1863

> *Frederick Douglass (1818–95) escaped from slavery in 1838. He settled in Massachusetts, and within a few years emerged as a prominent abolitionist. An impressive public speaker, Douglass also became an influential journalist.*

In 1848 he moved to Rochester, New York where he edited the North Star *and its successors,* Frederick Douglass' Paper *and the* Douglass Monthly. *Initially an advocate of nonviolence, by the late 1840s Douglass became convinced that black men had to assert their manhood by fighting for freedom. During the Civil War, he was among the first to link enlistment of black troops with making emancipation of the slaves a Union war objective. He criticized the Lincoln administration for its reluctance to adopt either of these policies. Following the Emancipation Proclamation on January 1, 1863, Douglass helped recruit black soldiers, beginning with the 54th Massachusetts regiment. Douglass knew well that many African Americans distrusted Lincoln's promise of freedom. To counteract that distrust, his "Men of Color to Arms!" editorial appeals to black masculinity, the military crisis, the struggle for racial justice, and the memory of black heroes who had earlier taken up arms against slavery.*

When first the rebel cannon shattered the walls of Sumter, and drove away its starving garrison, I predicted that the war then and there inaugurated would not be fought out entirely by white men. Every month's experience during these two dreary years, has confirmed that opinion. A war undertaken and brazenly carried on for the perpetual enslavement of colored men, calls logically and loudly upon colored men to help suppress it. Only a moderate share of sagacity was needed to see that the arm of the slave was the best defence against the arm of the slaveholder. Hence with every reverse to the National arms, with every exulting shout of victory raised by the slaveholding rebels, I have implored the imperiled nation to unchain against her foes her powerful black hand. Slowly and reluctantly that appeal is beginning to be heeded. Stop not now to complain that it was not heeded sooner. It may, or it may not have been the best that it should not. This is not the time to discuss that question. Leave it to the future. When the war is over, the country is saved, peace is established, and the black man's rights are secured, as they will be, history with an impartial hand, will dispose of this and sundry other questions. Action! action! not criticism is the plain duty of this hour. Words are now useful only as they stimulate to blows. The office of speech now is only to point out when, here and how, to strike to the best advantage. There is no time for delay. The tide is at its flood that leads on to fortune. From East to West, from North to South, the sky is written all over "NOW OR NEVER." Liberty won by white men would lose half its luster. Who would be free themselves must strike the blow. Better even die free, than to live slaves. This is the sentiment of every brave colored man amongst us. There are weak and cowardly men in all nations. We have them amongst us. They tell you that this is a "white man's war";—that you will be no "better off after, than before the war"; that the getting of you into the army is to "sacrifice you on the first opportunity." Believe them not – cowards themselves, they do not wish to have their cowardice shamed by your brave example. Leave them to their timidity, or to whatever motive may hold them back....

In good earnest then, and after the best deliberations, I now for the first time during this war feel at liberty to call and counsel you to arms. By every consideration which binds you to your enslaved fellow country men, and the peace and welfare of your country; by every aspiration which you cherish for the freedom and equality of yourselves and your children; by all the ties of blood and identity which makes us one with the brave black men, now fighting our battles in Louisiana, in South Carolina, I urge you to fly to arms, and smite with death the power that would bury the Government and your Liberty in the same hopeless grave. I wish I could tell you that the State of New York calls you to this high honor. For the moment her constituted authorities are silent on the subject. They will speak by and by, and doubtless on the right side; but we are not compelled to wait for her. We can get at the throat of treason and slavery, through the State of Massachusetts.

She was the first in the war of Independence, first to break the chains of her slaves; first to make the black man equal before the law; first to admit colored children to her common schools, and she was first to answer with her blood the alarm cry of the nation – when its capital was menaced by rebels. You know her patriotic Governor [John A. Andrew], and you know Charles Sumner – I need not add more.

Massachusetts now welcomes you to arms as her soldiers. She has but a small colored population from which to recruit. She has full leave of the General government to send one regiment to the war, and she has undertaken to do it. Go quickly and help fill up this first colored regiment from the north. I am authorized to assure you that you will receive the same wages, the same rations, the same equipments, the same protection, the same treatment and the same bounty secured to white soldiers. You will be led by able and skillful officers – men who will take especial pride in your efficiency and success. They will be quick to accord to you all the honor you shall merit by your valor – and see that your rights and feelings are respected by other soldiers. I have assured myself on these points – and can speak with authority. More than twenty years unswerving devotion to our common cause may give me some humble claim to be trusted at this momentous crisis.

I will not argue. To do so implies hesitation and doubt, and you do not hesitate. You do not doubt. The day dawns – the morning star is bright upon the horizon! The iron gate of our prison stands half open. One gallant rush from the North will fling it wide open, while four millions of our brothers and sisters shall march out into liberty. The chance is now given you to end in a day the bondage of centuries, and to rise in one bound from social degradation to the plane of common equality with all other varieties of men. Remember Denmark Vesey of Charleston. – Remember Nathaniel Turner of South Hampton [sic], remember Shields Green and [John] Copeland who followed noble John Brown, and fell as glorious martyrs for the cause of the slave. – Remember that in a contest with oppression, the Almighty has no attribute which can take sides with oppressors. The case is before you. This is our golden opportunity – let us accept it – and forever wipe out the dark reproaches unsparingly hurled against us by our enemies. [Let us] win for ourselves the gratitude of the country – and the best blessings of our posterity through all time. The nucleus of this first regiment is now in camp at Readville, a short distance from Boston. I will undertake to forward to Boston all persons adjudged fit to be mustered into the regiment, who shall apply to me at any time within the next two weeks.

Source: *Douglass Monthly* (Rochester, NY), 5 (March 1863): 802.

7. Abraham Lincoln
Gettysburg Address, November 19, 1863

> *Abraham Lincoln's Gettysburg Address, which he presented at a ceremony to dedicate a cemetery for Union troops killed at the Battle of Gettysburg, is one of the greatest orations in American history. Contrary to legend, he spent several weeks composing this brief explanation of the Civil War's meaning. The main speaker that day was the famed orator Edward Everet, who delivered a two hour speech. Lincoln spoke for two minutes and was twice interrupted by applause. The address had a significant contemporary impact, although few immediately recognized its transcendent importance. Lincoln had redefined the role of the American government, suggesting that it must continually expand freedom.*

Fourscore and seven years ago our fathers brought forth on this continent a new nation, conceived in Liberty, and dedicated to the proposition that all men are created equal.

Now we are engaged in a great civil war, testing whether that nation or any nation so conceived and so dedicated can long endure. We are met on a great battlefield of that war. We have come to dedicate a portion of that field as a final resting place for those who here gave their lives that that nation might live. It is altogether fitting and proper that we should do this.

But in a larger sense we cannot dedicate – we cannot consecrate – we cannot hallow – this ground. The brave men, living and dead, who struggled here, have consecrated it, far above our poor power to add or detract. The world will little note nor long remember what we say here, but it can never forget what they did here. It is for us the living, rather, to be dedicated here to the unfinished work which they who fought here have thus far so nobly advanced. It is rather for us to be here dedicated to the great task remaining before us – that from these honored dead we take increased devotion to that cause for which they gave the last full measure of devotion – that we here highly resolve that these dead shall not have died in vain – that this nation, under God, shall have a new birth of freedom – and that government of the people, by the people, for the people, shall not perish from the earth.

Source: John G. Nicolay and John Hay, eds., *Complete Works of Abraham Lincoln*, 12 vols. (New York: Century, 1894), 9:209–10.

8. Bromley and Company
Democratic Caricature of Republican Racial Policy, 1864

Political cartoons were common during the Civil War era. This lithograph, produced by Bromley and Company of New York City and sold in bulk by Currier and Ives, is part of a series commissioned by Democratic politicians during the presidential election campaign of 1864. Abraham Lincoln was running for reelection on the Union Party ticket supported by Republicans and some War Democrats. The Democratic nominee was former Union military commander George B. McClellan. Neither Lincoln nor the great majority of white Republicans advocated racial equality. But Lincoln and the Republicans were far more favorable to black rights than were their northern Democratic opponents, who hoped to appeal in the campaign to racial prejudice by caricaturing Lincoln and other leading Republicans as advocates and practitioners of miscegenation (interracial sex). In the lower left of this cartoon, Senator Charles Sumner introduces Lincoln to a black woman, whom Lincoln vows "to number among my intimate friends." At center Horace Greeley dines with a black woman, and on the right (even more shocking to white sensibilities) white Republican women embrace black men.

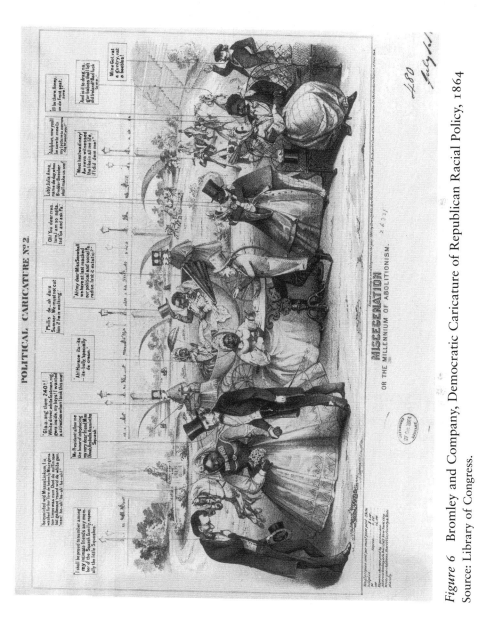

Figure 6 Bromley and Company, Democratic Caricature of Republican Racial Policy, 1864
Source: Library of Congress.

9. Robert Barnwell Rhett Jr.
War for Slavery, January 13, 1865

> *Since defense of slavery was the primary cause of secession, it is not surprising that hardly any African Americans were Confederate combat soldiers. Black men served in southern armies, but overwhelmingly as conscripted laborers, cooks, and teamsters. In some cases black body servants accompanied their white masters to war. Yet, as the Confederacy's need for fighting men grew desperate in late 1864 and early 1865, its leaders in Virginia – including Secretary of State Judah P. Benjamin, General of the Armies Robert E. Lee, and President Jefferson Davis – advocated arming slaves. They suggested that black men who fought for the Confederacy could be granted freedom. This raised basic questions about the "social institutions" white southerners fought to defend. Robert Barnwell Rhett Jr., who edited the* Charleston Mercury *from 1857 to its termination in 1868, responds vehemently to this threat to slavery and white supremacy in a column headed "Lunacy."*

The wild talk prevalent in the official and the semi-official organs at Richmond grates harshly upon the ear of South Carolina. It is still more grievous to her to hear the same unmanly proposition from those in authority in the old State of Virginia. Side by side Carolina and Virginia have stood together against all comers for near two centuries – the exemplars and authors of Southern civilization. Side by side it is our earnest hope they will stand to all time against the world. But we grieve to say there are counsels now brewing there that South Carolina cannot abet – that she will not suffer to be consummated, so far as *she* is concerned in them.

There are men in Virginia, and there are men in South Carolina, who have supposed that there is jealousy existing between these states, in the race of fame and ambition. These men are small pettifoggers and petty creatures. There is no State in the Union that has the solid calm respect for the merits of Virginia, than exists here in South Carolina. But we are not mouthers, or worshippers.... We are no *followers.*

In 1860 South Carolina seceded alone from the old union of States. Her people, in Convention assembled, invited the *slaveholding* States (none others) of the old Union to join her in erecting a separate Government of *Slave States*, for the protection of their common interests. All of the slave states, with the exception of Maryland and Kentucky, responded to her invitation. The Southern Confederacy of slave States was formed.

It was on account of encroachment upon the institution of *slavery* by the sectional majority of the old Union, that South Carolina seceded from that

Union. It is not at this late day, after the loss of thirty thousand of her best and bravest men in battle, that she will suffer it to be bartered away; or ground between the upper and nether mill stones, by the madness of Congress, or the counsels of shallow men elsewhere.

By the compact we made with Virginia and the other States of this Confederacy, South Carolina will stand to the bitter end of destruction. By that compact she intends to stand or to fall. Neither Congress, nor certain makeshift men in Virginia, can force upon her their mad schemes of weakness and surrender. She stands upon her institutions – and there she will fall in their defence. *We want no Confederate Government without our institutions.* And we will have none. Sink or swim, live or die, we stand by them, and are fighting for them this day. This is the ground of our fight – it is well that all should understand it at once. Thousands and tens of thousands of the bravest men, and the best blood of this State, fighting in the ranks, have left their bones whitening on the bleak hills of Virginia in this cause. We are fighting for our system of civilization – not for buncomb [bunkum], or for Jeff Davis. We intend to fight for *that*, or nothing. We expect Virginia to stand beside us in that fight, as of old, as we have stood beside her in this war up to this time. But such talk coming from such a source is destructive to the cause. Let it cease at once, in God's name, and in behalf of our common cause! It is paralizing [sic] to every man here to hear it. It throws a pall over the hearts of the soldiers from this State to hear it. The soldiers of South Carolina will not fight beside a nigger – to talk of emancipation is to disband our army. We are free men, and we chose to fight for ourselves – we want no slaves to fight for us. Skulkers, money-lenders, money-makers, and blood-suckers, alone will tolerate the idea. It is the man who wont fight himself, who wants his nigger to fight for him, and to take his place in the ranks. . . . Control your armies – put men of capacity in command, re-establish confidence – enforce thorough discipline – and there will be found men enough, and brave men enough, to defeat a dozen SHERMANS. Falter and hack at the root of the Confederacy – our institutions – our civilization – and you kill the cause as dead as boiled crab.

The straight and narrow path of our deliverance is in the reform of our government, and the discipline of our armies. Will Virginia stand by us as of old in this rugged pathway? We will not fail her in the shadow of a hair. But South Carolina will fight upon no other platform, than that she laid down in 1860.

Source: *Charleston Mercury*, January 13, 1865.

10. Abraham Lincoln
Second Inaugural Address, March 4, 1865

> *Abraham Lincoln's Second Inaugural Address rivals his Gettysburg Address in significance and literary power. He presented it on the verge of Union victory and six weeks before his death by assassination on April 15, 1865. It constitutes his maturing understanding of the relationship between slavery and the Civil War. In words at times reminiscent of the religious phraseology of John Brown's last speech, Lincoln ponders the purposes of God in United States history and the moral debt slavery entailed on white Americans – northerners as well as southerners. Lincoln, who had worked to secure Congress's passage of the Thirteenth Amendment to the US Constitution on January 31 (ratified the following December), remained flexible concerning the process of emancipation. But, despite his call for "malice toward none" in finishing "the work we are now in," he links the significance of the war to black freedom.*

FELLOW-COUNTRYMEN: . . . On the occasion corresponding to this four years ago, all thoughts were anxiously directed to an impending civil war. All dreaded it, all sought to avert it. While the inaugural address was being delivered from this place, devoted altogether to *saving* the Union without war, insurgent agents were in the city seeking to *destroy* it without war – seeking to dissolve the Union, and divide effects, by negotiation. Both parties deprecated war; but one of them would *make* war rather than let the nation survive; and the other would accept war rather than let it perish. And the war came.

One-eighth of the whole population were colored slaves, not distributed generally over the Union, but localized in the Southern part of it. These slaves constituted a peculiar and powerful interest. All knew that this interest was, somehow, the cause of the war. To strengthen, perpetuate, and extend this interest was the object for which the insurgents would rend the Union, even by war; while the Government claimed no right to do more than to restrict the territorial enlargement of it. Neither party expected for the war the magnitude or the duration which it has already attained. Neither anticipated that the *cause* of the conflict might cease with, or even before, the conflict itself should cease. Each looked for an easier triumph, and a result less fundamental and astounding. Both read the same Bible, and pray to the same God, and each invokes His aid against the other. It may seem strange that any men should dare to ask a just God's assistance in wringing their bread from the sweat of other men's faces, but let us judge not, that we be not judged. The prayers of both could not be answered. That of neither has been answered fully. The Almighty has His own purposes. "Woe unto the world because of offenses for it must needs be that offenses come, but woe to that man by whom the offense cometh." If we shall suppose that American slavery is one of those offenses which, in the providence of God, must needs come, but which, having continued through His appointed time, He now wills to remove, and that He gives to both North and South this terrible war, as the woe due to those by whom the offense came, shall we discern therein any departure from those divine attributes which the believers in a living God always ascribe to Him? Fondly do we hope, fervently do we pray that this mighty scourge of war may speedily pass away. Yet, if God wills that it continue until all the wealth piled by the bondsman's two hundred and fifty years of unrequited toil shall be sunk, and until every drop of blood drawn by the lash shall be paid by another drawn with the sword, as was said three thousand years ago, so still it must be said, "The judgments of the Lord are true and righteous altogether."

With malice toward none, with charity for all, with firmness in the right, as God gives us to see the right, let us strive on to finish the work we are in, to bind up the nation's wounds, to care for him who shall have borne the battle, and for his widow, and his orphan, to do all which may achieve and cherish a just and lasting peace among ourselves, and with all nations.

Source: James D. Richardson, ed., *A Compilation of the Messages and Papers of the Presidents*, 10 vols. (Washington, DC: Government Printing Office, 1897), 6:276–7.

Discussion Questions

1 What were the roles of emancipation and assertions of African-American rights during the Civil War?
2 In what ways do Lincoln's Emancipation Proclamation, Gettysburg Address, and Second Inaugural Address reflect the spirit of the Battle Hymn of the Republic? In what ways do they not?
3 What roles did dissent play in the Union and Confederacy during the Civil War?
4 How do you suppose Clement L. Vallandigham and Robert Barnwell Rhett Jr. would evaluate Frederick Douglass's call on black men to enlist in Union armies?

Chapter 7   The Trans-Mississippi West

1. US Congress
Homestead Act, May 20, 1862

> *Secession and the departure from Congress of most southern representatives
> and senators permitted Republicans to pass legislation long favored by their
> constituents. Much of this legislation, including the creation of a uniform
> national currency and a national bank, served the interests of northeastern
> industry. Nevertheless two pieces of legislation – the Homestead Act and the
> Pacific Railroad Act – had especial relevancy for the West. Opening
> government-owned western land to settlers from the East had been a popular
> issue in the North since the mid-1840s. But most southern politicians
> regarded efforts to provide cheap or free land as part of a scheme to exclude
> slavery and secure northern control of the western territories. Southern
> senators defeated a homestead bill in February 1859 and proslavery
> Democratic president James Buchanan vetoed a similar bill in early 1860.
> The act passed in May 1862 allowed any loyal citizen (or prospective citizen)
> to acquire 160 acres of land by either paying a minimal fee or by living on the
> land for five years. By the end of the Civil War, 20,000 farmers had taken
> advantage of the act, settling 3,000,000 acres. By 1900, 600,000 settlers had
> claimed 80,000,000 acres.*

An Act to secure Homesteads to actual Settlers on the Public Domain.

*Be it enacted by the Senate and House of Representatives of the United
States of America in Congress assembled,* That any person who is the head
of a family, or who has arrived at the age of twenty-one years, and is a
citizen of the United States, or who shall have filed his declaration of

intention to become such, as required by the naturalization laws of the United States, and who has never borne arms against the United States Government or given aid and comfort to its enemies, shall, from and after the first January, eighteen hundred and sixty-three, be entitled to enter one quarter section or a less quantity of unappropriated public lands, upon which said person may have filed a preemption claim, or which may, at the time the application is made, be subject to preemption at one dollar and twenty-five cents, or less, per acre; or eighty acres or less of such unappropriated lands, at two dollars and fifty cents per acre, to be located in a body, in conformity to the legal subdivisions of the public lands, and after the same shall have been surveyed: *Provided*, That any person owning and residing on land may, under the provisions of this act, enter other land lying contiguous to his or her said land, which shall not, with the land so already owned and occupied, exceed in the aggregate one hundred and sixty acres.

Sec. 2. *And be it further enacted*, That the person applying for the benefit of this act shall, upon application to the register of the land office in which he or she is about to make such entry, make affidavit before the said register or receiver that he or she is the head of a family, or is twenty-one years or more of age, or shall have performed service in the army or navy of the United States, and that he has never borne arms against the Government of the United States or given aid and comfort to its enemies, and that such application is made for his or her exclusive use and benefit, and that said entry is made for the purpose of actual settlement and cultivation, and not either directly or indirectly for the use of benefit of any other person or persons whomsoever; and upon filing the said affidavit with the register or receiver, and on payment of ten dollars, he or she shall thereupon be permitted to enter the quantity of land specified: *Provided, however*, That no certificate shall be given or patent issued therefor [sic] until the expiration of five years from the date of such entry; and if, at the expiration of such time, or at any time within two years thereafter, the person making such entry; or, if he be dead, his widow; or in case of her death, his heirs or devisee; or in case of a widow making such entry, her heirs or devisee, in case of her death; shall prove by two credible witnesses that he, she, or they have resided upon or cultivated the same for the term of five years immediately succeeding the time of filing the affidavit aforesaid, and shall make affidavit that no part of said land has been alienated, and that he has borne true allegiance to the Government of the United States; then, in such case, he, she, or they, if at that time a citizen of the United States, shall be entitled to a patent, as in other cases provided for by law: *And provided, further*, That in case of the death of both father and mother, leaving an infant child, or children, under twenty-one years of age, the right and fee shall enure [sic] to the benefit of said infant child or children. . . .

Sec. 3. *And be it further enacted,* That the register of the land office shall note all such applications on the tract books and plats of his office, and keep a register of all such entries, and make return thereof to the General Land Office, together with the proof upon which they have been founded.

Sec. 4. *And be it further enacted,* That no lands acquired under the provisions of this act shall in any event become liable to the satisfaction of any debt or debts contracted prior to the issuing of the patent therefor [sic].

Sec. 5. *And be it further enacted,* That if, at any time after the filing of the affidavit, as required in the second section of this act, and before the expiration of the five years aforesaid, it shall be proven after due notice to the settler, to the satisfaction of the register of the land office, that the person having filed such affidavit shall have actually changed his or her residence, or abandoned the said land for more than six months at any time, then and in that event the land so entered shall revert to the government.

Sec. 6. *And be it further enacted,* That no individual shall be permitted to acquire title to more than one quarter section under the provisions of this act; and that the Commissioner of the General Land Office is hereby required to prepare and issue such rules and regulations, consistent with this act, as shall be necessary and proper to carry its provisions into effect; and that the registers and receivers of the several land offices shall be entitled to receive the same compensation for any lands entered under the provisions of this act that they are now entitled to receive when the same quantity of land is entered with money, one half to be paid by the person making the application at the time of so doing, and the other half on the issue of the certificate by the person to whom it may be issued; but this shall not be construed to enlarge the maximum of compensation now prescribed by law for any register or receiver: *Provided,* . . . That all persons who may have filed their application for a preemption right prior to the passage of this act, shall be entitled to all privileges of this act: *Provided, further,* That no person who has served, or may hereafter serve, for a period of not less than fourteen days in the army or navy of the United States, either regular or volunteers under the laws thereof, during the existence of an actual war, domestic or foreign, shall be deprived of the benefits of this act on account of not having attained the age of twenty-one years.

[. . .]

Sec. 8. *And be it further enacted,* That nothing in this act shall be so construed as to prevent any person who has availed him or herself of the benefits of the first section of this act, from paying the minimum price, or the price to which the same may have graduated, for the quantity of land so entered at any time before the expiration of the five years, and obtaining a patent therefor [sic] from the government, as in other cases provided by law, on making proof of settlement and cultivation as provided by existing laws granting preemption rights....

Source: *US Statutes at Large*, 12 (1862): 392–3.

2. John S. Smith
Sand Creek Massacre, November 29, 1864

Encouragement of settlement in the trans-Mississippi West promoted violent clashes in that huge region. In some cases Union and Confederate forces fought each other. Far more common and deadly were struggles between white settlers and American Indians. At the Battle of Glorieta Pass, New Mexico Territory, on March 28, 1862, a tiny Union army of 1,300 men defeated a Confederate army of similar size, forcing the permanent withdrawal of southern forces west of Texas. Among the Union heroes of the battle was Major John M. Chivington, a Methodist minister turned soldier. Two-and-a-half years later Chivington, as colonel of Colorado Volunteers, led an attack on the Sand Creek Reservation in the southwestern portion of the territory, killing 450 Cheyenne and 40 Arapaho men, women, and children. The small reservation lacked the natural resources to sustain its population, and Cheyenne men had been raiding ranches and wagon trains for food. Chivington's attack came in retaliation. John S. Smith (d. 1871), in testimony given on March 14, 1865 before a congressional committee investigating the incident, was an experienced and respected white "Indian agent" and interpreter who was fluent in Cheyenne. Although his "half-breed" son had died in the attack, he provides remarkably dispassionate testimony.

Question. Will you state to the committee all that you know in relation to the attack of Colonel Chivington upon the Cheyenne and Arapahoe Indians in November last?

Answer. Major Anthony was in command at Fort Lyon at the time. Those Indians had been induced to remain in the vicinity of Fort Lyon, and were promised protection by the commanding officer at Fort Lyon. The commanding officer saw proper to keep them some thirty or forty miles distant from the fort, for fear of some conflict between them and the soldiers or the traveling population, for Fort Lyon is on a great thoroughfare. He advised them to go out on what is called Sand creek, about forty miles, a little east of north from Fort Lyon. Some days after they had left Fort Lyon when I had just recovered from a long spell of sickness, I was called on by Major

S.G. Colley, who asked me if I was able and willing to go out and pay a visit to these Indians, ascertain their numbers, their general disposition toward the whites, and the points where other bands might be located in the interior.

Question. What was the necessity for obtaining that information?

Answer. Because there were different bands which were supposed to be at war; in fact, we knew at the time that they were at war with the white population in that country; but this band had been in and left the post perfectly satisfied. I left to go to this village of Indians on the 26th of November last. I arrived there on the 27th and remained there the 28th. On the morning of the 29th, between daylight and sunrise – nearer sunrise than daybreak – a large number of troops were discovered from three-quarters of a mile to a mile below the village. The Indians, who discovered them, ran to my camp, called me out, and wanted to me to go and see what troops they were, and what they wanted. The head chief of the nation, Black Kettle, and head chief of the Cheyennes, was encamped there with us. Some years previous he had been presented with a fine American flag by Colonel Greenwood, a commissioner, who had been sent out there. Black Kettle ran this American flag up to the top of his lodge, with a small white flag tied right under it, as he had been advised to do in case he should meet with any troops out on the prairies. I then left my own camp and started for that portion of the troops that was nearest the village, supposing I could go up to the men. I did not know but they might be strange troops, and thought my presence and explanations could reconcile matters. Lieutenant Wilson was in command of the detachment to which I tried to make my approach; but they fired several volleys at me, and I returned back to my camp and entered my lodge.

Question. Did these troops know you to be a white man? . . .

Answer. They could not help knowing it. I had on pants, a soldier's overcoat, and a hat such as I am wearing now. I was dressed differently from any Indian in the country. . . . After I had left my lodge to go out and see what was going on, Colonel Chivington rode up to within fifty or sixty yards of where I was camped; he recognized me at once. They all call me Uncle John in that country. He said, "Run here, Uncle John; you are all right." I went to him as fast as I could. He told me to get in between him and his troops, who were then coming up very fast; I did so; directly another officer who knew me – Lieutenant Baldwin, in command of a battery – tried to assist me to get a horse; but there was no loose horse there at the time. He said, "Catch hold of the caisson, and keep up with us."

By this time the Indians had fled; had scattered in every direction. The troops were some on one side of the river and some on the other, following up the Indians. We had been encamped on the north side of the river; I followed along, holding on the caisson, sometimes running, sometimes walking. Finally, about a mile above the village, the troops had got a parcel of the Indians hemmed in under the bank of the river; as soon as the troops overtook them, they commenced firing on them; some troops had got above them, so that they were completely surrounded. There were probably a hundred Indians hemmed in there, men, women, and children; the most of the men in the village escaped. By the time I got up with the battery to the place where these Indians were surrounded there had been some considerable firing. Four or five soldiers had been killed, some with arrows and some with bullets. The soldiers continued firing on these Indians, who numbered about a hundred, until they had almost completely destroyed them. I think I saw altogether some seventy dead bodies lying there; the greater portion women and children. There may have been thirty warriors, old and young; the rest were women and small children of different ages and sizes.

The troops at that time were very much scattered. There were not over two hundred troops in the main fight, engaged in killing this body of Indians under the bank. The balance of the troops were scattered in different directions, running after small parties of Indians who were trying to make their escape....

The Indians had left their lodges and property; everything they owned. I do not think more than one-half of the Indians left their lodges with their arms. I think there were between 800 and 1,000 men in this command of United States troops. There was a part of three companies of the 1st Colorado, and the balance were what were called 100 days men of the 3rd regiment. I am not able to say which party did the most execution on the Indians, because it was very much mixed up at the time.

We remained there that day after the fight. By 11 o'clock, I think, the entire number of soldiers had returned back to the camp where Colonel Chivington had returned. On their return, he ordered the soldiers to destroy all the Indian property there, which they did, with the exception of what plunder they took away with them, which was considerable.

Question. How many Indians were there there?

Answer. There were 100 families of Cheyennes, and some six or eight lodges of Arapahoes.

Question. How many persons in all, should you say?

Answer. About 500 we estimate them at five to a lodge.

Question. 500 men, women and children?

Answer. Yes, sir.

Question. Do you know the reason for that attack on the Indians?

Answer. I do not know any exact reason. I have heard a great many reasons given. I have heard that that whole Indian war had been brought on for selfish purposes. Colonel Chivington was running for Congress in Colorado, and there were other things of that kind; and last spring a year ago he was looking for an order to go to the front, and I understand he had this Indian war in view to retain himself and his troops in that country, to carry out his electioneering purposes.

Question. In what way did this attack on the Indians further the purpose of Colonel Chivington?

Answer. It was said – I did not hear him say it myself, but it was said that he would do something; he had this regiment of three-months men, and did not want them to go out without doing some service. Now he had been told repeatedly by different persons – by myself, as well as others – where he could find the hostile bands.

The same chiefs who were killed in this village of Cheyennes had been up to see Colonel Chivington in Denver but a short time previous to this attack. He himself told them that he had no power to treat with them; that he had received telegrams from General [Samuel R.] Curtis directing him to fight all Indians he met with in that country. Still he would advise them, if they wanted any assistance from the whites, to go to their nearest military post in their country, give up their arms and the stolen property, if they had any, and then they would receive directions in what way to act. This was told them by Colonel Chivington and by Governor [John] Evans, of Colorado. I myself interpreted for them and for the Indians.

Question. Did Colonel Chivington hold any communciation with these Indians, or any of them, before making the attack upon them?

Answer. No, sir, not then. He had some time previously held a council with them at Denver city. When we first recovered the white prisoners from the Indians, we invited some of the chiefs to go to Denver, inasmuch as they had sued for peace, and were willing to give up these white prisoners.... Governor Evans and Colonel Chivington were in Denver, and were present at this council. They told the Indians to return with Major [Edward W.] Wynkoop, and whatever he agreed on doing with them would be recognized by them.

I returned with the Indians to Fort Lyon. There we let them go out to their villages to bring in their families, as they had been invited through the proclamation or circular of the governor during the month of June, I think. They were gone some twelve or fifteen days from Fort Lyon, and then they returned with their families....

Then Major Anthony, through me, told the Indians that he did not have it in his power to issue rations to them, as Major Wynkoop had done. He said that he had assumed command at Fort Lyon, and his orders were positive from headquarters to fight the Indians in the vicinity of Fort Lyon, or at any other point in the Territory where they could find them. He said that he had understood that they had been behaving very badly. But on seeing Major Wynkoop and others there at Fort Lyon, he was happy to say that things were not as had been presented, and he could not pursue any other course than that of Major Wynkoop except the issuing rations to them. He then advised them to [go] out to some near point, where there was buffalo, not too far from Fort Lyon or they might meet with troops from the Platte, who would not know them from the hostile bands. This was the southern band of Cheyennes; there is another band called the northern band. They had no apprehensions in the world of any trouble with the whites at the time this attack was made.

Question. Had there been, to your knowledge, any hostile act or demonstration on the part of these Indians or any of them?

Answer. Not in this band. But the northern band, the band known by the name of Dog soldiers of Cheyennes, had committed many depredations on the Platte.

Question. Do you know whether or not Colonel Chivington knew the friendly character of these Indians before he made the attack upon them?

Answer. It is my opinion that he did.

Question. On what is that opinion based?

Answer. On this fact, that he stopped all persons from going on ahead of him. He stopped the mail, and would not allow any person to go on ahead of him at the time he was on his way from Denver city to Fort Lyon. He placed a guard around old Colonel Bent, the former agent there; he stopped a Mr. Hagues and many men who were on their way to Fort Lyon. He took the fort by surprise, and as soon as he got there he posted pickets all around the fort, and then left at 8 o'clock that night for this Indian camp.

Question. Was that anything more than the exercise of ordinary precaution in following Indians?

Answer. Well, sir, he was told that there were no Indians in the vicinity of Fort Lyon, except Black Kettle's band of Cheyennes and Left Hand's band of Arapahoes....

[...]

Question: Did you tell Colonel Chivington the character and disposition of these Indians at any time during your interviews on this day?

Answer. Yes, sir.

Question. What did he say in reply?

Answer. He said he could not help it; that his orders were positive to attack the Indians.

Question. From whom did he receive these orders?

Answer. I do not know; I presume from General Curtis....

Question. Were the women and children slaughtered indiscriminately, or only so far as they were with the warriors?

Answer. Indiscriminately.

Question. Were there any acts of barbarity perpetrated there that came under your own observation?

Answer. Yes, sir; I saw the bodies of those lying there cut all to pieces, worse mutilated than any I ever saw before; the women cut all to pieces....

Question. How cut?

Answer. With knives; scalped; their brains knocked out; children two or three months old; all ages lying there, from sucking infants up to warriors....

Question. Did you see them when they were mutilated?

Answer. Yes, sir.

Question. By whom were they mutilated?

Answer. By the United States troops.

Question. Do you know whether or not it was done by the direction or consent of any of the officers.

Answer. I do not; I hardly think it was....

Question. Did you speak of these barbarities to Colonel Chivington?

Answer. No sir; I had nothing at all to say about it, because at that time they were hostile towards me, from the fact of my being there. They probably supposed that I might be compromised with them in some way or other.

Question. Who called on you to designate the bodies of those who were killed?

Answer. Colonel Chivington himself asked me if I would ride out with Lieutenant Colonel Bowen, and see how many chiefs or principal men I could recognize.

Question. Can you state how many Indians were killed – how many women and how many children?

Answer. Perhaps one-half were men, and the balance were women and children. I do not think that I saw more than 70 lying dead then, as far as I went. But I saw parties of men scattered in every direction, pursuing little bands of Indians....

Question. How large a body of troops?

Answer. I think that probably there may have been about 60 or 70 warriors who were armed and stood their ground and fought. Those that were unarmed got out of the way as they best could.

Question. How many of our troops were killed and how many wounded?

Answer. There were ten killed on the ground, and thirty-eight wounded; four of the wounded died at Fort Lyon before I came on east.

Source: Senate Report No. 142, 38th Cong., 2d sess. *Report of the Joint Committee on the Conduct of the War*, 3 vols. (Washington: Government Printing Office, 1865), 1:"Massacre of Cheyenne Indians," 4–12.

3. United States and Sioux Nation
Treaty of Fort Laramie, April 29, 1868

Several factors contributed the Treaty of Fort Laramie, Wyoming, signed in April 1868. They included American Indian resistance to white encroachment in the northern Great Plains region, railroad interests, and an ultimately unsuccessful effort within the United States government to adopt a more enlightened "Indian Policy." The discovery of gold near Bannack, Montana, in 1863, increasing numbers of white migrants, and the establishment of US Army posts in the region had precipitated Red Cloud's War in 1866. Red Cloud, a powerful Sioux (Lakota) war leader, and his followers were most determined to mount a forceful resistance. But Cheyenne (some of whom had been at Sand Creek), Arapaho, Kiowa, and Comanche bands also took action. They attacked white firewood cutters, settlers, and traders. On December 21, 1866, 3,000 Sioux surrounded, killed, and mutilated the bodies of 80 US soldiers under the command of Captain William Fetterman. As violence spread, President Andrew Johnson appointed a peace commission to negotiate with Indian leaders. At Medicine Lodge Creek, Kansas, on October 21, 1867, the commission signed a treaty with leaders of the Kiowa and Comanche. The following April the commission signed a similar but more generous treaty with Red Cloud at Fort Laramie. In a clear victory for Red Cloud, it committed the United States to abandoning several forts in the region and recognized Sioux possession of the western half of South Dakota and large portions of Montana and Wyoming. In a characteristically paternalistic manner, the treaty also committed the United States to provide educational and agricultural aid to the Sioux and other Indian nations. It committed the Sioux to refrain from violence against settlers and railroads. The main provisions of the treaty lasted only to 1874 when prospectors discovered gold in the Black Hills of western South Dakota. This led to another war, George Armstrong Custer and the US 7th Cavalry's defeat at the Battle of the Little Bighorn on June 25, 1876, the capitulation of the Sioux and Cheyenne shortly thereafter, and US acquisition of the Black Hills in February 1877.

Articles of a treaty made and concluded by and between Lieutenant General William T. Sherman, General William S. Harney, General Alfred H. Terry, General O. O. Augur, J. B. Henderson, Nathaniel G. Taylor, John G. Sanborn, and Samuel F. Tappan, duly appointed commissioners on the part of the United States, and the different bands of the Sioux Nation of Indians, by their chiefs and headmen, whose names are hereto subscribed, they being duly authorized to act in the premises.

ARTICLE 1. From this day forward all war between the parties to this agreement shall for ever cease. The government of the United States desires peace, and its honor is hereby pledged to keep it. The Indians desire peace, and they now pledge their honor to maintain it.

If bad men among the whites, or among other people subject to the authority of the United States, shall commit any wrong upon the person or property of the Indians, the United States will, upon proof made to the agent, and forwarded to the Commissioner of Indian Affairs at Washington city, proceed at once to cause the offender to be arrested and punished according to the laws of the United States, and also reimburse the injured person for the loss sustained. If bad men among the Indians shall commit a wrong or depredation upon the person or property of any one, white, black, or Indian, subject to the authority of the United States, and at peace therewith, the Indians herein named solemnly agree that they will, upon proof made to their agent, and notice by him, deliver up the wrongdoer to the United States, to be tried and punished according to its laws, and, in case they willfully refuse so to do, the person injured shall be reimbursed for his loss from the annuities, or other moneys due or to become due to them under this or other treaties made with the United States; and the President, on advising with the Commissioner of Indian Affairs, shall prescribe such rules and regulations for ascertaining damages under the provisions of this article as in his judgment may be proper, but no one sustaining loss while violating the provisions of this treaty, or the laws of the United States, shall be reimbursed therefor [sic].

ARTICLE 2. The United States agrees that the following district of country, to wit, viz: commencing on the east bank of the Missouri river where the 46th parallel of north latitude crosses the same, thence along low-water mark down said east bank to a point opposite where the northern line of the State of Nebraska strikes the river, thence west across said river, and along the northern line of Nebraska to the 104th degree of longitude west from Greenwich, thence north on said meridian to a point where the 46th parallel of north latitude intercepts the same, thence due east along said parallel to the place of beginning; and in addition thereto, all existing reservations of the east bank of said river, shall be and the same is, set apart for the absolute and undisturbed use and occupation of the Indians herein named, and for such other friendly tribes or individual Indians as from time to time they may be willing, with the consent of the United States, to admit amongst them; and the United States now solemnly agrees that no persons, except those herein designated and authorized so to do, and except such officers, agents, and employees of the government as may be authorized to enter upon Indian reservations in discharge of duties enjoined by law, shall ever be permitted to pass over, settle upon, or reside in the territory described in this article, or in such territory as may be added to this reservation for the use of said Indians, and henceforth they will and do hereby relinquish all claims or right in and to any portion of the United States or Territories, except such as is embraced within the limits aforesaid, and except as hereinafter provided.

ARTICLE 3. If it should appear from actual survey or other satisfactory examination of said tract of land that it contains less than 160 acres of tillable land for each person who, at the time, may be authorized to reside on it under the provisions of this treaty, and a very considerable number of such persons shall be disposed to commence cultivating the soil as farmers, the United States agrees to set apart, for the use of said Indians, as herein provided, such additional quantity of arable land, adjoining to said reservation, or as near to the same as it can be obtained, as may be required to provide the necessary amount.

ARTICLE 4. The United States agrees, at its own proper expense, to construct, at some place on the Missouri river, near the centre of said reservation where timber and water may be convenient, the following buildings, to wit, a warehouse, a store-room for the use of the agent in storing goods belonging to the Indians, to cost not less than $2,500; an agency building, for the residence of the agent, to cost not exceeding $3,000; a residence for the physician, to cost not more than $3,000; and five other buildings, for a carpenter, farmer, blacksmith, miller, and engineer – each to cost not exceeding $2,000; also, a school-house, or mission building, so soon as a sufficient number of children can be induced by the agent to attend school, which shall not cost exceeding $5,000. The United States agrees further to cause to be erected on said reservation, near the other buildings herein authorized, a good steam circular saw-mill, with a grist-mill and shingle machine attached to the same, to cost not exceeding $8,000.

ARTICLE 5. The United States agrees that the agent for said Indians shall in the future make his home at the agency building; that he shall reside among them, and keep an office open at all times for the purpose of prompt and diligent inquiry into such matters of complaint by and against the Indians as may be presented for investigation under the provisions of their treaty stipulations, as also for the faithful discharge of other duties enjoined on him by law. In all cases of depredation on person or property he shall cause the evidence to be taken in writing and forwarded, together with his findings, to the Commissioner of Indian Affairs, whose decision, subject to the revision of the Secretary of the Interior, shall be binding on the parties to this treaty.

ARTICLE 6. If any individual belonging to said tribes of Indians, or legally incorporated with them, being the head of a family, shall desire to commence farming, he shall have the privilege to select, in the presence and with the assistance of the agent then in charge, a tract of land within said reservation, not exceeding three hundred and twenty acres in extent, which tract, when so selected, certified, and recorded in the "Land Book" as herein directed, shall cease to be held in common, but the same may be occupied and held in the exclusive possession of the person selecting it, and of his family, so long as he or they may continue to cultivate it.

Any person over eighteen years of age, not being the head of a family, may in like manner select and cause to be certified to him or her, for purposes of cultivation, a quantity of land, not exceeding eighty acres in extent, and thereupon be entitled to the exclusive possession of the same as above directed.

For each tract of land so selected a certificate, containing a description thereof and the name of the person selecting it, with a certificate endorsed thereon that the same has been recorded, shall be delivered to the party entitled to it, by the agent, after the same shall have been recorded by him in a book to be kept in his office, subject to inspection, which said book shall be known as the "Sioux Land Book." . . .

ARTICLE 7. In order to insure the civilization of the Indians entering into this treaty, the necessity of education is admitted, especially of such of them as are or may be settled on said agricultural reservations, and they, therefore, pledge themselves to compel their children, male and female, between the ages of six and sixteen years, to attend school, and it is hereby made the duty of the agent for said Indians to see that this stipulation is strictly complied with; and the United States agrees that for every thirty children between said ages, who can be induced or compelled to attend school, a house shall be provided, and a teacher competent to teach the elementary branches of an English education shall be furnished, who will reside among said Indians and faithfully discharge his or her duties as a teacher. The provisions of this article to continue for not less than twenty years.

ARTICLE 8. When the head of a family or lodge shall have selected lands and received his certificate as above directed, and the agent shall be satisfied that he intends in good faith to commence cultivating the soil for a living, he shall be entitled to receive seeds and agricultural implements for the first year, not exceeding in value one hundred dollars, and for each succeeding year he shall continue to farm, for a period of three years more, he shall be entitled to receive seeds and implements as aforesaid, not exceeding in value twenty-five dollars. And it is further stipulated that such persons as commence farming shall receive instruction from the farmer herein provided for, and whenever more than one hundred persons shall enter upon the cultivation of the soil, a second blacksmith shall be provided, with such iron, steel, and other material as may be needed.

ARTICLE 9. At any time after ten years from the making of this treaty, the United States shall have the privilege of withdrawing the physician, farmer, blacksmith, carpenter, engineer, and miller herein provided for, but in case of such withdrawal, an additional sum thereafter of ten thousand dollars per annum shall be devoted to the education of said Indians, and the Commissioner of Indian Affairs shall, upon careful inquiry into their condition, make such rules and regulations for the expenditure of said sums as will best promote the education and moral improvement of said tribes.

ARTICLE 10. In lieu of all sums of money or other annuities provided to be paid to the Indians herein named under any treaty or treaties heretofore made, the United States agrees to deliver at the agency house on the reservation herein named, on or before the first day of August of each year, for thirty years, the following articles, to wit:

For each male person over 14 years of age, a suit of good substantial woollen clothing, consisting of coat, pantaloons, flannel shirt, hat, and a pair of home-made socks.

For each female over 12 years of age, a flannel shirt, or the goods necessary to make it, a pair of woollen hose, 12 yards of calico, and 12 yards of cotton domestics.

For the boys and girls under the ages named, such flannel and cotton goods as may be needed to make each a suit as aforesaid, together with a pair of woollen hose for each.

And in order that the Commissioner of Indian Affairs may be able to estimate properly for the articles herein named, it shall be the duty of the agent each year to forward to him a full and exact census of the Indians, on which the estimate from year to year can be based.

And in addition to the clothing herein named, the sum of $10 for each person entitled to the beneficial effects of this treaty shall be annually appropriated for a period of 30 years, while such persons roam and hunt, and $20 for each person who engages in farming, to be used by the Secretary of the Interior in the purchase of such articles as from time to time the condition and necessities of the Indians may indicate to be proper. And if within the 30 years, at any time, it shall appear that the amount of money needed for clothing, under this article, can be appropriated to better uses for the Indians named herein, Congress may, by law, change the appropriation to other purposes, but in no event shall the amount of the appropriation be withdrawn or discontinued for the period named. And the President shall annually detail an officer of the army to be present and attest the delivery of all the goods herein named, to the Indians, and he shall inspect and report on the quantity and quality of the goods and the manner of their delivery. And it is hereby expressly stipulated that each Indian over the age of four years, who shall have removed to and settled permanently upon said reservation, shall receive one pound of meat and one pound of flour per day, provided the Indians cannot furnish their own subsistence at an earlier date. And it is further stipulated that the United States will furnish and deliver to each lodge of Indians or family of persons legally incorporated with the, who shall remove to the reservation herein described and commence farming, one good American cow, and one good well-broken pair of American oxen within 60 days after such lodge or family shall have so settled upon said reservation.

ARTICLE 11. In consideration of the advantages and benefits conferred by this treaty and the many pledges of friendship by the United States, the tribes who are parties to this agreement hereby stipulate that they will relinquish all right to occupy permanently the territory outside their reservations as herein defined, but yet reserve the right to hunt on any lands north of North Platte, and on the Republican Fork of the Smoky Hill river, so long as the buffalo may range thereon in such numbers as to justify the chase. And they, the said Indians, further expressly agree:

1st. That they will withdraw all opposition to the construction of the railroads now being built on the plains.

2d. That they will permit the peaceful construction of any railroad not passing over their reservation as herein defined.

3d. That they will not attack any persons at home, or travelling, nor molest or disturb any wagon trains, coaches, mules, or cattle belonging to the people of the United States, or to persons friendly therewith.

4th. They will never capture, or carry off from the settlements, white women or children.

5th. They will never kill or scalp white men, nor attempt to do them harm.

6th. They withdraw all pretence of opposition to the construction of the railroad now being built along the Platte river and westward to the Pacific ocean, and they will not in future object to the construction of railroads, wagon roads, mail stations, or other works of utility or necessity, which may be ordered or permitted by the laws of the United States. But should such roads or other works be constructed on the lands of their reservation, the government will pay the tribe whatever amount of damage may be assessed by three disinterested commissioners to be appointed by the President for that purpose, one of the said commissioners to be a chief or headman of the tribe.

7th.   They agree to withdraw all opposition to the military posts or roads now established south of the North Platte river, or that may be established, not in violation of treaties heretofore made or hereafter to be made with any of the Indian tribes.

[. . .]

ARTICLE 16. The United States hereby agrees and stipulates that the country north of the North Platte river and east of the summits of the Big Horn mountains shall be held and considered to be unceded Indian territory, and also stipulates and agrees that no white person or persons shall be permitted to settle upon or occupy any portion of the same; or without the consent of the Indians, first had and obtained, to pass through the same; and it is further agreed by the United States, that within ninety days after the conclusion of peace with all the bands of the Sioux nation, the military posts now established in the territory in this article named shall be abandoned, and that the road leading to them and by them to the settlements in the Territory of Montana shall be closed.

Source: *Indian Affairs. Laws and Treaties*, comp. and ed. Charles J. Kappler, 7 vols. (Washington: Government Printing Office, 1904–79), 2:998–1003.

4. Andrew J. Russell
Joining of the Rails, Promontory, Utah, May 10, 1869

That the United States could construct a transcontinental railroad across huge distances over difficult terrain at the same time it fought the Confederacy testifies to the strength of its industrializing economy. Congress had begun considering plans for a government-subsidized railroad from the Mississippi River to the Pacific Ocean in 1845. But disagreements between northern and southern congressmen concerning the railroad route prevented action until after secession. On July 1, 1862, under Republican leadership, Congress passed the Pacific Railroad Act, providing extensive land grants and government loans to two private companies for the construction of a railroad between Omaha and San Francisco. Beginning in 1863, the Union Pacific Railroad Company built westward from Nebraska, and the Central (later Southern) Pacific built eastward from California. Andrew J. Russell (1829–1902), working for Frank Leslie's Illustrated News, *photographed the May 1869 ceremonies that marked the joining of the two rail lines at Promontory, Utah. Russell, who served as a military photographer during the Civil War, captures in this photograph the excitement and significance of the occasion. The crowded scene suggests the huge number of workers involved in the project and (in the form of the locomotives) the technological power and innovation required. In neither this photograph nor any of the others Russell produced at Promontory is there the slightest indication that railroads more than any other factor were responsible for the destruction of the Indian nations of the Great Plains and Rocky Mountain regions.*

Figure 7 Andrew J. Russell, Joining of the Rails, Promontory, Utah, 1869
Source: Andrew Russell photograph—Joining of the Rails, Promontory, Utah, May 10, 1869. Library of Congress.

Discussion Questions

1 What do the documents in this chapter indicate concerning the relationship of events in the Trans-Mississippi West during the 1860s to the Civil War?
2 Do the documents in this chapter support the Neo-Confederate contention that the North was by nature economically, culturally, and militarily aggressive?
3 In what ways are all the documents in this chapter interrelated?

Chapter 8   Reconstruction

1. Abraham Lincoln
Presidential Reconstruction, December 8, 1863

*At the start of the Civil War, Abraham Lincoln began planning for
reestablishing (or reconstructing) loyal governments in the Confederate states.
He never officially admitted that those states were out of the Union and
wanted to encourage them to return quickly to their "proper" place in it.
His Reconstruction policies were, like his emancipation policies, war measures
designed to end the "rebellion." In 1861 he recognized a loyal government
in exile for Virginia. In 1862 he attempted to create, without success, loyal
governments in portions of Tennessee, North Carolina, and Texas. Lincoln's
most fully articulated Reconstruction plan appears in his Proclamation of
Amnesty and Reconstruction of December 1863. Relying on his power as
commander-in-chief, he encourages the rapid formation of loyal governments.
He requires that such governments abolish slavery but sets no standards for
action concerning the rights and status of former slaves.*

Whereas in the Constitution of the United States it is provided that the
President "shall have the power to grant reprieve and pardons for offences
against the United States, except in cases of impeachment;" and

Whereas a rebellion now exists whereby the loyal State Governments of
several States have for a long time been subverted, and many persons have
committed and are now guilty of treason against the United States; and

Whereas, with reference to said rebellion and treason, laws have been
enacted by Congress declaring forfeitures and confiscation of property and
liberation of slaves, all upon terms therein stated, and also declaring that the

President was thereby authorized at any time thereafter, by proclamation, to extend to persons who may have participated in the existing rebellion in any State or part thereof pardon and amnesty, with such exceptions and at such times and on such conditions as he may deem expedient for the public welfare; and

Whereas the Congressional declaration for limited and conditional pardon accords with well-established judicial exposition of the pardoning power; and

Whereas, with reference to said rebellion, the President of the United States has issued several proclamations with provisions in regard to the liberation of slaves; and

Whereas it is now desired by some persons heretofore engaged in said rebellion to resume their allegiance to the United States and reinaugurate loyal State governments within and for their respective States:

Therefore: I, Abraham Lincoln, President of the United States, do proclaim, declare, and make known to all persons who have, directly or indirectly, participated in the existing rebellion, except as hereinafter excepted, that a full pardon is hereby granted to them and each of them, with restoration of all rights of property, except as to slaves, and in property cases where the rights of third parties shall have intervened, and upon condition that every person shall take and subscribe to an oath, and thenceforward keep and maintain that said oath inviolate; and which oath shall be registered for permanent preservation, and shall be of the tenor and effect following, to wit:

"I, _____ _____, *do solemnly swear, in the presence of Almighty God, that I will henceforth faithfully support, protect, and defend the Constitution of the United States and the Union of the States thereunder; that I will in like manner, abide by and faithfully support all acts of Congress passed during the existing rebellion with reference to slaves, so long and so far as not repealed, modified, or held void by Congress, or by decision of the Supreme Court; and that I will, in like manner, abide by and faithfully support all proclamations of the President made during the existing rebellion having reference to slaves, so long and so far not modified or declared void by decision of the supreme court. So help me God.*

The persons excepted from the foregoing provisions are all who are or shall have been civil or diplomatic officers or agents of the so-called Confederate Government; all who have left judicial stations under the United States to aid the rebellion; all who are military or naval officers of said so-called Confederate Government above the rank of colonel in the army or lieutenant in the navy; all who left seats in the United States Congress to aid the rebellion; all who resigned commissions in the Army or Navy of the United States and afterwards aided the rebellion; and all who have engaged in any way in treating colored persons, or white persons in charge of such, otherwise than lawfully as prisoners of war, and which persons may have been found in the United States service as soldiers, seamen, or in any capacity.

And I do further proclaim, declare and make known that whenever, in any of the states of Arkansas, Texas, Louisiana, Mississippi, Tennessee, Alabama, Georgia, Florida, South Carolina, and North Carolina, a number of persons, not less than one-tenth in number of the votes cast in such State at the Presidential election of the year AD 1860, each having taken the oath aforesaid, and not having since violated it, and being a qualified voter by the election law of the State existing immediately before the so-called act of secession, and excluding all others, shall reestablish a State government which shall be republican and in no wise contravening said oath, such shall be recognized as the true government of the State, and the State shall receive thereunder the benefits of the constitutional provision which declares that "the United States shall guaranty to every state in this Union a republican form of government and shall protect each of them against invasion, and on application of the legislature, or the executive (when the legislature cannot be convened), against domestic violence."

And I do further proclaim, declare, and make known that any provision which may be adopted by such State government in relation to the freed people of such State, which shall recognize and declare their permanent freedom, provide for their education, and which may yet be consistent as a temporary arrangement with their present condition as a laboring, landless, and homeless class, will not be objected to by the National Executive.

And it is suggested as not improper that, in concentrating a loyal State government in any State, the name of the State, the boundary, the subdivisions, the constitution, and the general code of laws, as before the rebellion, be maintained, subject only to the modifications made necessary by the conditions hereinbefore stated, and such others, if any, not contravening said conditions, and which may be deemed expedient by those framing the new state government.

To avoid misunderstanding, it may be proper to say that this proclamation, so far as it relates to State governments, has no reference to States wherein loyal State governments have all the while been maintained. And for the same reason it may be proper to further say, that whether members sent to Congress from any State shall be admitted to seats constitutionally rests exclusively with the respective Houses, and not to any extent with the Executive. And still further, that this proclamation is intended to present the people of the states wherein the national authority has been suspended and loyal State governments have been subverted, a mode in and by which the national authority and loyal State governments may be reestablished within said states, or in any of them; and while the mode presented is the best the Executive can suggest, with his present impressions, it must not be understood that no other possible mode would he acceptable.

Source: James D. Richardson, ed., *A Compilation of the Messages and Papers of the Presidents*, 10 vols. (Washington, DC: Government Printing Office, 1897), 6: 213–15.

2. Alexander Gardner
African-American Refugees amid Ruins of Richmond, April 1865

Figure 8   Alexander Gardner, African-American Refugees amid Ruins of Richmond, 1865

Source: Library of Congress.

Alexander Gardner (1821–82) migrated from Scotland to the United States in 1856. Shortly thereafter he began working at Mathew Brady's photographic studio in New York City. Within a few years he gained prominence as a portrait photographer in Washington, DC, and in 1861 he joined Brady's project to create a photographic history of the Civil War. In late 1862, Gardner left Brady to establish his own studio. His photograph of black refugees, embarked with their possessions on canal boats passing through the

ruins of Richmond shortly after the Confederate capital surrendered to the
Union Army of the Potomac, captures two major themes of Reconstruction.
The first was to formulate policies in regard to an impoverished and often
dislocated black population, most of which had just emerged from slavery.
The second was to rebuild a southern economy and infrastructure destroyed
by the war. Although the available photographic technology required long
exposures and posing, Gardner achieves an impression of black people in
motion through a shattered urban landscape.

---

3. State Convention of the Colored People of South Carolina
Memorial to the Senate and House of Representatives of the United States,
November 24, 1865

In a Republican attempt to attract Democratic and Border South voters in the
1864 national election, Abraham Lincoln's vice-presidential running mate was
Andrew Johnson, a Democrat and former slaveholder from Tennessee. On
Lincoln's assassination in April 1865, Johnson became president. During that
spring and summer, Johnson adopted (with minor changes) Lincoln's mild
Reconstruction policy, and put it into effect. Like Lincoln, Johnson insisted
that reconstructed southern state governments abolish slavery, while allowing
those governments to determine the social, economic, and political status of
the former slaves. Johnson, however, was far more committed to white
supremacy and far more dismissive of black rights than Lincoln had been.
As new state governments formed in the South during the summer of 1865
amid considerable antiblack violence, they excluded black men from the polls,
passed black codes reestablishing slavery in all but name, and returned
Confederate leaders to power. African Americans across the South responded
by holding conventions to assert their citizenship rights. The meeting of
fifty-two black men at the Zion Presbyterian Church in Charleston, South
Carolina in November 1865 is typical of these conventions. It issued a public
address and sent this petition to Congress.

Gentlemen:

We, the colored people of the State of South Carolina, in Convention assembled, respectfully present for your attention some prominent facts in relation to our present condition, and make a modest yet earnest appeal to your considerate judgment.

We, your memorialists, with profound gratitude to almighty God, recognize the great boon of freedom conferred upon us by the instrumentality of our late President, Abraham Lincoln, and the armies of the United States.

> "The fixed decree, which not all Heaven can move,
> Thou, Fate, fulfill it; and, ye Powers, approve."

We also recognize with liveliest gratitude the vast services of the Freedmen's Bureau together with the efforts of the good and wise throughout the land to raise up an oppressed and deeply injured people in the scale of civilized being, during the throbbings of a mighty revolution which must affect the future destiny of the world.

Conscious of the difficulties that surround our position, we would ask for no rights or privileges but such as rest upon the strong basis of justice and expediency, in view of the best interests of our entire country.

We ask first, that the strong arm of law and order be placed alike over the entire people of this State; that life and property be secured, and the laborer as free to sell his labor as the merchant his goods.

We ask that a fair and impartial instruction be given to the pledges of the government to us concerning the land question.

We ask that the three great agents of civilized society – the school, the pulpit, the press – be as secure in South Carolina as in Massachusetts or Vermont.

We ask that equal suffrage be conferred upon us, in common with the white men of this State.

This we ask, because "all free governments derive their just powers from the consent of the governed"; and we are largely in the majority in this State, bearing for a long period the burden of an odious taxation, without a just representation. We ask for equal suffrage as a protection for the hostility evoked by our known faithfulness to our country and flag under all circumstances.

We ask that colored men shall not in every instance be tried by white men; and that neither by custom or enactment shall we be excluded from the jury box.

We ask that, inasmuch as the Constitution of the United States explicitly declares that the right to keep and bear arms shall not be infringed – and the Constitution is the Supreme law of the land – that the late efforts of the Legislature of this State to pass an act to deprive us of arms be forbidden, as a plain violation of the Constitution, and unjust to many of us in the highest degree, who have been soldiers, and purchased our muskets from the United States Government when mustered out of service.

We protest against any code of black laws the Legislature of this State may enact, and pray to be governed by the same laws that control other men. The right to assemble in peaceful convention, to discuss the political questions of the day; the right to enter upon all the avenues of agriculture, commerce, trade; to amass wealth by thrift and industry; the right to develop our whole being by all the appliances that belong to civilized society, cannot be questioned by any class of intelligent legislators.

We solemnly affirm and desire to live orderly and peacefully with all the people of this State; and commending this memorial to your considerate judgment.

Thus we ever pray.

Charleston, S. C., November 24, 1865.
Zion Presbyterian Church.

Source: *Proceedings of the Colored People's Convention of the State of South Carolina, held in Zion Church, Charleston, November 1865* (Charleston: South Carolina Leader Office, 1865), 30–1.

4. Thaddeus Stevens
Congressional Reconstruction, December 18, 1865

Most Republicans were willing to allow Andrew Johnson time to pursue a mild Reconstruction policy that indulged the interests and prejudices of white southerners. They hoped that it could be modified as time passed. But African-American leaders, white abolitionists, and Radical Republican politicians perceived that Johnson's willingness to allow newly formed governments in the former Confederate states to deny black men the right to vote would lead not only to a practical reestablishment of slavery but to a political debacle for the Republican Party. If black men could not vote, Democrats would dominate southern state governments and very likely regain control of the national government. Thaddeus Stevens (1792–1868) led the Radical Republicans in the House of Representatives. Long associated with the antislavery movement, Stevens represented a district in southeastern Pennsylvania. Both Lincoln and Johnson maintained that the Confederate states had not been out of the Union and therefore could be restored by the president to their proper places in it with a minimum of change. In his December 1865 speech on Reconstruction, Stevens argues that the Confederate states had been out of the Union and reduced by United States armies to "conquered provinces" or "dead states" under the control of Congress. He calls for a long and harsh Reconstruction policy directed by Congress rather than the president; federal protection for black economic, political, and social rights; and protection of the political dominance of the Republican Party.

. . . The President assumes, what no one doubts, that the late rebel States have lost their constitutional relations to the Union, and are incapable of representation in Congress, except by permission of the Government. . . . It is very plain that it requires the action of Congress to enable them to form a state government and send representatives to Congress. Nobody, I believe, pretends that with their old constitutions and frames of government they can be permitted to claim their old rights under the Constitution. They have torn their constitutional States into atoms, and built on their foundations fabrics of a totally different character. Dead men cannot raise themselves. Dead States cannot restore their own existence "as it was." Whose especial duty is it to do it? In whom does the Constitution place the power? Not in the judicial branch of Government, for it only adjudicates and does not prescribe laws. Not in the Executive, for he only executes and cannot make laws. Not in the Commander-in-Chief of the armies, for he can only hold them under military rule until the sovereign legislative power of the conqueror shall give them law.

There is fortunately no difficulty in solving the question. There are only two provisions in the Constitution, under one of which the case must fall. The fourth article says: New States may he admitted by the Congress into this Union.

In my judgment this is the controlling provision in the case. Unless the law of nations is a dead letter, the late war between the two acknowledged belligerents severed their original compacts, and broke all the ties that bound them together. The future condition of the conquered power depends on the will of the conqueror. They must come in as new States or remain as conquered provinces. Congress – the Senate and the House of Representatives, with the concurrence of the President – is the only power that can act in this matter. . . .

To prove that they are and for four years have been out of the Union for all legal purposes, and now being conquered, subject to the absolute disposal of Congress, I will suggest a few ideas and adduce a few authorities. If the so-called "confederate States of America" were an independent belligerent, and were so acknowledged by the United States and by Europe, or had assumed and maintained an attitude which entitled them to be considered and treated as a belligerent, then, during such time, they were precisely in the condition of a foreign nation with whom we were at war; nor need their independence as a nation be acknowledged to produce that effect. . . .

The idea that the States could not and did not make war because the Constitution forbids it, and that this must be treated as a war of individuals, is a very injurious and groundless fallacy. Individuals cannot make war. They may commit murder, but that is no war. . . .

But why appeal to reason to prove that the seceded States made war as States, when the conclusive opinion of the Supreme Court is at hand? In the prize cases . . . the Supreme Court say:

Hence, in organizing this rebellion, they have acted as States claiming to be sovereign over all persons and property within their respective limits, and asserting a right to absolve their citizens from their allegiance to the Federal Government. Several of these States have combined to form a new confederacy, claiming to be acknowledged by the world as a sovereign State. Their right to do so is now being decided by wager of battle. The ports and territory of each of these States is no loose, unorganized insurrection, having no defined boundary or possession. It has a boundary marked by lines of bayonets, and which can be crossed only by force. South of this line is the enemies' territory, because it is claimed and held in possession by an organized hostile and belligerent power.

[...]

The theory that the rebel States, for four years a separate power and without representation in Congress, were all the time here in the union, is a good deal less ingenious and respectable than the metaphysics of Berkeley, which proved that neither the world nor any human being was in existence. If this theory were simply ridiculous, then it could be forgiven; but its effect is deeply injurious to the stability of the nation. I cannot doubt that the late confederate States are out of the Union to all intents and purposes for which the conqueror may choose so to consider them.

[...]

But suppose these powerful but now subdued belligerents, instead of being out of the Union, are merely destroyed, and are now lying about, a dead corpse, or with animation so suspended as to be incapable of action, and wholly unable to heal themselves by any unaided movements of their own. Then they may fall under the provision of the Constitution which says "the United States shall guaranty to every State a republican form of government." Under that power can the judiciary, or the President, or the Commander-in-Chief of the Army, or the Senate or House of Representatives, acting separately, restore them to life and readmit them into the Union? I insist that if each acted separately, though the action of each was identical with all the others, it would amount to nothing. Nothing but the joint action of the two Houses of Congress and the concurrence of the President could do it. If the Senate admitted their Senators, and the House their members, it would have no effect on the future action of Congress....

Congress alone can do it. But Congress does not mean the Senate, or the House of Representatives, and President, all acting severally. Their joint action constitutes Congress. Hence a law of Congress must be passed before any new State can be admitted or any dead ones revived. Until then no member can be lawfully admitted into either House. Hence it appears with how little knowledge of constitutional law each branch is urged to admit members separately from these destroyed States. The provision that "each House shall be the judge of the elections, returns, and qualifications of its own members," has not the most distant bearing on this question. Congress must create States and declare when they are entitled to be represented. Then each House must judge whether the members presenting themselves from a recognized State possess the requisite qualifications of age, residence, and citizenship and whether the election and returns are according to the law. The Houses, separately, can judge of nothing else. It seems amazing that any man of legal education could give it any larger meaning.

It is obvious from all this that the first duty of Congress is to pass a law declaring the condition of these outside the Union or defunct States, and providing proper civil governments for them.... As there are no symptoms that the people of these provinces will he prepared to participate in the constitutional government for some years, I know of no arrangement so proper for them as territorial governments. There they can learn the principles of freedom and eat the fruit of foul rebellion. Under such governments while electing members to the Territorial Legislatures, they will necessarily mingle with those to whom Congress shall extend the right of suffrage. In Territories Congress fixes the qualifications of electors; and I know of no better place nor better occasion for the conquered rebels and the conqueror to practice justice to all men, and accustom themselves to make and obey equal laws.

As these fallen rebels cannot at their option reenter the heaven which they have disturbed, the Garden of Eden which they have deserted, and flaming swords are set at the gates to secure their exclusion, it becomes important to the welfare of the nation to inquire when the doors shall be reopened for their admission.

According to my judgment they ought never to be recognized as capable of acting in the union or of being counted as valid States, until the Constitution shall have been so amended as to make it what its framers intended; and so as to secure perpetual ascendancy to the party of the Union; and so as to render our republican Government firm and stable forever. The first of those amendments is to change the basis of representation among the States from Federal numbers to actual voters. Now all the colored freemen in the slave States, and three fifths of all slaves, are represented, though none of them have votes. The States have nineteen representatives of colored slaves. If the slaves are now free and [the former Slave states] can add, for the other two-fifths, thirteen more, making the representation of non-voting people of color about thirty-seven. The whole number of representatives now from the slave States is seventy. Add the other two-fifths and it will be eighty-three.

If the [14th] amendment prevails, and those States withhold the right of suffrage from persons of color, it will deduct about thirty-seven, leaving them but forty-six. With the basis unchanged, the eighty-three southern members, with the Democrats that will always in the best of times be elected from the North, will always give them a majority in Congress and in the Electoral College. They will at the very first election take possession of the White House and the halls of Congress. I need not depict the ruin that would follow. Assumption of the rebel debt or repudiation of the Federal debt would be sure to follow. The oppression of the freedmen; the re-amendment of their State constitutions, and the reestablishment of slavery would be the inevitable result. . . . If they should grant the right of suffrage to persons of color, I think there would always be Union white men enough in the South, aided by blacks, to divide the representation, and thus continue the Republican ascendancy. If they should refuse to thus alter their election laws it would reduce the representatives of the late slave States to about forty-five and render them powerless for evil.

It is plain that this [14th] amendment must he consummated before the defunct States are admitted to be capable of State action, or it never can be.

[. . .]

But this is not all we ought to do before these inveterate rebels are invited to participate in our legislation. We have turned, or are about to turn, loose four million slaves without a hut to shelter them or a cent in their pockets. The infernal laws of slavery have prevented them from acquiring an educa-tion, understanding the commonest laws of contract, or of managing the ordinary business of life. This Congress is bound to provide for them until they can take care of themselves. If we do not furnish them with home-steads, and hedge them around with protective laws; if we leave them to the legislation of their late masters, we had better have left them in bondage. Their condition would be worse than that of our prisoners at Andersonville. If we fail in this great duty now, when we have the power, we shall deserve and receive the execration of history and of all future ages.

Two things are of vital importance.

1. So to establish a principle that none of the rebel States shall be counted in [ratifying] any of the amendments of the Constitution until they are duly admitted into the family of States by the law-making power of the con-queror. For more than six months the amendment of the Constitution abolishing slavery has been ratified by the Legislatures of three-fourths of the States that acted on its passage by Congress, and which had Legislatures, or which were States capable of acting, or required to act, on the question.

I take no account of the . . . white-washed rebels, who without any legal authority have assembled in the capitals of the late rebel States and simu-lated legislative bodies. . . .

2. It is equally important to the stability of this republic that it should now be solemnly decided that no power [but Congress] can revive, recreate, and reinstate these provinces into the family of States, and invest them with the rights of American citizens. It is time that Congress should assert its sovereignty, and assume something of the dignity of a Roman senate....

This Congress owes it to its own character to set the seal of reprobation upon a doctrine which is becoming too fashionable, and unless rebuked will be the recognized principle of our Government. Governor [Benjamin F.] Perry [of South Carolina] and the other provisional governors and orators proclaim that "this is the white man's Government." The whole copperhead party, pandering to the lowest prejudices of the ignorant, repeat the cuckoo cry, "This is the white man's Government." Demagogues of all parties, even some in high authority gravely shout, "This is the white man's Government." What is implied by this? That one race of men are to have the exclusive right forever to rule this nation, and to exercise all acts of sovereignty, while all other races and nations and colors are to be their subjects, and have no voice in making the laws and choosing the rulers by whom they are to be governed. Wherein does this differ from slavery? Does not all this contradict all the distinctive principles of the Declaration of Independence? When the great and good men promulgated that instrument, and pledged their lives and sacred honors to defend it, it was supposed to form an epoch in civil government. Before that time it was held that the right to rule was vested in families, dynasties or races, not because of superior intelligence or virtue, but because of a divine right to enjoy exclusive privileges.

Our fathers repudiated the whole doctrine of the legal superiority of families or races, and proclaimed the equality of men before the law. Upon that they created a revolution and built up the Republic. They were prevented by slavery from perfecting the superstructure whose foundations they had thus broadly laid. For the sake of the Union they consented to wait, but never relinquished the idea of its final completion. The time to which they looked forward with anxiety has come. It is our duty to complete their work. If this Republic is not now made to stand upon their great principles, it has no honest foundation, and the Father of all men will shake it to its center. If we have not yet been sufficiently scourged for our national sin to teach us to do justice to all God's creatures, without distinction of race or color, we must expect the still more heavy vengeance of an offended Father, still increasing his inflictions as he increased the severity of the plagues of Egypt until the tyrant consented to do justice. And when that tyrant repented of his reluctant consent, and attempted to re-enslave the people, as our southern tyrants are attempting to do now, he filled the Red sea with broken chariots and drowned horses, and strewed the shores with dead carcasses.

Mr. Chairman, I trust the Republican party will not he alarmed at what I am saying. I do not profess to speak for their sentiments, nor must they be held responsible for them. I speak for myself, and take the responsibility, and will settle with my intelligent constituents.

This is not a "white man's Government," in the exclusive sense in which it is used. To say so is political blasphemy, for it violates the fundamental principles of our gospel of liberty. This is a man's Government; the Government of all men alike; not that all men will have equal power and sway within it. Accidental circumstances, natural and acquired endowment and ability, will vary their fortunes. But equal rights to all the privileges of the Government is innate in every immortal being, no matter what shape or color of the tabernacle which it inhabits.

If equal privileges were granted to all, I should not expect any but white men to be elected to office for long ages to come. The prejudice engendered by slavery would not soon permit merit to be preferred to color. But it would still be beneficial to the weaker races. In a country where political divisions will always exist, their power, joined with just white men, would greatly modify, if it did not entirely prevent, the injustice of majorities. Without the right of suffrage in the slave States, (I do not speak of the free States,) I believe the slaves had far better been left in bondage.…

How shameful is it that men of influence should mislead and miseducate the public mind! They proclaim, "This is white man's Government," and the whole coil of copperheads echo the same sentiment, and upstart, jealous Republicans join the cry. Is it any wonder ignorant foreigners and illiterate natives should learn this doctrine, and be led to despise and maltreat a whole race of their fellow-men?…

Source: *Congressional Globe*, 39th Cong., 1st sess. (December 18, 1865), 72–5.

5. United States
Reconstruction Amendments, Ratified December 18, 1865–March 30, 1870

*The Thirteenth, Fourteenth, and Fifteenth Amendments to the US
Constitution embody the development of national Reconstruction policy from
1864 to1870. The Thirteenth Amendment reflects the limited goals of
Presidential Reconstruction, while the Fourteenth and Fifteenth are products
of Congress's increasing concern with protecting black rights. In June 1864 the
Senate Judiciary Committee drafted the Thirteenth Amendment, abolishing
slavery throughout the United States. The amendment's clear language is
borrowed from Congress's 1787 ban on slavery in the Northwest Territory.
The amendment passed Congress in January 1865 and by the following*

December had been ratified by the required three-quarters of the state legislatures. The Fourteenth Amendment, drafted by the Joint Committee on Reconstruction during the spring of 1866, became the core of Congressional Reconstruction. It guarantees federal protection for black equality before the law, encourages states to enfranchise black men, and disfranchises former Confederate leaders. In February 1869, after several southern states had either refused to enact black suffrage or to ratify the Fourteenth Amendment, Congress passed the Fifteenth Amendment, designed to protect the voting rights of black men. During the 1870s the US Supreme Court accepted interpretations of the Fourteenth and Fifteenth Amendments that gravely diminished the protections they provided to African Americans. Not until the 1930s did civil rights lawyers begin a long but largely successful effort to restore them.

Amendment XIII.

Section 1. Neither slavery nor involuntary servitude, except as a punishment for crime whereof the party shall have been duly convicted, shall exist within the United States, or any place subject to their jurisdiction.

Section 2. Congress shall have power to enforce this article by appropriate legislation. [Ratified Dec. 18, 1865]

Amendment XIV.

Section 1. All persons born or naturalized in the United States and subject to the jurisdiction thereof, are citizens of the United States and of the State wherein they reside. No State shall make or enforce any law which shall abridge the privileges or immunities of citizens of the United States; nor shall any State deprive any person of life, liberty, or property, without due process of law; nor deny any person within its jurisdiction the equal protection of the laws.

Section 2. Representatives shall be apportioned among the several States according to their respective numbers, counting the whole number of persons in each State, excluding Indians not taxed. But when the right to vote at any election for the choice of electors for President and Vice President of the United States, Representatives in Congress, the Executive and Judicial officers of a State, or the members of the Legislature thereof, is denied to any of the male inhabitants of such State, being twenty-one years of age, and citizens of the United States, or in any way abridged, except for participation in rebellion, or other crime, the basis of representation therein shall be reduced in the proportion which the number of such male citizens shall bear to the whole number of male citizens twenty-one years of age in such State.

Section 3. No person shall be a Senator or Representative in Congress, or elector of President and Vice President, or hold any office, civil or military, under the United States, or under any State, who, having previously taken an oath, as a member of Congress, or as an officer of the United States, or as a member of any State legislature, or as an executive or judicial officer of any State, to support the Constitution of the United States, shall have engaged in insurrection or rebellion against the same, or given aid or comfort to the enemies thereof. But Congress may by a vote of two-thirds of each House, remove such disability.

Section 4. The validity of the public debt of the United States, authorized by law, including debts incurred for payment of pensions and bounties for services in suppressing insurrection or rebellion, shall not be questioned. But neither the United States nor any State shall assume or pay any debt or obligation incurred in aid of insurrection or rebellion against the United States, or any claim for the loss or emancipation of any slave; but all such debts, obligations and claims shall be held illegal and void.

Section 5. The Congress shall have power to enforce by appropriate legislation, the provisions of this article. [Ratified July 28, 1868]

Amendment XV.
Section 1. The right of citizens of the United States to vote shall not be denied or abridged by the United States or by any State on account of race, color, or previous condition of servitude.

Section 2. The Congress shall have power to enforce this article by appropriate legislation. [Ratified March 30, 1870]

Source: US Statutes at Large 13 (1865): Appendix 774–5; 15 (1868): Appendix 708–9; 16 (1870): Appendix 1131.

6. National Woman Suffrage and Educational Committee, Washington, DC
An Appeal to the Women of the United States, April 19, 1871

Black rights and women's rights had been linked since the 1830s, when women gained prominence in the antislavery movement. Male abolitionists, such as William Lloyd Garrison and Frederick Douglass, became strong advocates of equal rights for women. But debates over the Fourteenth and Fifteenth Amendments divided leading white feminists and advocates of voting rights for black men. The Fourteenth Amendment proposed only to protect the voting rights of "male inhabitants." When the Fifteenth Amendment stated that states could not deny the right to vote on the basis of "race, color, or previous condition of servitude," it did not mention sex. These omissions led to antagonism between the more militant advocates of woman suffrage, such as Elizabeth Cady Stanton and Susan B. Anthony, on one side, and such advocates of black suffrage as Douglass, on the other. The issue also split the woman's movement. Stanton and Anthony formed the National Woman Suffrage Association, dedicated to immediate voting rights for women. Another group, led by Lucy Stone and Julia Ward Howe, formed the American Woman Suffrage Association, which was willing to defer woman suffrage until after voting rights for black men had been fully guaranteed. This appeal, circulated by the National Woman Suffrage and Educational Committee in 1871, represents the views of the former organization.

DEAR FRIENDS: – The question of your rights as citizens of the United States, and of the grave responsibilities which a recognition of those rights will involve, is becoming the great question of the day in this country, and the culmination of the great question which has been struggling through the ages for solution, that of the highest freedom and of the largest personal responsibility of the individual under such necessary and wholesome restraints as are required by the welfare of society. As you shall meet and act upon this question, so shall these great questions of freedom and responsibility sweep on, or be retarded, in their course.

This is pre-eminently the birthday of womanhood. The material has long held in bondage the spiritual; henceforth the two, the material refined by the spiritual, the spiritual energized by the material are to walk hand in hand for the moral regeneration of mankind. Mothers, for the first time in history, are able to assert, not only their inherent first right to the children they have borne, but their right to have a protective and purifying power in the political society into which those children are to enter. To fulfil [sic] therefore, their whole duty of motherhood, to satisfy their whole capacity in that divine relation, they are called of God to participate, with man, in all the responsibilities of human life, and to share with him every work of brain and of heart, refusing only those physical labors that are inconsistent with the exalted duties and privileges of maternity, and requiring these of men as the equivalent of those heavy yet necessary burdens which women alone can bear.

Under the constitution of the United States justly interpreted, you were entitled to participate in the government of the country, in the same manner as you were held to allegiance and subject to penalty. But in the slow development of the great principles of freedom, you. and all, have failed both to recognize and appreciate this right but; to-day, when the rights and responsibilities of women are attracting the attention of thoughtful minds throughout the whole civilized world, this constitutional right, so long unobserved and unvalued, is becoming one of prime importance, and calls upon all women who love their children and their country to accept and rejoice in it. Thousands of years ago God uttered this mingled command and promise, "Honor thy father AND THY MOTHER, that thy days may be long upon the land which the Lord thy God giveth thee." May we not hope that in the general recognition of this right and this duty of woman to participate in government, our beloved country may find her days long and prosperous in this beautiful land which the Lord hath given her.

To the women of this country who are willing to unite with us in securing the full recognition of our rights, and to accept the duties and responsibilities of a full citizenship, we offer for signature the following Declaration and Pledge, in the firm belief that our children's children will with fond veneration recognize in this act our devotion to the great doctrines of liberty in their new and wider and more spiritual application, even as we regard with reverence the prophetic utterances of the Fathers of the Republic in their Declaration of Independence:

Declaration and Pledge of the Women of the United States
concerning their Right to and their Use of the Elective Franchise.

"We, the undersigned, believing that the sacred rights and privileges of citizenship in this Republic were guaranteed to us by the original Constitution, and that these rights are confirmed and more clearly established by the Fourteenth and Fifteenth Amendments, so that we can no longer refuse the solemn responsibilities thereof, do hereby pledge ourselves to accept the duties of the franchise in our several States, so soon as all legal restrictions are removed.

"And believing that character is the best safe-guard of national liberty, we pledge ourselves to make the personal purity and integrity of candidates for public office the *first* test of fitness.

"And lastly, believing in God as the Supreme Author of the American Declaration of Independence, we pledge ourselves in the spirit of that memorable Act, to work hand in hand with our fathers, husbands, and sons, for the maintenance of those equal rights on which our Republic was originally founded, to the end that it may have, what is declared to be the first condition of just government, *the consent of the governed.*"

You have no new issue to make, no new grievances to set forth. You are taxed without representation, tried by a jury *not* of your peers, condemned and punished by judges and officers not of your choice, bound by laws you have had no voice in making, many of which are specially burdensome upon you as women; in short, your rights to life, liberty and the pursuit of happiness are daily infringed simply because you have heretofore been denied the use of the ballot, the one weapon of protection and defence under a republican form of government. Fortunately, however, you are not compelled to resort to force in order to secure the rights of a complete citizenship. These are provided for by the original Constitution, and by the recent amendments you are recognized as citizens of the United States, whose rights, including the fundamental right to vote, may not be denied or abridged by the United States, nor by any State. The obligation is thus laid upon you to accept or reject the duties of citizenship, and to your own consciences and your God you must answer if the future legislation of this country shall fall short of the demands of justice and equality.

The participation of woman in political affairs is not an untried experiment. Woman suffrage has within a few years been fully established in Sweden and Austria, and to a certain extent in Russia. In Great Britain women are now voting equally with men far all public officers except members of Parliament....

In this country, which stands so specially on equal representation, it is hardly possible that the same equal suffrage would not be established by law if the matter were to be left merely to the progress of public sentiment and the ordinary course of legislation. But as we confidently believe, and as we have before stated, the right already exists in our national constitution, and especially under the recent amendments.... The original Constitution provides in express terms that the representatives in Congress shall be elected "by the PEOPLE of the several States" – with no restriction whatever as to the application of that term. This right, thus dearly granted to all the people, is confirmed and placed beyond reasonable question by the fourteenth and fifteenth amendments. The act of May, 1870, the very title of which, *"An Act to enforce the rights of citizens of the United States to vote,"* is a concession of all that we claim, provides that the officers of elections throughout the United States shall give an equal opportunity to all citizens of the United States to become qualified to vote by the registry of their names or other pre-requisite; and that, where upon the application of any citizen, such pre-requisite is refused, such citizen may vote without performing such pre-requisite; and imposes a penalty upon the officers refusing either the application of the citizen to be qualified or his subsequent application to vote.... All this may be accomplished without the necessity of bringing suits for the penalty imposed upon public officers by the act referred to: but should it be thought best to institute prosecutions where the application of women to register to vote is refused, the question would thereby at once be brought into the Courts.... Whatever mode of testing the question shall be adopted, we must not be in the slightest degree discouraged by adverse decisions, for the final result in our favor is certain, and we have besides great reason to hope that Congress at an early day will pass a Declaratory Act affirming the interpretation of the Constitution which we claim.

…As soon as the conviction possesses the public mind that women are to be voters at an early day, as they certainly are to be, the principles and the action of public parties will be shaping themselves with reference to the demands of this new constituency. Particularly in nominations for office will the moral character of candidates become a matter of greater importance.

To carry on this great work a Board of six women has been established, called "The National Woman Suffrage and Educational Committee," whose office at Washington it is proposed to make the centre of all action upon Congress and the country, and with whom through their Secretary, resident there, it is desired that all associations and individuals interested in the cause of woman suffrage should place themselves in communication. The committee propose to circulate the very able and exhaustive Minority Report of the House Judiciary Committee on the constitutional right of woman to the suffrage and other tracts on the general subject of woman suffrage. They also propose ultimately, and as part of their educational work, to issue a series of tracts on subjects vitally affecting the welfare of the country, that women may become intelligent and thoughtful on such subjects, and the intelligent educators of the next generation of citizens....

A large printing fund will therefore be needed by the Committee, and we appeal first to the men of this country, who control so large a part of its wealth, to make liberal donations toward this great educational work. We also ask every thoughtful woman to send her name to the Secretary to be inserted in the Pledge Book, and if she is able, one dollar. But as many working women will have nothing to send but their names, we welcome these as a precious gift, and urge those who are able, to send us their fifties and hundreds, which we promise faithfully to use and account for....

Source: National Woman Suffrage and Educational Committee, *An Appeal to the Women of the United States* (Washington, DC: [NWSEC], 1871).

7. Elias Hill
Ku Klux Klan Terrorism, May 5, 1871

During the election campaign of 1868, the Democratic Party, in the southern states and at the national level, stood for white supremacy, "the white man's government," and black subservience. In the South that year the terrorist Ku Klux Klan emerged as the Democrats' military wing. Mounted and hooded Klansmen, many of whom were Confederate veterans, used murder, arson, and intimidation to keep black and white Republicans from voting. Although Klan tactics hurt the Democrats in the North, they produced Democratic election victories in Louisiana and Georgia, and reduced Republican victory margins in other southern states. After 1868 the Klan continued to attack African Americans and their white allies. Klansmen often singled out black school teachers and political leaders. When Reconstruction governments in the southern states were unable to destroy the Klan, Congress in 1870 and 1871 authorized President Ulysses S. Grant to suspend the writ of habeas corpus and employ federal marshals and troops to arrest thousands of Klansmen. Congress also conducted hearings in regard to Klan activities. Among those who testified was Elias Hill (b. 1819), a self-educated and crippled black minister and school teacher who engaged in Republican politics in York County, South Carolina. Hill describes common Klan tactics and attitudes.

YORKVILLE, SOUTH CAROLINA, July 25, 1871.

Question. State whether at any time men in disguise have come to the place where you live, and, if so, what they did and said. First, state when it was.

Answer. On the night of the 5th of last May, after I had heard a great deal of what they had done in that neighborhood, they came. It was between 12 and 1 o'clock at night, when I was awakened and heard the dogs barking, and something walking very much like horses. As I had often laid awake listening for such persons . . . I supposed that it was them. They came in a very rapid manner, and I could hardly tell whether it was the sound of horses or men. At last they came to my brothers [sic] door, which is in the same yard, and broke open the door and attacked his wife, and I heard her screaming and mourning. I could not understand what they said, for they were talking in an outlandish and unnatural tone, which I had heard they generally used at a negro's house. I heard them knocking around in her house. I was lying in my little cabin in the yard. At last I heard them have her in the yard. She was crying, and the Ku-Klux were whipping her to make her tell where I lived. I heard her say, "Yon is his house." . . . They were then in the yard, and I had heard them strike her five or six licks when I heard her say this. Some one then hit my door. It flew open. One ran in the house, and stopping about the middle of the house, which is a small cabin, he turned around as it seemed to me as I lay there, awake, and said "Who's here?" Then I knew they would take me, and I answered, "I am here." He shouted for joy as it seemed, "Here he is! Here he is! We have found him!" and he threw the bed-clothes off of me and caught me by one arm, while another man took me by the other and they carried me into the yard between the houses, my brother's and mine, and put me on the ground beside a boy. The first thing they asked me was, "Who did that burning? Who burned our houses?"

gin-houses, dwelling-houses and such. Some had been burned in the neighborhood. I told them it was not me; I could not burn houses; it was unrea-
sonable to ask me. Then they hit me with their fists, and said I did it, I ordered
it. They went on asking me didn't I tell the black men to ravish all the white
women. No, I answered them. They struck me again with their fists on my
breast and then they went on, "When did you hold a night-meeting of the
Union League, and who were the officers? Who was the president?" I told
them I had been the president, but that there had been no Union League
meeting held at that place where they were formerly held since away in the
fall. This was the 5th of May. They said that Jim Raney, that was hung, had
been at my house since the time I had said the League was last held, and that
he had made a speech. I told them he had not, because I did not know the
man. I said, "Upon honor." They said I had no honor and hit me again. They
went on asking me hadn't I been writing to Mr. A. S. Wallace, in Congress, to
get letters from him. I told them I had. They asked what I had been writing
about? I told them "Only tidings." They said, with an oath, "I know the
tidings were d – d good, and you were writing something about the Ku-Klux,
and haven't you been preaching about the Ku-Klux?" One asked, "Haven't
you been preaching political sermons?" Generally, one asked me all the
questions, but the rest were squatting over me – some six men I counted as
I lay there. Said one, "Didn't you preach against the Ku-Klux," and wasn't
that what Mr. Wallace was writing to me about. "Not at all," I said. "Let me
see the letter," said he; "What was it about?" I said it was on the times. They
wanted the letter. I told them if they would take me back into the house, and
lay me in the bed, which was close adjoining my books and papers, I would
try and get it. They said I would never go back to that bed, for they were going
to kill me – "Never expect to go back; tell us where the letters are." I told them
they were on the shelf somewhere, and I hoped they would not kill me. Two of
them went into the house. My sister says that as quick as they went into the
house they struck the clock at the foot of the bed. I heard it shatter. One of the
four around me called out, "Don't break any private property, gentlemen, if
you please; we have got him we came for, and that's all we want." I did not
hear them break anything else. They staid in there a good while hunting
about and then came out and asked me for a lamp. I told them there was a
lamp somewhere. They said" Where?" I was so confused I said I could not tell
exactly. They caught my leg – you see what it is – and pulled me over the yard
and then left me there, knowing I could not walk nor crawl, and all six went
into the house. . . . After they had staid in house for a considerable time, they
came back to where I lay and asked if I wasn't afraid at all. They pointed
pistols at me all around my head once or twice, as if they were going to shoot
me, telling me they were going to kill me, wasn't I ready to die? and willing to

die? didn't I preach? that they came to kill me – all the time pointing pistols at me. . . . I told them that I was not exactly ready; that I would rather live; that I hoped they would not kill me that time. They said they would; I had better prepare. One caught me by the leg and hurt me, for my leg for forty years has been drawn each year, more and more year by year, and I made moan when it hurt so. One said G-d d – n it, hush!" He had a horsewhip, and he told me to pull up my shirt and he hit me. He told me at every lick "Hold up your shirt." I made a moan every time he cut with the horsewhip. I reckon he struck me eight cuts right on the hip bone; it was almost the only place he could hit my body, my legs are so short – all my limbs drawn up and withered away with pain. I saw one of them standing over me or by me motion to them to quit. They all had disguises on. I then thought they would not kill me. . . . One of them said, "Now you see I've burned up the d – d letter of Wallace's and all," and he brought out a little book and says, "What's this for?" I told I did not know; to let me see with a light and I could read it. They brought a lamp and I read it. It was a book in which I had kept an account of the school. I had been licensed to keep a school. I read them some of the names. He said that would do, and asked if I had been paid for those scholars I had put down? I said no. He said I would now have to die. I was somewhat afraid, but one said not to kill me. They said "Look here! Will you put a card in the paper next week like June Moore and Sol Hill?" They had been prevailed on to put a card in the paper to renounce all republicanism and never vote. I said, "If I had the money to pay the expense I could." They said I could borrow, and gave me another lick. They asked me, "Will you quit preaching?" I told them I did not know. I said that to save my life. They said I must stop that republican paper that was coming to Clay Hill. It has only a few weeks since it stopped. The republican weekly paper was then coming to me from Charleston. It came to my name. They said I must stop it, quit preaching, and put a card in the newspaper renouncing republicanism, and they would not kill me; but if I did not they would come back the next week and kill me. With that one of them went into the house where my brother and my sister-in-law lived, and, brought her to pick me up. As she stooped down to pick me up one of them struck her, and as she was carrying me into the house another struck her with a strap. She carried me into the house and laid me on the bed. Then they gathered around and told me to pray for them. I tried to pray. They said "Don't you pray against Ku-Klux, but pray that God may forgive Ku-Klux. Don't pray against us. Pray that God may bless and save us." I was so chilled with cold lying out of doors so long and in such pain I could not speak to pray, but I tried to, and they said that would do very well, and all went out of the house except one. He handed me back a little book, that schoolbook, saying, "Here's that little book;" but it seemed that he forgot to speak in that outlandish tone that they use to disguise their voices. He spoke in his common, plain voice, and then he went out.

Question. Was that the end of it with you?

Answer. Yes, sir. . . .

Question. How were they disguised?

Answer. With coverings over their faces. Some had a kind of check disguise on their heads. One had black oil-cloth over his head, and something like gloves covering his hands and wrists. When they brought the lamp to read that little book I could see his face all around his eyes, and he seemed a red-whiskered man.

Question. Did you know any of them?

Answer. No, sir, I cannot say I know any one of them.

Source: US Congress, *Testimony Taken by the Joint Select Committee to Inquire into the Condition of Affairs in the Late Insurrectionary States*, 5 vols. (Washington: Government Printing Office, 1872), 3:1406–8.

8. Albion W. Tourgee
Failure of Reconstruction, 1879

Historians traditionally recognize 1877 as the year in which Reconstruction ended in failure. Early that year Democratic congressmen agreed to accept Republican candidate Rutherford B. Hayes as the victor in the disputed presidential election of 1876. In return Republicans pledged to withdraw the last US troops from the South. By then Republican governments, on which African Americans depended for protection, remained in power only in South Carolina, Florida, and Louisiana. With the withdrawal of the troops these governments fell, and with them went the last hope for meaningful black suffrage and progress. For a nearly a century thereafter white supremacy prevailed in a South characterized by widespread poverty and racial segregation. Albion W. Tourgee (1838–1905) uses his semi-autobiographical novel, A Fool's Errand (1879), to analyze why Reconstruction failed to secure its goals. The protagonist in the novel is Comfort Servosse (the Fool), an initially idealistic Union veteran who moves south after the war to help create a racially just society. In this passage, Servosse has just left the South and is discussing with an old friend what he has learned.

It was shortly after the rupture of his home-life and his departure from Warrington, that Servosse visited, by special invitation, Doctor Enos Martin, the ancient friend who had been at first his instructor, and afterward his revered and trusted counselor. . . . A score of years had passed since they had met. To the one, these years had been full of action. He had been in the current, had breasted its buffetings, and been carried away out of the course which he had marked out for himself on life's great chart, by its cross-currents and counter-eddies. He had a scar to show for every struggle.... The other had watched with keenest apprehension those movements which had veered and whirled about in their turbid currents the life of the other, himself but little moved, but ever seeking to draw what lessons of value he might from such observation....

This constant and observant interest in the great social movements of the world which he overlooked from so serene a height had led him to note with peculiar care the relations of the nation to the recently subjugated portion of the South, and more especially the conditions of the blacks. In so doing, he had been led to consider especially that transition period which comes between Chattelism, or some form of individual subordination and dependence, and absolute individual autonomy. This is known by different names in different lands and ages, – villenage [sic] in England, serfdom in Russia. In regard to this, his inquiries had been most profound, and his interest in all those national questions had accordingly been of the liveliest character: hence his keen desire to see his old pupil, and to talk with one in whom he had confidence as an observer, in regard to the phenomena he had witnessed and the conclusions at which he had arrived, and to compare the same, not only with his own more remote observations, but also with the facts of history. They sat together for a long time in the library where the elder had gathered the intellectual wealth of the world and the ages, and renewed the personal knowledge of each other which a score of years had interrupted....

"And so," said the elder gravely, "you think, Colonel Servosse, that what has been termed Reconstruction is a magnificent failure?"

"Undoubtedly," was the reply, "so far as concerns the attainment of the result intended by its projectors, expected by the world, and to be looked for as a logical sequence of the war."

"I do not know that I fully understand your limitation," said Martin doubtfully.

"I mean," said the younger man, "that Reconstruction was a failure so far as it attempted to unify the nation, to make one people in fact of what had been one only in name before the convulsion of civil war. It was a failure, too, so far as it attempted to fix and secure the position and rights of the colored race. They were fixed, it is true, on paper, and security of a certain sort taken to prevent the abrogation of that formal declaration. No guaranty whatever was provided against their practical subversion, which was accomplished with an ease and impunity that amazed those who instituted the movement."

"You must at least admit that the dogma of 'State Rights' was settled by the war and by that system of summary and complete national control over the erring commonwealths which we call Reconstruction," said Martin.

"On the contrary," answered Servosse, "the doctrine of 'State Rights' is altogether unimpaired and untouched by what has occurred, except in one particular; to wit, *the right of peaceable secession.* The war settled that. The Nation asserted its right to defend itself against disruption."

"Did it not also assert its right to re-create, to make over, to reconstruct?" asked the elder man.

"Not at all," was the reply. "Reconstruction was never asserted *as a right*, at least not formally and authoritatively. Some did so affirm; but they were accounted visionaries. The act of reconstruction was *excused* as a necessary sequence of the failure of attempted secession: it was never defended or promulgated as a *right of the nation*, even to *secure its own safety.*"

[. . .]

"You do not regard the struggle between the North and the South as ended, then," said Martin.

"Ended?" ejaculated the Fool sharply. "It is just begun! I do not mean the physical tug of war between definitely defined sections. That is a mere incident of a great underlying struggle, – a conflict which is ever going on between two antagonistic ideas. It was like a stream with here and there an angry rapid, before the war; then, for a time, it was like a foaming cascade; and since then it has been the sullen, dark, but deep and quiet whirlpool, which lies below the fall, full of driftwood and shadows, and angry mutterings, and unseen currents, and hidden forces, whose farther course no one can foretell, only that it must go on. . . . "

"Do you mean to say that the old battle between freedom and slavery was not ended by the extinction of slavery?" asked the doctor in surprise.

"I suppose it would be," answered the Fool, with a hint of laughter in his tones, "if slavery were extinct. I do not mean to combat the old adage that 'it takes two to make a quarrel'; but that is just where our mistake – the mistake of the North, for the South has not made one in this matter – has been. We have *assumed* that slavery was dead, because we had a Proclamation of Emancipation, a Constitutional Amendment, and 'laws passed in pursuance thereof,' all reciting the fact that involuntary servitude, except for crime, should no more exist. Thereupon, we have thrown up our hats, and crowed lustily for what we had achieved, as we had a good right to do. The [American] Antislavery Society met, and congratulated itself on the accomplishment of its mission, on having no more worlds to conquer, no more oppression to resist, and no more victims to succor. And thereupon, in the odor of its self-laudation, it dissolved its own existence, dying full of good works, and simply for the want of more good works to be done. It was an end that smacks of the millennium; but, unfortunately, it was farcical in the extreme. I don't blame [William Lloyd] Garrison and [Wendell] Phillips and yourself, and all the others of the old guard of abolitionists. It was natural that you should at least wish to try on your laurels while alive."

[. . .]

"It was our fault, – the then youngsters who had just come out of the furnace-fire in which the shackles were fused and melted away from the cramped and shriveled limbs. We ought to have seen and known that only the shell was gone. Slavery as a formal state of society was at an end: as a force, a power, a moral element, it was just as active as before. Its conscious evils were obliterated: its unconscious ones existed in the dwarfed and twisted natures which had been subjected for generations to its influences, – master and slave alike. As a form of society, it could be abolished by proclamation and enactment: as a moral entity, it is as indestructible as the souls on which it has left its mark."

"You think the 'irrepressible conflict' is yet confronting us, then?" said Martin.

"Undoubtedly. The North and the South are simply convenient names for two distinct, hostile, and irreconcilable ideas, – two civilizations they are sometimes called, especially at the South. At the North there is somewhat more of intellectual arrogance; and we are apt to speak of the one as civilization, and of the other as a species of barbarism. These two must always be in conflict until the one prevails, and the other falls. To uproot the one, and plant the other in its stead, is not the work of a moment or a day. That was our mistake. We tried to superimpose the civilization, the idea of the North, upon the South at a moment's warning. We presumed, that, by the suppression of rebellion, the Southern white man had become identical with the Caucasian of the North in thought and sentiment; and that the slave, by emancipation, had become a saint and a Solomon at once. So we tried to build up communities there which should be identical in thought, sentiment, growth, and development, with those of the North. It was A FOOL'S ERRAND." . . .

"I am not sure but you are right," said the elder. "It looks like it now, and every thing which has happened is certainly consistent with your view. But, leaving the past, what have you to say of the future?"

"Well," answered Servosse thoughtfully, "the battle must be fought out. If there is to remain one nation on the territory we now occupy, it must be either a nation unified in sentiment and civilization, or the one civilization must dominate and control the other. As it stands now, that of the South is the most intense, vigorous, and aggressive. The power of the recent slave has been absolutely neutralized. The power of the Southern whites has been increased by exactly two-fifths of the colored adults, who were not counted in representation before the war. Upon all questions touching the nation and its future they are practically a unit, and are daily growing more and more united as those who once stood with us succumb to age or the force of their surroundings."

[...]

"But why do you think the South more likely to rule than the more populous and more enterprising North?"

"Because they are thoroughly united, and are instinctive, natural rulers. They are not troubled with scruples, nor do they waste their energies upon frivolous and immaterial issues. They are monarchical and kinglike in their characteristics. Each one thinks more of the South than of himself, and any thing which adds to her prestige or glory is dearer to him than any personal advantage. The North thinks the Southern people are especially angry because of the loss of slave-property: in truth, they are a thousand times more exasperated by the elevation of the freed negro to equal political power. The North is disunited: a part will adhere to the South for the sake of power; and, just as before the civil war, the South will again dominate and control the nation."

"And when will this end?" asked the elder man, with a sigh of weariness.

"When the North learns to consider facts, and not to sentimentalize; or when the South shall have worked out the problem of race-conflict in her own borders, by the expiration or explosion of a system of unauthorized and illegal serfdom. The lords of the soil are the lords of the labor still, and will so remain until the laborers have grown, through the lapse of generations, either intelligent or desperate."

"Ah! my young friend," said the old man, with a glow of pride in his countenance, "there you are coming upon my ground, and, I must say, striking at my fears for the future too. The state of the newly-enfranchised freedmen at the South is most anomalous and remarkable. I can not help regarding it with apprehension. There are but few cases in history of an enslaved race leaping at once from absolute chattelism to complete self-rule. Perhaps the case of the ancient Israelites affords the closest analogy. Yet in their case, under divine guidance, two things were found necessary: First, an exodus which took them out from among the race which had been their masters, away from the scenes and surroundings of slavery; and, second, the growth of a new generation who had never known the lash of the task-master, nor felt in their own persons the degradation of servitude. The flight from Egypt, the hardships of the wilderness, the forty years of death and growth away from and beyond the ken of the Egyptian, all were necessary to fit the children of Israel for self-government and the exercise of national power, even without the direct and immediate interposition of divine aid and the daily recurrence of miraculous signs and wonders. Can the African slave of America develop into the self-governing citizen, the co-ordinate of his white brother in power, with less of preparation?"

"The analogy of the Israelitish people is so striking, that it seems to recur to almost every mind," said Servosse. "It is a favorite one with the colored people themselves. The only important difference which I can see is the lack of a religious element, – the want of a prophet."

"That is the very thing!" said the old Doctor, with animation.... The instinct of the slave is to flee from the scene of servitude when his soul begins to expand with the aspirations of independent manhood. That this spirit has not manifested itself before, in our case, I think a matter of surprise: that it will come hereafter, I fear is a certainty. I can not see how a race can become prepared for absolute autonomy, real freedom, except by the gradual process of serfdom or villenage [sic], or by the scath [harshness] and tribulation of the sojourn in the wilderness, or its equivalent of isolated self-support, by which individual self-reliance, and collective hardihood and daring, may be nourished and confirmed."

"They are likely to have their forty years," said Servosse, "and to leave more than one generation in the wilderness, before they regain the rights which were promised them, and which they for a little time enjoyed."

[. . .]

"If they were of the same stock as the dominant race [Servosse continued], there might be a chance for the line of separation to disappear with the lapse of time. Marked as they are by a different complexion, and one which has long been accounted menial and debased, there is no little of truth in the sad refrain of their universal story, 'Niggers never can have a white man's chance here.'"

"But what can be done for their elevation and relief, or to prevent the establishment of a medieval barbarism in our midst?" asked the doctor anxiously.

"Well, Doctor," said the Fool jocosely, "that question is for some one else to answer, and it must be answered in deeds, too, and not in words.... The remedy...is one that must be applied from the outside. The sick man can not cure himself. The South will never purge itself of the evils which affect it. Its intellect, its pride, its wealth, in short, its power, is all arrayed against even the slow and tedious development which time and semi-barbarism would bring. Hour by hour, the chains will be riveted closer. Look at the history of slavery in our land! See how the law-makers, the courts, public sentiment, and all the power of the land, grew year by year more harsh and oppressive on the slave and his congener, the 'free person of color,' in all the slave States!... In direct conflict with all the predictions of statesmen, the thumb-screws of oppression were given a new and sharper turn with every passing year. . . . "

"I see the prospect, and admit the truth of your prevision; but I do not get your idea of a remedy," said the elder man doubtfully.

[. . .]

[The Fool replied,] "The Nation nourished and protected slavery. The fruit-age of slavery has been the ignorant freedman, the ignorant poor-white man, and the arrogant master. The impotence of the freedman, the ignorance of the poor-white, the arrogance of the late master, are all the result of national power exercised in restraint of free thought, free labor, and free speech. Now, let the Nation undo the evil it has permitted and encouraged. Let it educate those whom it made ignorant, and protect those whom it made weak. It is not a matter of favor to the black, but of safety to the Nation. Make the spelling-book the scepter of national power. Let the Nation educate the colored man and the poor-white man *because* the Nation held them in bondage, and is responsible for their education; educate the voter *because* the Nation can not afford that he should be ignorant. Do not try to shuffle off the responsibility, nor cloak the danger. Honest ignorance in the masses is more to be dreaded than malevolent intelligence in the few. It furnished the rank and file of rebellion and the prejudice-blinded multitudes who made the Policy of Repression effectual. Poor-Whites, Freedmen, Ku-Klux, and Bulldozers are all alike the harvest of ignorance. The Nation can not afford to grow such a crop."

"But how," asked the doctor, "shall these citizens of the States be edu-cated by the Government without infringement of the rights of the States?"

[. . .]

"Perhaps you are right, Doctor," said the Fool. " . . . At any rate, I leave your question for the Wise Men to answer. I will only say two words about it. The South – that *pseudo* South which has the power – does not wish this thing to be done to her people, and will oppose it with might and main. If done at all, it must be done by the North – by the Nation moved, instigated, and controlled by the North, I mean – in its own self-defense. It must be an act of sovereignty, an exercise of power. That Nation expected the liberated slave to be an ally of freedom. It was altogether right and proper that it should desire and expect this. But it made the fatal mistake of expecting the freedman to do successful battle on his part of the line, without training or knowledge. This mistake must be remedied. As to the means, I feel sure that when the Nation has smarted enough for its folly, it will find a way to undo the evil, whether the States-Rights Moloch stand in the way, or not."

Source: Albion W. Tourgee, *A Fool's Errand: By One of the Fools* (New York: Howard and Hubert Ford, 1879), 335–48.

Discussion Questions

1   What do the documents in this chapter suggest about the realities and theories of Reconstruction?
2   In what ways are the goals for Reconstruction set by Lincoln, the State Convention of Colored People of South Carolina, and Thaddeus Stevens similar? In what ways are they different?
3   What does the Appeal to the Women of the United States indicate about the relationship between the Civil War and Reconstruction on the one hand and the women's rights movement on the other?
4   Based on the other documents in this chapter, how accurate is Albion W. Tourgee's analysis of what went wrong during Reconstruction?

Suggested Reading

Attie, Jeanie. *Patriotic Toil: Northern Women and the American Civil War*. Ithaca, NY: Cornell University Press, 1998.

Blight, David W. *Frederick Douglass' Civil War: Keeping Faith in Jubilee*. Baton Rouge: Louisiana State University Press, 1989.

Campbell, Jacqueline. *When Sherman Marched North from the Sea: Resistance on the Confederate Home Front*. Chapel Hill: University of North Carolina Press, 2003.

Fahs, Alice. *The Imagined Civil War: Popular Literature of the North and South 1861–1865*. Chapel Hill: University of North Carolina Press, 2001.

Faust, Drew Gilpin. *Mothers of Invention: Women of the Slaveholding South in the Civil War Era*. Chapel Hill: University of North Carolina Press, 1998.

Foner, Eric. *Reconstruction: America's Unfinished Revolution 1863–1877*. New York: Oxford University Press, 1988.

Glatthaar, Joseph T. *Forged in Battle: The Civil War Alliance of Black Soldiers and White Officers*. New York: Free Press, 1990.

Guelzo, Allen C. *The Crisis of the American Republic: A History of the Civil War and Reconstruction Era*. New York: St. Martin's, 1995.

Harrold, Stanley. *American Abolitionists*. Harlow, UK: Longman, 2001.

Leonard, Elizabeth. *All the Daring of a Soldier: Women of the Civil War Armies*. New York: Penguin, 1999.

Litwack, Leon. *Been in the Storm So Long: The Aftermath of Slavery*. New York: Knopf, 1979.

McPherson, James M. *Battle Cry of Freedom: The Civil War Era*. New York: Oxford University Press, 1988.

Neely, Mark. *The Fate of Liberty: Abraham Lincoln and Civil Liberties*. New York: Oxford University Press, 1991.

Perman, Michael L. *The Coming of the American Civil War*. 3d ed. Lexington, MA: D. C. Heath, 1993.

Index